Send This Jerk
the Bedbug Letter

Send This Jerk the Bedbug Letter

How Companies,
Politicians, and the
Mass Media Deal
with Complaints and
How to Be a More
Effective Complainer

JOHN BEAR, PH.D

Ten Speed Press
Berkeley, California

1⊖

Ten Speed Press
P.O. Box 7123
Berkeley, California 94707

Distributed in Australia by E. J. Dwyer Pty. Ltd., in Canada by Publishers Group West, in New Zealand by Tandem Press, in South Africa by Real Books, and in the United Kingdom and Europe by Airlift Books.

Cover design by Cale Burr
Interior design by Catherine Jacobes

Library of Congress Cataloging-in-Publication Data
Bear, John, 1938-
    Send the jerk the bedbug letter: how companies, politicians, and
the mass media deal with complaints, and how to be a more effective
complainer / John Bear.
        p.   cm.
    Includes bibliographical references and index.
    ISBN 0-89815-811-7 (pbk.)
    1. Consumer complaints.   2. Complaint letters.   3. Customer
services--Management.   4. Consumer satisfaction.   I. Title.
HF5415.52.B43   1996
381.3--dc20   96-1526
                                                          CIP

First printing, 1996
Printed in Canada

1 2 3 4 5 6 7 8 9 10 — 00 99 98 97 96

For Marina Bear.
No major complaints in thirty-three years.

Acknowledgments

IN THIS, MY ELEVENTH BOOK for Ten Speed Press, it's about time I properly thanked the people there who make me possible. Phil Wood and George Young took me to lunch in 1979 (and a few times since), and their support, enthusiasm, and good will have meant a lot to me. They also had the good sense soon after that to hire a talented young kid for after-school donkey work, and said kid, eldest daughter Mariah Bear, has grown splendidly to become Ten Speed's managing editor, my sometime co-author, and a true colleague. May everyone live long enough to be edited by his or her children.

Bedbug evolved from the doctoral work I did at Michigan State University many years ago. I am forever grateful to Professors Jean Kerrick (without whom I would never have begun), Malcolm MacLean (without whom I would never have continued, and Erwin Bettinghaus (without whom I would never have finished). To them, and to Professor David Berlo, the best teacher I ever had, who died the month this book went to press, my grateful thanks.

Many people contributed stories, anecdotes, and case histories in response to my written and electronically published requests for assistance. To a man (and woman), they said, in effect, "For God's sake, don't use my name in the book." And so I thank these anonymous unindicted coconspirators here; may they all be victorious in tilting against their various corporate and political windmills. Next, my thanks to then-graduate-student and now Doctor Donna Reid for her assistance with academic and library research. Finally, it cannot be easy living with a chronic complainer. I am grateful that my daughters did not run away from home any earlier than they did; that we all remain good friends; and that they never sought Power of Attorney to have me sent to the Home for the Terminally Indignant.

Table of Contents

My Epiphany: You Mean I Could Really Do That?

A S YOU WILL LEARN in the ensuing pages, I have been a pretty good complainer for most of my life. I've had a few grand and satisfying successes along with a bundle of annoying failures. But it was not until I read an article about Richard Feinberg, head of the Department of Consumer Sciences and Retailing at Purdue University, that it came to me that I'd gotten it all wrong.

Sure, I identified with the "I'm mad as hell..." character in *Network,* and sure I had observed more than a few squeaky wheels getting their grease, but until Feinberg pointed it out, it had simply never occurred to me that *it isn't my fault.* The things that I complain about are not my fault. The things that go wrong, resulting in the need to complain, are not my fault. And, most important of all, the people who can make things right, whether the president of Chrysler or the clerk at my neighborhood hardware store, are not doing me a favor by condescending to listen to my begging. They have an obligation to make things right, because they work for me. They would be out of work if it were not for me, and therefore *they have no right to ignore my complaint.* They have no right because *it's not my fault.*

Such a simple, if novel, idea. Empires are built, or crumble, because of such simple ideas, and this surely is a simple idea that has the power to crumble empires of indifference, pomposity, apathy, or downright nastiness.

Let's go to your friendly (or possibly not-so-friendly) neighborhood bank. You have a question about an error on your statement, which the automatic machines cannot answer. It is lunch hour, and the lines at the two open teller windows are fairly long. But at the same time, you see three other employees standing around chatting, and through the glass you see the vice president sitting at his big mahogany desk shuffling paper.

What do you do? Are you, as was I, one of those well-meaning wimps whose mother taught him or her never to make a scene, and who will, therefore, stand there at the end of the long line like a dope, the well-paid, college-educated, generous, benevolent, sensitive, caring person, suffering the abuse or neglect or intimidation of a minimum-wage clerk or thoughtless manager inflicting on you an abusive company policy developed and enforced by an uncaring management?

Or do you have, in the words of "Fight Back" guru David Horowitz, "the psychological stamina to slash through the red tape, penetrate the bureaucratic brier patch, and cope with other people's ineptness and bumbling, all of which rob you of your dollars and your self-esteem"?

Mr. Feinberg of Purdue's solution is simple and elegant. In this situation at your bank, do one of two things:

1. Walk up to one of the closed windows. Stand there politely. When someone says, as they surely will, "Excuse me, that window is closed," reply, "Then open it, please." When they say, "We can't do that," say, "Why not?" Like the horse standing in the bathtub in that old shaggy dog story, you are too large and too visible to be ignored. After a minute or two, you might even invite other customers to stand in that line with you.

2. Go to the vice president's door, knock on it, and invite him to come out and open a new window. "I can't do that now." "Why not, there are three employees standing over there chatting." "They are on their lunch break." "So am I. Perhaps you could help me. I have a question about my statement. Do you know how to operate your bank's computer?"

Supermarkets. Car dealerships. Medical offices. Government agencies. Department stores. Wherever and whenever people are doing things that make it necessary for you to complain, your mantra must be "These people all work for me. They would be out of work if it were not for me. I will not let them push me around."

"It may sound radical," says Richard Feinberg, "but that's exactly what consumers need to do to get the attention they deserve."

THINGS ARE NOT GOOD

In his comprehensive academic study, *When Consumers Complain,* Arthur Best summarizes matters thus:

> Scrutiny of both willful and random business techniques of refusing reasonable consumer requests shows the need for exposing the techniques to further criticism; their application in many cases is unsupported by logic or fairness. Unfortunately, however, the power of individuals to force such scrutiny is slight.

In other words, nothing works and nobody cares.

In their fine book, *Getting What You Deserve: A Handbook for the Assertive Consumer,* the authors, two high-powered consumer attorneys, lament that

> the much-vaunted consumer revolution has made people more aware of problems that have been around a long time. Yet its accomplishments have in truth been modest. The marketplace is still a minefield for the unwary consumer. Consumer ripoffs continue on a large scale across the country and the legal remedies are generally inadequate....Very often consumers accept bad treatment as one of the inevitable frustrations of modern life.

Researchers Claes Fornell at Northwestern University and Robert Westbrook at the University of Arizona suggest that the problem is both serious and disturbing, since organizations "appear to behave in a dysfunctional manner with respect to consumer complaints."

BUT THERE MAY BE HOPE

As Eric Reisfeld writes in his charming treatise *Consumer Karate: A Guide for Economic Survival,*

> The average businessman—owner or manager—does not want trouble. He wants to operate his business with a minimum of untoward incidents...because troubles take time and effort to resolve, hence he will cut down on the net results,

the profitability of his undertaking. If therefore you can show him just how it came about that you were screwed in his place, and present the case in a calm, logical manner, he like as not will resolve it in short order in your favor....

If, however, he doesn't agree,

be this through his intractability, plain stupidity, because his wife gave him a hard time at home...your next remedy is to convince this guy that you are not going to shut up and take it; that you are capable of giving him trouble, plenty of it, and redetermined to invest the time and effort required to deliver it.

Social commentator David Hapgood puts it this way, in *The Average Man Fights Back:*

A falling standard of living and a rising tide of skepticism provide promising conditions for efforts to reverse the screwing of the average man. Much more information is available about how screwings can be avoided, and many more people are absorbing that information and acting on it....People are finding that even as lone individuals they can stand up to an expert and ward off a swindle. People in groups are achieving similar results on a somewhat larger scale....[T]he struggle is to decide who—ourselves or others—shall design the shape of our lives....[A] growing number of us have come to realize that our present rules can no longer be trusted to determine the circumstances under which we live.

These people all work for me. They would be out of work if it were not for me. I will not let them push me around.

Why it is even official U.S. government policy: "People don't realize that being heard and expecting results are fundamental consumer rights" (Polly Baca, director, U.S. Office of Consumer Affairs).

Fundamental rights. What a nice concept, just like those in the Constitution. Indeed, if George Washington had bought a nonfunctioning musket from a mail-order house, or Ben Franklin had had to stand in line endlessly at his bank, we might well have found these five basic consumers' rights embedded in the Constitution along with bearing arms and speaking freely.

TOP FIVE RIGHTS OF COMPLAINERS
AND POTENTIAL COMPLAINERS

(adapted from Richard Feinberg's consumerist top ten)

1. The right to complain and get satisfaction. A complaint is the organization's chance to make things right.

2. The right, after complaining, to hear "Yes." Not "We can't do that" or "I'll have to ask my manager." People who deal with the public need the power to solve problems *now*.

3. The right not to wait too long, whether in line, or to be noticed in a store, or to get an answer from a business or agency, or to be dealt with promptly by telephone (or to have someone offer to call you back after no more than a minute on hold).

4. The right to a "wow." Being a consumer should be fun. Feinberg says, "Believe it or not, it is possible to provide such incredible customer service that the consumer says, 'Wow, that was one of the greatest experiences of my life.'"

5. The right to have everyone and anyone in the business serve you. Presidents and vice presidents and supervisors must remember that without customers, there are no presidents, vice presidents, or supervisors.

These people all work for me. They would be out of work if it were not for me. I will not let them push me around.

On the other hand, much as we might wish to, we cannot go through life complaining about every injustice, every instance of poor treatment or shoddy merchandise or being abandoned in someone's voice mail system. If sensible complaining is our job, our investment, then, as with any investment, we want to expend our time and energy and perhaps money in those places most likely to produce a satisfactory result, whether that be a refund, an apology, a righted wrong, or even the pleasure that some people get from a case of creative revenge.

How to Decide in Advance Whether It Is Worth Complaining

SOME PEOPLE COMPLAIN for the sheer joy of complaining, or to get even with some organization. But the vast majority of complaints are from people who genuinely feel that someone—a store, a car dealer, a doctor, a government agency—has done something inappropriate to them, and they would like matters set right.

Since complaining is a time-consuming activity (not to mention money and emotional energy), wouldn't it be nice to be able to know, in advance, whether any given complaint is likely to produce a satisfactory result? There is, alas, no magic wand we can wave to achieve this knowledge, but a careful analysis of dozens and dozens of doctoral research projects, hundreds of academic papers on complaining, and thousands of actual case studies does point to the existence of a method that will work in many instances.

This is art, not science. It won't give you a precise answer. But it will definitely help you evaluate the likelihood of a satisfactory response, and thus might help you decide whether or not it is worth complaining, and the way in which you should complain.

FOUR FACTORS

There are four main factors that interact in determining the eventual response (or lack of response) to a complaint.

1. How big a deal is it?

The bigger the project or idea is, the less likely that complainers will have any effect in changing it. The reasons are as likely to be financial as ideological. If a great deal of money has been invested in something, it is usually considered to be bad business to retract it without overpowering reasons.

When Xerox Corporation started getting complaint letters after committing $4 million to promoting the United Nations one year, that sum represented 50 percent of their advertising budget—clearly a big deal. If a larger company like Procter & Gamble had committed $4 million to a special project, that would have been less than 2 percent of their ad budget, and thus not such a big deal.

For a first-term member of Congress, a bill to build a bridge might be the most important thing he or she has ever done, and it would take a great deal to have an effect on it, while the same bridge bill might be very low on the priority (and interest) list of an experienced long-time politician.

If I am the chairman of Ford, and I have committed millions of dollars of my company's money to the creation of a brand-new car, and I have very clear ideas on exactly what that car should be like, and what it should be named, then no number of complaint letters from dealers, the investment community, automotive writers, or the public are likely to persuade me that the Edsel is not a good idea.

2. Level of commitment

The more firmly the recipient of a complaint—whether a company, a network, a politician, or your next-door neighbor—is committed to a course of action, the less likely you are to persuade them into wavering from that course. Personal commitment (personal belief, credo, etc.) is probably more unshakable than impersonal commitment (corporate policy, election mandate, etc.).

If I am a physician who believes that abortions are absolutely and unequivocally wrong, then no number of complaint letters from pro-choice people are likely to change my mind. But if I am a bit uncertain about my position, or if I have only taken my position because of the views of the hospital I work for, and I receive a letter from the mother of a twelve-year-old pregnant victim of rape-incest who may die without an abortion, I am more likely to reconsider my position.

If I am the chairman of KPMG, the huge international accounting firm, and I believe firmly in the right of Israel to exist as a nation, and I receive complaint letters from some Arab clients, suggesting that because I have opened an office in Israel I am likely to lose their business, I am quite unlikely to take action because of those complaints.

If, however, a client complains that my white presentation folders are a problem for him because white is considered a very unlucky or ill-fated color in his country, then, hey, no big deal, I'll change the color of my report covers.

3. Quality of the complaint

Time and again, people who deal with complaint letters mention quality before quantity. One or two high-quality letters can have greater effect than thousands of low-quality letters. "Quality" is a difficult concept to define precisely, but it seems to be something that people who have received a lot of complaint letters can always identify. Intelligence and sincerity seem to be the two key qualities. Either or both of these in a letter that is clearly not part of a mass letter-writing campaign constitute quality mail.

Appearance is linked with intelligence, or, more significantly, with perceived intelligence. A complaint letter in pencil, with misspellings, on yellow lined paper, may well be both sincere and intelligent, but it also is much less likely to be read.

Legibility should go without saying, but it doesn't. A lawyer I know, a member of Mensa to boot, writes letters with a thick pen in small block capital letters, and they are, for many people, literally impossible to read. The receiver of his letters cannot know if they are complaints, praise, or something entirely different.

A very important component of quality is uniqueness. If one person writes a wonderful and brilliant letter to Georgia-Pacific opposing the closing of a lumber mill and moving the jobs to Mexico, at least that letter will be read, possibly circulated throughout the executive wing, and might even have an effect. But if ten or fifty or a thousand copies of that same letter arrive, perhaps in different handwritings or typefaces, perhaps with minor changes in wording, none of them is likely to have any influence at all.

◆ ◆ ◆ ◆ ◆ ◆ ◆ ◆ ◆ ◆ ◆ ◆

CASE STUDY

Sorry, Pillsbury, Your Funny Face Isn't Very Funny

The large food products company introduced a heavily advertised line of artificially sweetened fruit-flavored powdered drink mixes, presumably to compete with Kool-Aid. The Funny Face line featured six flavors:

Loud Mouth Lime, Freckle-Faced Strawberry, Rootin' Tootin' Raspberry, Goofy Grape, Chinese Cherry, and Injun Orange. Each drink packet had an intended-to-be-humorous cartoon drawing of the smiling fruit: a strawberry with freckles, an orange in a war bonnet, a cherry with buck teeth and slanting eyes, and so on.

After less than a year on the market, two of the flavors were withdrawn, and their names changed. Can you guess which two? Indeed, Chinese Cherry became Choo Choo Cherry, and Injun Orange became Jolly Olly Orange.

When I asked why, Pillsbury wrote me that "those who designed and approved the original Funny Face labels [believed] the characters are so abstract, so removed from reality, that they would not likely be related to an actual person, and second, the characters are friendly and likable, not unpleasant or unkind."

Pillsbury was, however "seriously troubled" by the mail they received. "I should point out," the product publicity manager wrote, "that the quality of the letters was more impressive to us than the quantity." They only received a few letters, but "they were highly articulate, literate letters which expressed sincere concern for the damage which could be done by ethnic stereotyping, particularly in the minds of children."

There was no evidence of any organized campaign. "Each of the letters was different and personal. Many in fact were at pains to point out that they were not members of either of the minority groups involved, but felt a citizen's concern for them."

The absence of any organized complaining was confirmed by the politically active Chinese Chamber of Commerce in San Francisco, which once launched a major complaint-letter drive when Barry Goldwater said, of an opponent, "He's got no more chance than a one-legged Chinaman."

Pillsbury's decision to destroy millions of preprinted packets and revamp their marketing campaign was, it turned out, based on perhaps a dozen sincere letters. For them, the scope was relatively minor, the commitment was not huge, and the quality of the complaints was high.

◆ ◆ ◆ ◆ ◆ ◆ ◆ ◆ ◆ ◆ ◆ ◆

4. Quantity of complaints

Contrary to the beliefs of many political and social organizations, a vast amount of complaint mail, by itself, is unlikely to have any effect whatsoever. It is only in conjunction with other factors that the size of the response is likely to have any effect at all. For instance, if two similar companies have about the same commitment to a venture of comparable scope—say setting up a manufacturing plant in China—and one gets one or two excellent letters, while the other gets hundreds, perhaps even thousands, of excellent letters, it is the second company that is more likely to take them to heart and reconsider its decision.

On the other end of the scale, a large quantity of low-quality mail—either because the letters are poorly written, or because they are clearly a part of an organized complaint drive—is likely to have quite the opposite effect of the desired one. To be sure, some politicians seek photo opportunities with great stacks of mail, if it supports a position they have already taken, but if their minds are already made up, especially on a big issue, or one that is really important to them, then, as one senator put it, "A ton of mail isn't going to have an ounce of effect. If they wanted me to weigh my mail, they should have elected a butcher."

The perception of quantity depends on the situation. For an obscure company that never gets any complaint mail, a dozen letters would be an avalanche, while giant corporations or prominent politicians might regard a thousand letters as just routine for the day.

Four factors means sixteen possibilities

Whether you are complaining about the U.S. policy toward China, or a dry cleaner who lost a button from your vest, these same four factors will come into play in determining what kind of response you will get: scope (how big a deal is it?), commitment to the idea, quality of complaints, and quantity of complaints.

Each of those factors can have a high level and a low level. It can be a big deal or a small one. There can be a high level of commitment or a modest one; there can be a high quality of complaints or a low quality; and there can be many complaints or few. Thus we have sixteen categories of possibilities that could be operating:

- Big deal, strong commitment, high-quality complaints, and many complaints
- Big deal, weak commitment, high-quality complaints, and many complaints

- Small deal, strong commitment, low-quality complaints, and many complaints

And so on. You get the idea. And in case you're the sort who would like to visualize this, here is a a chart. This one just has numbers, one to sixteen; we will return to this chart shortly to predict the chances of success in each of the sixteen boxes.

		FOR THE TARGET OF THE COMPLAINT			
		STRONG COMMITMENT		WEAK COMMITMENT	
		BIG DEAL	SMALL DEAL	BIG DEAL	SMALL DEAL
LOW QUALITY COMPLAINTS	SMALL VOLUME	1	2	3	4
	LARGE VOLUME	5	6	7	8
HIGH QUALITY COMPLAINTS	SMALL VOLUME	9	10	11	12
	LARGE VOLUME	13	14	15	16

ASSESSING YOUR COMPLAINT SITUATION

In order to get a pretty good idea of whether any given complaint has a chance of succeeding, it is necessary to come up with a rough guess about how big a deal it is, and how committed the person or organization you're writing to might be. Of course you cannot know, but often it is possible to make an educated guess.

As for the quality of complaints, reading through the case histories in this book should help you to assess them. The quantity may be as small as one, if it is "just" you making a complaint by mail, phone, or in person. Or it may be as large as your organizing or public relations skills can make possible.

You may wish to take the following simple quiz, and respond to the four items to the best of your ability. Of course there are no "right" or "wrong" answers:

1. How big a deal is the topic of my complaint for the person or organization I'm complaining to? ☐ Big deal ☐ Not such a big deal

2. How committed is the person or organization to this matter about which I'm complaining? ☐ Strong commitment ☐ Weak commitment

3. Is my complaint (or complaints, if a group effort) of high quality (personal, non–form letter, nonpetition, clear, legible, etc.)? ☐ High quality ☐ Not such high quality

4. How many complaints are likely to be sent on this matter? ☐ Many ☐ Few, or just mine

		FOR THE TARGET OF THE COMPLAINT			
		STRONG COMMITMENT		**WEAK COMMITMENT**	
		BIG DEAL	SMALL DEAL	BIG DEAL	SMALL DEAL
LOW QUALITY COMPLAINTS	SMALL VOLUME	extremely unlikely to work	very unlikely to work	unlikely to work	unlikely to work
	LARGE VOLUME	very unlikely to work	unlikely to work	hard to say has a chance	likely to work
HIGH QUALITY COMPLAINTS	SMALL VOLUME	unlikely to work	somewhat unlikely to work	likely to work	quite unlikely to work
	LARGE VOLUME	unlikely to work but has chance	hard to say might work	extremely unlikely to work	extremely unlikely to work

Your four answers will direct you to one of the sixteen boxes on the chart. Here's the chart again, with my best guess, based on research (mine and others), experience, hunch, and common sense, about what is likely to happen. But do remember that there is no certainty in this world, especially not in the way in which companies, politicians, or the mass media respond to complaints.

It is often helpful to read about real-world case histories, to see how the theory turns into practice. So I have selected sixteen case histories, one to illustrate each of the sixteen boxes. A brief overview of them follows, and the full stories appear in Appendix A.

1. Big deal, strong commitment, few complaints, low quality:

The decency brigades versus the "dirty dictionary"

When the *American Heritage Dictionary* included the "four-letter" words, some "decency" groups organized a complaint-letter drive. The publisher, with a strong commitment to a major publishing venture, was unmoved by the modest number of form letters received.

2. Small deal, strong commitment, few complaints, low quality:

The American Legion versus UNICEF

When Legion members urged Congress to withdraw support for this "subversive" organization, the legislators' strong commitment to this small budget item was unaffected by the small number of form letters received.

3. Big deal, weak commitment, few complaints, low quality:

"Sho 'nuff, Massa Colgate"

CASE STUDIES

Colgate insisted that its Darkie toothpaste, very popular in Hong Kong, featuring a widely grinning top-hatted blackface minstrel man, symbolized nothing more than a man with clean white teeth. Bring up the banjo music, maestro. Following what Colgate regarded as a small number of irrelevant complaints, they changed the name. Their weak commitment to the marketing strategy for a major product resulted in the change.

4. Small deal, weak commitment, few complaints, low quality:

The DAR and the patriotic girdles

When the Treo Company, almost as a gag, marketed a Stars 'n Stripes girdle (red, white and blue with stars and stripes), the National Chairman of the Daughters of the American Revolution Flag of the United

States of America Committee organized a modest complaint campaign. Because of the company's weak commitment to this small deal, they recalled 3,000 girdles and the campaign was discontinued.

5. Big deal, strong commitment, many complaints, low quality:

Xerox versus the John Birch Society

When Xerox Corporation announced a major contribution to the United Nations, the Birchers launched a massive protest letter writing campaign. But Xerox had a firm resolve in this major financial matter and the tens of thousands of form letters had no effect at all.

6. Small deal, strong commitment, many complaints, low quality:

CASE STUDIES

The "Communist front" known as the *Ladies Home Journal*

The *Journal* published a short story about what could happen in a classroom if the Communists took over the U.S. While nearly everyone saw it as a strong anti-Communist message, the John Birch Society urged its members to flood the *Ladies Home Journal* with complaint letters. The *Journal's* strong commitment to this story was unmoved by the thousands of form letters received.

7. Big deal, weak commitment, many complaints, low quality:

United Airlines reneging on its promise to a hero pilot

A pilot rewarded by the airline for skill and bravery persuaded the company to put the United Nations logo on its planes and UN literature on the plane. But when a large number of complaint form letters were received by anti-UN organizations, the weak commitment to this big policy change crumbled, and the UN symbols were quietly removed.

8. Small deal, weak commitment, many complaints, low quality

The supermarket and the "slave labor" hams

The Jewel Tea Company chain of supermarkets was urged, in a pressure-group-organized complaint-letter campaign, not to sell "slave labor Polish hams" in their stores. It was a small deal to the market—there was no real commitment to those products—and a flurry of form letters was enough to get the offending hams removed from the shelves.

9. Big deal, strong commitment, few complaints, high quality:

But for 17 miles it was a helluva fine car—
the flaming Cadillac

After only seventeen miles of driving, a Midwestern man's brand new Cadillac burst into flames. General Motors offered to repair the car, but not replace it. The company's commitment to the no-replacement policy was enough to deny the sincere complaint. (But in this instance, following a lawsuit, the company was ordered to replace the car.)

10. Small deal, strong commitment, few complaints, high quality:

The all-day turkey

Stew Leonard's has a commitment to a policy that says the customer is always right, even when they're not. And so when a woman complained that a turkey, which she had cooked for twelve hours, was tough and stringy, the store immediately offered her a choice of a refund or a new turkey.

11. Big deal, weak commitment, few complaints, high quality:

Time-Warner and cop killer rap

CASE STUDIES

A small number of complainers suggested it was inappropriate for Time-Warner to be reaping profits from an album including the selection called "Cop Killer." Giving in on editorial policy was a big deal, but their resolve was not that strong. When they sold their interest in the offending record company, they insisted the deal was good business, and unrelated to the "Cop Killer" flap.

12. Small deal, weak commitment, few complaints, high quality:

The weary businessman versus Holiday Inn

When a salesman who had guaranteed his room with a credit card arrived at midnight, the hotel claimed the credit card was invalid (they were one digit off on the number) and they had rented their room to someone else. The salesman headed to the men's room, and emerged in his pajamas, settling in on a large sofa in the lobby. The hotel somehow managed to find a room. It was a small deal for the big hotel, and there was no major commitment to a 'get tough' policy, so the innovative high-quality complaint did the job.

13. Big deal, strong commitment, many complaints, high quality:

Bed companies do the darndest things

Art Linkletter's television commercials helped sell hundreds of thousands of Craftmatic electric folding beds, mostly to senior citizens. Thousands complained about unprovable medical claims, misstated Medicare reimbursement claims, and 'bait and switch' tactics to the $6,000 top of the line bed. Following several major lawsuits, Craftmatic evolved a strong commitment to make things right, agreeing to binding arbitration for all complaints that could not otherwise be settled.

14. Small deal, strong commitment, many complaints, high quality:

Pink birds, si; golf, no

CASE STUDIES

When the Venezuelan government announced plans for a commercial development in the middle of a large flamingo habitat, Global Response, an international letter-writing network, generated a large high-quality protest. The government was committed to the project, but it was a small deal in the grander scheme of things. Embarrassed by the international complaints, they decided that the new golf course, highway, and factory area were not that important after all and the project was canceled.

15. Big deal, weak commitment, many complaints, high quality:

Classic Motor "miscarriages"

Classic Motor Carriages of Florida sold thousands of expensive kits to build replicas of famous sports cars on the chassis of inexpensive American cars. The kits had many flaws, the advertising was misleading, and the company ignored complaints. This was a big deal—the company had only one product—but, as it turned out, they had a weak commitment to making things right, even after agreeing to comply with the demands of Florida regulators. The complainers ultimately prevailed in the sense that Classic finally threw in the towel and faded away, albeit leaving a wake of anger, hostility, and unsettled claims.

16. Small deal, weak commitment, many complaints, high quality:

"Did we say a free television? We meant to say 'a useless coupon book.'"

Homeowners in Boston were invited to visit a nearby vacation resort, have a lovely day, listen to a one-hour sales presentation, and come home with a free television set. But the high-pressure sales presentation lasted four hours, after which people were given a coupon book good for some discounts in Hawaii. What about the television? "So sorry," they were told, "There must have been a misprint in our brochure." Many complaints ensued, to the company and the Office of Consumer Protection. The perpetrators had other schemes going, so closing down this one and making good was no big deal. So they offered a 13-inch color television to everyone who had suffered through their sales pitch.

CHAPTER 2

Who Complains

THE SAD FACT IS THAT MOST PEOPLE DON'T

IN EVERY STUDY AND SURVEY that has ever been done on complaining, the findings in one key area are essentially the same: a great many people have something to complain about, and a very small percentage of them actually do anything about it.

The number of complaints made each year seems awfully high: well over a billion. Many of the companies that release complaint statistics report rising numbers as the public becomes more consumer-oriented. Scott Paper got 1,000 complaint letters the year they established a consumer relations department. Ten years later, it was up to 70,000. General Foods gets over 100,000 letters a year, and nearly 40 percent are complaints. Best Foods has several dozen people handling more than 60,000 letters each year, two thirds of them complaints. Scott Lawn Care got 200,000 letters one year, 30,000 of them complaints.

But the Federal Trade Commission has estimated that buyers in the United States are unhappy with 75 million purchases every year, from chewing gum to luxury cars and "as few as 4 percent ever complain."

One researcher asked consumers how they felt about various products they had purchased from a television shopping channel. The dissatisfaction levels were remarkably high for such items as "miracle" stain remover (48 percent were unhappy), a "permanently sharp" kitchen knife set (33 percent unhappy), and a treadmill exercise device (35 percent unhappy). Yet only 15 percent of the dissatisfied people took any action: 5 percent returned the goods for a refund, and 10 percent wrote a complaint letter but did not follow it up. Another 10 percent of the unhappy people complained only to family or friends, and the vast majority, seven in ten, did nothing whatsoever.

When the Massachusetts Office of Consumer Affairs asked a large number of people about their complaining behavior, 95 percent said they had something to complain about, but fewer than 10 percent had actually complained.

A. R. Andreasan discovered that 23 percent of the people in his survey had a complaint about their medical doctor. Of the people who were not satisfied or had a problem, only 11 percent complained to anyone, although many more than that either switched physicians or planned to do so.

THE COMPLAINERS, THE CONSUMERS, AND THE DOPES

Who are these people: those who complain and those who don't? Here's an interesting way to look at these people, based on the work of Rex Warland at Penn State University.

Let's start with two factors: (1) whether or not you are the sort of person who complains, and (2) whether or not you are a concerned citizen: someone interested in the consumer movement, someone who knows about Ralph Nader, someone who reads *Consumer Reports,* and encourages others to take a more active role in making this a better world.

Thus we can divide the world up into four kinds of people (plus a fifth to be described shortly):

- *The Concerned Complainers:* People who actively complain, and who feel it is important to encourage others to do the same; who distrust big business and big government. The rallying cry might come from the movie *Network:* "We're mad as hell and we're not going to take it any more." Some research suggests that about 25 percent of people fit into this category.

- *The Unconcerned Complainers:* People who actively complain about things important to them, but don't especially like the Nader ideology; don't think that more laws and more regulation will help matters; and who think business generally knows what it's doing. Perhaps 10 percent of us are in this particular bin.

- *The Concerned Noncomplainers:* They sympathize with the consumerist movement; they like Ralph Nader; they read

Consumer Reports; they just don't relate to complaining as one of the things one does in life. Figure roughly another 10 percent.

- *The Unconcerned Noncomplainers:* They are aware of the consumer movement, but neither that, nor complaining about things, are their cups of tea. About 15 percent of people are in that particular lifeboat.

- *The Dopes:* About six people in ten would identify with one of those four groups. So what about the other 40 percent? Well, they fall into a category that the academics politely call "uninformed unconcerned noncomplainers." I am less polite. I call them dopes. They've never heard of Ralph Nader. Some of them may be dimly aware of *Consumer Reports,* but they've never read it. And of course they never, never complain, nor read books about complaining, which is why I'm not concerned with insulting readers of this book. They'll never see it. If this group had a motto, it might well be Dorothy Parker's quatrain: "See the happy moron, doesn't give a damn. I wish I were that moron. My God, perhaps I am."

Now that we have all of humankind neatly arrayed in one of five categories, it is time to look at the kinds of people who live in those five fields. What do we look at? We look at the two most important things that help define who you are: your personality and your demographics (age, sex, religion, and so on).

Personality and complaining

The psychologists have been let loose in the world of complaining, and they love it. Let's give people personality tests, and let's learn about their complaining behaviors, and let's see how they relate to one another. The problem with this has been that the results have been awfully inconclusive. Because complaining can take so many forms, there may be something there for nearly everyone:

- The shy and reclusive woman, who would never, ever engage in a face-to-face argument with someone, may be the terror of the postal system, firing off one angry and vigorous complaint after another.

- The power-seeking hard-driving executive may avoid complaining entirely, because he knows he might not emerge triumphant and would not take well to such an ego blow.

- The gentle scholar might resort only to gentle, reasoned arguments, until a threshold is passed, whereupon he registers his complaint by launching the most ingenious and diabolical, but utterly secretive, kind of revenge imaginable.

◆ ◆ ◆ ◆ ◆ ◆ ◆ ◆ ◆ ◆ ◆ ◆

CASE STUDY

"Oh, no, no, no, but surely you don't think I ..."
The case of *Lust Ranch* in the children's library

Bernie L. was a mild-mannered fellow who owned a medium-sized video rental store in a medium-sized midwestern city. While he did not stock hard-core pornography, he did carry some foreign art films, as well as epics like *Porky's* for the local college crowd. A rather pompous and flamboyant local minister took it upon himself to cleanse the town of the "filth" of Bernie's shop, and indeed of Bernie himself. "We don't need the likes of him in our town."

The minister and his flock made life miserable for Bernie, with posters, picketing, and boycotting. It was the injustice of it all that finally pushed Bernie over the threshold, since there was a big chain video store in town renting much worse stuff than he carried.

He drove to the nearby big city, where he visited an adult bookstore and purchased a dozen extremely racy novels, ranging from Henry Miller and Fanny Hill to out-and-out hard-core stuff, of which *Lust Ranch* was the tamest. They were *not* illustrated books; Bernie had his limits. Next, he used his personal computer to design a simple bookplate, and ran off a dozen of them on sticky paper. They declared that "this book is a gift to the Town Library, through the generosity of [the minister's name]."

Finally, mild-mannered Bernie carried the books into the library, and judiciously placed them on the shelves, all over the place: in the juvenile room, among the religious books, the cookbooks, the "how-to" books, whatever. And that's all he did, other than quietly enjoy thinking about what must have unfolded over the ensuing weeks and months. Oh, and for whatever reason, the minister and his flock finally turned their moral cannons on other targets, and Bernie's video store survived quite nicely.

◆ ◆ ◆ ◆ ◆ ◆ ◆ ◆ ◆ ◆ ◆ ◆

One of the biggest studies we have of the personality profile of complainers comes from the work of Judy Zaichkowsky and John Liefield. They interviewed hundreds of known complainers: people who had written complaint letters either to a government agency or to the Better Business Bureau.

Personality profile of the complainers

In a nutshell, when the complainers were compared to the noncomplainers, they were found to be more outgoing, less shy, more sober and conscientious, more tough-minded, more apprehensive, more willing to be experimental, and more self-controlled. But the most important factor that separated the complainers from the noncomplainers was imagination.

To the extent people can be categorized as either imaginative or practical, the complainers were imaginative. They were intensely subjective; they had an active inner life, and less of a regard for the rules or procedures of the groups in which they lived or worked. They might not be well accepted in their groups, but that doesn't bother them.

Other research has suggested that the complainers have a higher level of inner anxiety, a level of internal conflict, and, possibly as a result of this, they are more accident-prone than the noncomplainers.

THE LIFE AND LIFESTYLE OF COMPLAINERS

Everybody and her sister seems to have attempted to examine the demographic aspects of complainers. There are some factors, especially age and wealth, that regularly seem to be a predictor of complaining behavior. And there are lots of others, including gender, education, and marital status, that are completely unpredictable: sometimes they relate to complaining, and often they don't.

- In one study, people who complained about medical services were richer, better educated, and younger.

- Of 568 people who complained about problems with their new Chevrolet to an Ohio dealer, neither age, wealth, nor education were a factor, but men complained much more than women, and the more vigorous complainers tended to have larger families.

- Of people who called the Wisconsin Consumer Protection Hotline, there were higher percentages of women, married people, and educated people, and lower percentages of poor people and those over age fifty-five.

- A Kansas researcher found that whites were twice as likely to complain about government services than blacks, and people under sixty-five were five times more likely to complain than those over that age.

- A Ph.D. thesis at USC found that education level and job had nothing to do with complaining, and that while blacks and older people complain less, they tend to be more satisfied with the outcome of their complaint than whites and younger people.

- An oil company found that their more affluent customers—those with credit cards—complained more about money matters, made smaller claims for what they felt they were owed, and seemed happier with the result of their complaint.

- Two researchers investigated a large number of people who complained about appliances they had bought. The complainers tended to be wealthier and older, but their age, marital status, or educational level had nothing to do with their likelihood of complaining.

- Three scholars at the University of Guelph in Canada surveyed nearly 10,000 people who complained about various matters to the federal government, the Better Business Bureau, and a woman's magazine. They found the complainers were much less likely to be under twenty-five or over fifty-four; that widows complain less than married, divorced or single people; that men and women are equally likely to complain; and that professionals, managers, and the unemployed complain more than office workers, clerks, or salespeople.

- The results of one small study suggest that both lower- and upper-class whites are more likely to complain about various matters than comparable blacks, but middle-class blacks are more likely to complain than middle-class whites.

- Of forty-four people who wrote a total of 385 complaint letters to a southern newspaper, only two were under forty, and only two were women. They tended to be well-educated conservatives who had lived in the area for an average of eighteen years.

- Forty people who wrote complaint letters to an Oregon newspaper were compared with the local population who didn't complain. They were found to be older, better educated, less mobile, more religious, more mature, and more imaginative. They had more children, and they read more books.

WHY POOR PEOPLE DON'T COMPLAIN

It is well documented that poor people, whom many researchers call economically disadvantaged people, complain a lot less than those with more resources. The obvious explanation is that complaining takes time and money. One state's consumer telephone hotline surveyed the public to find out why people weren't using it, and they learned, not surprisingly, that many poor people work unusually hard and long hours, and don't have time to make phone calls during the day, even if they have ready access to a phone (which many didn't).

Some experts suggest that people who are lower on the socioeconomic scale are more likely to notice clerical problems ("My check is made out for the wrong amount...") but less likely to be aware of problems requiring judgment: "Is this gown from CheapMart supposed to have sagging seams and a nonfunctioning zipper? Well, I suppose it's OK." Further, the traditional view of poor people is that they suffer from irrational fears of what may happen if they complain, and they are not familiar with the complaining process.

Well, maybe in some cases, but this unflattering view is contradicted by the doctoral work of David Stephenson at the University of Colorado, who spent four years as a consumer fraud investigator. Contrary to even his own predictions, he found that poor people's complaining behavior is often a rational, calculated response to the amount of time, money, and "psychological costs" that complaining would require. Stephenson goes on to suggest that instead of blaming the poor for not complaining enough, society should be blaming those who nourish an "ethic of deceit" in their deceptive or evasive practices that particularly victimize the poor.

WHY OLDER PEOPLE DON'T COMPLAIN

Every bit of research suggests that people over sixty complain much less than average, even though they are victimized just as much as younger people, often more so. The reasons are, for the most part, the obvious ones. Older people have less money. They are often more dependent on others, which makes them increasingly compliant, and willing to overlook or live with problems. They are more inward-focused on matters of getting through the day—dressing, bathing, preparing meals—which somehow occupies a great deal of their time.

People who are in the business of encouraging older people to be more assertive suggest that these people often have the wrong priorities. One Gray Panther activist wrote about a terrible nursing home, later closed by the state, in which the complaints received were mostly about the small portions of desserts and the movies shown in the lounge, while at that very time, some patients were being tied to their beds and physically abused by a hostile staff.

The encouraging news is that older people can be very effective complainers, and their very age can be a factor in their success, because who wants to offend someone's grandmother? Saul Alinsky, himself a "senior citizen" at the time, had considerable success in Chicago training people to be more effective complainers, in a most practical way. "It is all well and good," he suggested, "to generate another thousand letters to Washington protesting Medicare cuts, but the important complaining, and the opportunities for success, are right here in the neighborhood: meals on wheels for the elderly, stop signs installed at dangerous intersections, enhanced funding for senior drop-in centers, and so forth."

ARE COMPLAINERS IN OTHER COUNTRIES DIFFERENT FROM AMERICANS?

In a word, yes, for reasons that range from the basic politeness of the English to the Norwegians' wish to avoid an unpleasant situation. Of course, one cannot define an entire nation with a simple set of qualities or virtues ("Americans tend to be loud, pushy, and shallow"), but various researchers have found some interesting differences in the way people complain (or don't) in various cultures.

Geert Hofstede analyzed questionnaires filled out by over 100,000 IBM employees living in fifty-three different cultures, and found the biggest differences in these four qualities:

- Individualism. Some cultures are much more individualistic, in which people act on their own (the United States is a case in point), while others, many of them in Asia, are more collective, and complaining behavior would only be done as a group effort, or with group approval.

- Sex differences. There are cultures (more than a few in Latin America, less than a few in Scandinavia) where being a male means one is much more likely to be assertive, aggressive, competitive, self-reliant, and oriented to things and money. Females in such places manifest less of these qualities and tend to be more people-oriented.

- Power and prestige. In some cultures, especially but not limited to some African countries, consumers tend to feel that they are in a weak position when treated badly by those they see as having more prestige and power: businesses, government officials. When there is a problem in faulty goods and services, they shrug their shoulders, and say that is just a fact of life.

- Attitude toward uncertainty. There are places where there is much resistance to change and much fear of taking risks, because it is somehow more comfortable to keep the status quo, even if there are problems, than take the chance of making changes or creating possible conflict. Some cultures in the Middle East and Asia have common concerns in such matters.

Norway: "I'm not happy, but, hey, that's OK."

When a home shopping channel came to Norway a few years ago, there was a fair amount of unhappiness with the quality of the products, the prices, and the delivery time. But the vast majority of dissatisfied Norwegians didn't complain. Why? Half of them said it was just too much bother; a quarter felt that nothing would happen anyway, and it is unpleasant to have to complain, so why waste the time. Many of the rest blamed themselves for being stupid or felt that they had taken a risk in buying, and if it wasn't satisfactory, well, that's life. When asked if they would use the television shopping channel again, 90 percent of the satisfied customers said yes and, inexplicably, more than half of the dissatisfied ones also said yes. Something to do during those long, dark winters, perhaps.

China: "If I complain, you'll think less of me, so I won't."

Two Washington academics studied the complaining behaviors of Chinese and American students at their university. They concluded that the Chinese have a certain sense of fatalism, that others have more control over their destiny than they do, and thus complaining is often inappropriate. A study of consumers at the University of Hong Kong found that most dissatisfied buyers don't complain because of "losing face" when required to criticize another, especially in a face-to-face setting. This finding applied to both men and women, but only the men were likely to stop buying the product or using the service in question.

Tanzania: "If my neighbors complain, then so will I."

A Tanzanian researcher discovered that in this African nation, the best predictor of complaining behavior was not age or wealth or sex or job but, simply, where a person lived. For instance, people living in poorer neighborhoods did not complain much, but equally poor people who happened to live in a better neighborhood complained a good deal more. They learned complaining skills, and they had come to appreciate that complaining is an appropriate behavior, that one should not accept injustices just because one is poorer.

Korea: "We village people have nothing to complain about, but, oh, when Mr. Park moved to Seoul, how he changed."

A Korean dissertation author, writing on consumer behavior, characterized his countrymen and -women as conservative, cautious buyers, sophisticated but not innovative, and loyal to brands and to certain stores and services. This is especially true in the smaller towns and villages, where complaining is rare. But in the cities, people have grown just a little more aggressive about complaining, even though their cautious buying behavior often means they have less to complain about.

WHAT DOES THIS ALL MEAN?

As we have known all along, we do not live in a great homogeneous melting pot of a global village. We are all individualists, some of us much more subject to (or victims of) the vagaries of our upbringing, the pressures of our society, and the expectations of our peers. The good news, for those of us who think complaining is an important thing to do, is that there is no "noncomplaining gene," no innate biological reason why people do not or cannot complain.

Even though there are many older people, poorer people, less educated people, timid people, Norwegian people, and so on, who don't complain, there are always distinct subsets of these groups who are regular and effective complainers. No one is required to complain by family, peers, employers, or the government. But equally so, it is clear that one cannot get away with an excuse such as "I'm too old to do that" or "I'm too poor" or "I'm too Norwegian."

We may not live in a global village, but no one, not the Chinese student nor the Norwegian housewife nor the Tanzanian merchant nor the Chicago homeowner, needs to end up in that category earlier identified as "dopes." Every one of us has access at least to pen and paper or the telephone, as well as the ability to tell others about a problem and to communicate with the causer of the problem, if only by "sending a message" by avoiding that product or service in the future. For whatever reason, you may choose to be a noncomplainer or a nonconsumerist, or both, but a person has no valid reason to choose to be a dope.

WHY MAYA ANGELOU DOESN'T COMPLAIN

Maya Angelou wrote an eloquent essay for the *Ladies Home Journal* in 1994, on why she does not complain. She tells the story of her grandmother who raised her in Stamps, Arkansas. People came into the grandmother's store full of complaints about the heat, the humidity, the plowing, whatever, and her grandmother said:

> Sister, did you hear what Brother So and So or Sister Much
> to Do complained about? You heard that? ...Sister, there are
> people who went to sleep all over the world last night, poor
> and rich and white and black, but they will never wake again.

Sister, those who expected to rise did not, their beds became their cooling boards and their blankets became their winding sheets. And those dead folks would give anything, anything at all for just five minutes of this weather or ten minutes of that plowing that person was grumbling about.

So you watch yourself about complaining, Sister. What you're supposed to do when you don't like a thing is change it.

If you can't change it, change the way you think about it.

Don't complain.

CHAPTER 3

Why People Complain (and Why They Don't)

A MAN WHOSE NAME I shall mercifully withhold earned a Ph.D. from a large southern university for a dissertation whose sole conclusion was that "people are more likely to complain when they are dissatisfied." Thanks a lot, Doc. There is, needless to say, a lot more to this matter of complaining than just that. Indeed, researchers in departments of business, psychology, sociology, political science, and communication research have been looking at this phenomenon for several decades. Here are the main reasons people complain, followed by some of the reasons they don't.

REASONS WHY PEOPLE COMPLAIN

"My expectations were not met."

For many people, the thing that is important is not just what happened, but how the thing that happened compared with what they thought was going to happen. If you buy a $3 watch at the drug store, your expectations about performance are quite different than they would be for the $300 watch from the department store or the $3,000 watch from Tiffany's. Thus two people could buy the identical product or service, and have the identical problem, and respond very differently. One would say, "What the heck; I didn't expect much from a chiropractor anyway," while the other would go into high complaint gear, because she fully expected her treatment to relieve her back pain promptly.

Diane Halstead at the University of Kentucky looked at 404 people nationwide who had bought the same brand of carpet. About half of them had complained to the company; the other half had not. Even though the carpet was identical in all cases, the complainers were people whose expectations were not met: the carpet was not as plush as they expected; it was wearing out faster; or it was not as stain resistant.

Veronica Liljander interviewed several hundred people who either were or were not happy about one of three major restaurant chains. The likelihood of complaining related closely to their expectations and how well they were met. The most important expectation, by far, was the quality of service. Did the service meet their expectations? None of the other factors examined seemed to have anything to do with the predisposition to complain: waiting time, time for food to come, smells, decor, the quality of customers, cleanliness, restrooms, menu variation, appearance of food, portion size, price, noisiness, background music, furniture, or even, surprisingly, the taste of the food.

❖ ❖ ❖ ❖ ❖ ❖ ❖ ❖ ❖ ❖ ❖

CASE STUDY

The case of the man who couldn't do math

Robert K., an Ohio man, was considering a correspondence course in electronics from Bell & Howell Schools, but he was concerned that he didn't have good enough math skills to handle it. The salesman reassured him, and he went ahead and bought it. After the first few lessons, it was very clear to Robert that his expectations were not met; he could not handle the math, so he stopped making his installment payments. The school dunned him for its payments. Eventually a small claims judge determined that Robert's expectations were based on having been misled by the salesman, and so not only did he not have to make further payment, he was entitled to a full refund.

◆ ◆ ◆ ◆ ◆ ◆ ◆ ◆ ◆ ◆ ◆ ◆

"This is very important to me."

People are much more likely to complain when there is a problem with something that is really important to them. That much is easy to say, but there is little consistency, and often little logic, in determining which things are important. Often, importance is a situational matter. If you get six shirts back from the laundry and one has a rip, no big deal. But if you go to your one and only clean shirt, the one you've been saving for the concert this evening, and find that it has a rip down the front, there's going to be a major complaint.

"$2 a pill is OK, but only if it works."

Two Ohio State researchers surveyed hundreds of customers of pharmacies in twenty-one cities in the Midwest. While they found almost equal levels of dissatisfaction with the cost of drugs and with their effectiveness, it was the case that the people who were unhappy with the cost almost never complained, while those concerned about the effectiveness of the drugs complained a good deal.

"This is really important. My clown doesn't blow bubbles."

Many of the people who complained to a television shopping channel took pains to explain why something was really important to them, even though someone else might think it trivial. "You may not understand why I am so upset that my bubble-blowing clown doesn't work. I know it only cost $14.95, but it was going to be a birthday present for my dear nephew Willie, but I can't give him something that doesn't work." More than two-thirds of the complaints received dealt with products that didn't work as promised or, often, didn't work at all. Seven percent of the complaints dealt with the cost: once people had the product in hand, they didn't feel they had good value for money; 3 percent dealt with slow delivery or nondelivery.

"Let me tell you what I found in the chef's surprise."

A State University of New York graduate student collected data on complaining behavior among his fellow graduate students with regard to dining in the school cafeteria. While attitude toward complaining in general, and knowledge of how to complain were relevant factors, the big one was the intensity of their feelings. Some people discover a mystery object in their stew and consider that par for the course in a school cafeteria, while others are deeply offended, distressed, or outraged, and launch a complaint.

The cost-benefit model of complaining

"If my time is worth $12 an hour..."

Complaining can be a costly activity in terms of time, money, and other factors. A full-fledged complaint effort might involve time off from work, travel, telephone calls, postage, and paying for third-party advice and professional help. If the main reason for complaining is reimbursement, not revenge, personal satisfaction, or other factors, then it makes sense for some people to sit down for a few minutes with calculator in hand, and treat the launching of a complaint as a small business venture. What is it likely to cost, and what am I likely to get?

Complaining to bolster one's ego

One subset of complainers are those people who feel a need to let the world, or a small portion thereof, know how important they are, and that is why it is especially reprehensible that this particular product or service was not acceptable. In restaurants and in theater lines, such people have been known to say, "Do you know who I am?" In sending forth their complaints, they make clear who they are.

A psychologist looking at this phenomenon suggests that some of these people may have fragile egos beneath their blustery veneer and be basically insecure when writing to a giant corporation. As Henry Fairlie writes, "Abuse is the simplest way of putting yourself on someone's level....Scratch an Englishman and you will find a lord....Scratch a [complaint] letter and become a lord."

For some of these complainers, there is also a vicarious sense of power: "I am writing a letter which is actually going to be read by Senator Such-and-such, or by the president of General Motors." These are often the people who get back an autotyped machine-signed form letter from the senator, which they have framed and hang on the wall.

Complaining as a hobby, a game, or a career

Some people really enjoy the process of complaining. They justify whatever reasonable time and money it takes because they're having fun. There's nothing wrong with this, as long as the complaints are valid. Some people, like "Lazlo Toth," the alter ego of comedian Don Novello, also do well by publishing books of their clever complaint letters and the responses received.

Complaining as a way to get rich

There are more than a few "urban legends" about people who earn a handsome income by writing endless numbers of complaint letters and receiving carloads of free samples, free trips, and cash payoffs to keep them from suing. Their hero is a man named Ralph Charrell, who, in 1973, published a book called *How I Turn Ordinary Complaints into Thousands of Dollars*. Charrell specialized in hiring actors instead of lawyers to act on his behalf: everything from "supercilious pinstriped Englishmen to shrill overbearing dwarfs." Perhaps there is money to be made in these borderline ethical ways, but clearly not for long. Charrell's book has long been out of print. Then, of course, it could take only one successful mega-complaint to retire for life. Consider, for instance, the matter of the woman who complained that a minor cable car accident in San Francisco turned her into a nymphomaniac and graciously accepted a million-dollar-plus settlement from the San Francisco Municipal Railway Company.

Poison pen therapy

Paddy Calistro of the *Los Angeles Times* captures the spirit: When you have been wronged,

> Your fury knows no bounds. You resolve to take action.
> You're going to write a letter. In a very few minutes, pen in
> hand, you reconstruct the crime, get mad all over again,
> shout a few deletable expletives and vent your frustrations
> as you demand satisfactory reparation. You seal the enve-
> lope, lick the stamp and feel better as you drop it in the
> mailbox. But does that letter get results? Or was your
> [32]-cent exercise merely an economical substitute for a
> visit to the psychiatrist?

Psychiatrists believe there is substantial benefit in cathartic release of repressed material. The technique is used primarily for the cure of a neurotic disposition. Many patients derive much help simply by unburdening themselves.

There is a subset of psychoanalytic literature in which catharsis or release is achieved by writing sufficiently vicious complaint letters. This area has been called autoanalysis, graphocatharsis, semantic therapy, and, perhaps most graphically, by John Watkins, writing in the *American Journal of Psychotherapy,* poison pen therapy.

CASE STUDY

◆ ◆ ◆ ◆ ◆ ◆ ◆ ◆ ◆ ◆ ◆

The case of Mayor Daley and the 1,000 black balloons

When the first Mayor Daley ruled Chicagoland, one of his many abuses of power was to appoint his elderly family obstetrician as the well-paid medical advisor to the Air Pollution Control Board. Dozens of complaint letters from outraged citizens were easily ignored, and the local media seemed to have no interest in this matter. The opponents' opportunity came on Earth Day, when the mayor arranged for 100 little girls in white dresses to release 100 white balloons into the air, to celebrate the success of Chicago's clean air program. As the moment arrived, with TV cameras rolling, reporters present, and the 100 large white balloons rising into the air, several hundred anti-Daley volunteers stepped out of doorways, cars, and alleys, and released 1,000 larger black balloons, each with a tag attached explaining what the mayor had done. In the furor that followed this, the mayor made a more reasonable appointment to the pollution board.

◆ ◆ ◆ ◆ ◆ ◆ ◆ ◆ ◆ ◆ ◆

WHY PEOPLE DON'T COMPLAIN

Some people complain often or occasionally, but most people complain seldom or never. In one large survey of the reasons people don't complain, nearly half said it was just too time-consuming, a quarter felt that nothing would ever come of it anyway, while smaller percentages found the act of complaining personally unpleasant; they didn't know how or where to complain, they felt their time was too valuable to waste on such things, they believed they had only themselves to blame for the problem, or they believed the dollar amount was too small or the problem was otherwise too trivial to bother about.

"It's my own fault."

Quite often, people manage to put all the blame one themselves, saying, for instance: I never should have bought it; I should have known better; I should have listened to my mother; I am such a sucker for a smooth sales pitch; I should have looked it up in *Consumer Reports*; I could kick myself. And so on.

Watkins had his neurotic patients write letters to persons, groups, or organizations with whom they had a serious complaint. "The general release value appears to be in proportion to the viciousness of the attack and the adequacy with which the patient expresses himself emotionally."

Complaining and personality

"I am not a crank. I am not a crank."

Marjorie Wall at the University of Guelph writes persuasively that the likelihood of complaining is really not related to dissatisfaction with a product or service, but is, instead, dependent on the personal characteristics of the person. People with the sort of personality that makes them more likely to complain might be characterized as self-confident, assertive, likely to blame others for problems, have few fears that complaining will lead to hassles, and do not worry about being stigmatized as a crank.

There may also be some "right brain, left brain" factors at work here. One doctoral dissertation from Texas Tech University suggests that right-brain people—the ones who tend to be more intuitive and creative—are likely only to complain about problems that are clear, coherent, basic, and straightforward, such as the quality of a food product or the result of a car repair. The more analytical, academic, scientific left-brain people are more likely to complain about cerebral matters, such as performance by a stockbroker or treatment by a physician.

Could the complaint conceivably have an effect?

"Dear General Motors: please stop making gasoline-powered cars."

Researchers such as Jeffrey Blodgett at the University of Mississippi suggest that even the least sophisticated or the most unrealistic would-be complainer takes into account, at some level, whether the complaint has a snowball's chance in hell of succeeding. That is, of course, a matter of opinion. Many people explain their noncomplaining behavior by saying, "You can't fight city hall." And others have fought city hall very successfully.

♦ ♦ ♦ ♦ ♦ ♦ ♦ ♦ ♦ ♦ ♦

The case of the leaking stove and the shy consumer who nearly died

A St. Louis woman bought a gas range. She detected a nauseating odor from the oven, but wondered if she was just too sensitive. She did call her dealer, who suggested she was overly sensitive, and if there was a small problem, it would "burn itself out." The woman spent many hours in her backyard to avoid the stove odor. She didn't mention this to her friends, for fear they would think less of her. When things didn't improve, and her health seemed to be suffering, she phoned the Consumer Product Safety Commission, which urged her to call the company and be firm. Finally her faulty oven was fixed.

♦ ♦ ♦ ♦ ♦ ♦ ♦ ♦ ♦ ♦ ♦ ♦

"Keep your damn jack."

There is a shaggy dog story having to do with the traveling salesman who has a flat tire on a remote country road and finds he has no jack. As he trudges back to a farmhouse he spotted earlier, he finds himself thinking that the farmer probably has a lovely young daughter, and he'll be invited to stay the night, and he'll fall in love with her, and they'll get married, but she won't like life in the city, and she'll fool around with other men and make his life miserable, and on and on. When the kindly old farmer opens his door, the salesman's first words are "Keep your damn jack."

So it is that many would-be complainers work through the whole scenario in their mind, of how unpleasant or complicated the complaint will be, or how the company will fight back, or how their friends will think less of them, or how much money it will cost, so they do nothing because they believe they already know what will happen if they do something. One is reminded of the lovely slogan once used by the Guinness Stout people of Ireland: "I've never tried it because I don't like it."

"I don't know how to complain, and I'd rather not admit that."

Self-explanatory. An awful lot of people just don't know how or where to begin, and they are too shy or embarrassed to admit this, or they don't even know whom to admit it to. I can only hope some of these will be reading the "plain brown wrapper" edition of this book in the privacy of their homes.

"I'd like to complain, but I simply can't."

Hard as it is for us dyed-in-the-wool frequent complainers to remember, there are many people who are familiar with the concept of complaining, but simply do not have the wherewithal to do so. They don't have the time, or the money, or the library access. They feel their English is not good enough or their handwriting clear enough. Their physical or mental health is not up to the task. They can't type.

"I'm not that sort of person"

There is a whole subset of people who are very much aware of the complaining process, but they simply do not see themselves as the sort of person who does that sort of thing. Sometimes it is a personality thing; sometimes it is a skepticism about whether the process really can work; sometimes it is a wish to avoid confrontations or hassles. But what many of these people don't realize is that they do complain in a powerful way, since a common behavior for such folks is the "silent exit" followed by a long period of not only avoiding the product or service in question, but also telling friends, family, and others about the bad experience.

"I should make a federal case over one penny?"

CASE STUDY   **Well, if you are sufficiently motivated, why not?**
The case of the million-dollar federal case over one penny

Back in the days when coffee cost a dime a cup, a man sat down in a diner in a state that had a 4 percent sales tax. When he was charged a dime plus one penny in tax, he complained that 4 percent of ten cents was less than half a penny, and therefore he should not pay any tax. The implications of charging tax on small purchases, and which way to round off the amounts, had multi-million dollar implications reaching to the very core of our taxation system, and before that matter was resolved in the federal courts, huge sums had been expended on legal costs, all for the sake of a penny.

QUOTH THE MAVEN: THE TWO-STEP COMPLAINT

In the 1950s, Paul Lazarsfeld at Columbia University made a startling discovery about the way in which people make up their minds to act, whether to buy, to sell, or to complain. His breakthrough was the finding that most people depend on the opinion of another person, rather than on direct information about the product or service in question. These key people consider the facts, read the ads, study the literature, talk to companies, and then pass their wisdom along to others. These so-called "mavens" (influential middlemen and middlewomen) often take the role of urging, encouraging, or helping their "flock" to register complaints.

Mavens are not necessarily people of great stature or important titles. Sometimes they are "the lady at the candy store" or "that guy in the locker room at the club" or "my hairdresser," rather than "my boss" or "my doctor" or "my senator."

Are mavens different from ordinary folk with regard to their complaining behavior? Indeed they are. In a research paper called *Consumer Complaint Behaviors of Market Mavens,* Mark Slama and his colleagues confirmed Lazarfeld's basic finding that a great many buying decisions, both of products and services, are made with the advice of a maven. It can be as direct as a golf pro maven saying, "Hey, I hear that new Chevy is really something." It can be as indirect as a garden club member who conducts a transplanting demonstration using a particular brand of fertilizer.

Seeking out mavens may be a good way for businesses, from restaurants to psychiatrists, to get new clients, since the research of Feick and Price determined that 46 percent of shoppers knew a maven, and 57 percent of these considered the maven's views crucial in making a purchase decision. But there is a risk here, since research shows a much greater tendency on the part of mavens to engage in both private and third-party complaint behaviors.

How do we know this? In one research project, self-identified and group-identified mavens, along with nonmavens, were told a story about a situation in which someone bought a new jacket at a store. In normal use, the jacket ripped, and the store would do nothing about it, claiming it was the fault of the buyer.

In this study, mavens were more likely than nonmavens to

1. tell their friends what happened

2. convince their friends not to shop at that store

3. report what happened to a consumer agency in order to protect others

4. write to the local newspaper

5. take formal action in the courts or with arbitration

The only result that turned out to be the same for both mavens and nonmavens was that both groups expressed a determination not to shop at that store again, and in their unwillingness to ask a third party to intervene. The latter, presumably, is for two quite different reasons. The mavens don't need a third party because they are a third party. And the nonmavens may well be too shy or intimidated to take such a action.

It isn't easy to set up a real-world research situation in which the role of the maven can be measured, so such things are examined in simulated circumstances. In one study attempting to address this matter, experimental subjects were asked to read a story about a complaint-producing situation, in which "you are having a very busy day at the office, and were really looking forward to a short lunch break at a nearby busy restaurant. After a short wait, the order was taken, but when it came, it was the wrong sandwich, one you could not eat."

Four different versions of this story were told to different subjects from this point on. In one, your mature friend, whom you respect, urged you to complain to the waiter, the manager, or the restaurant owner. In the second, the friend advised not complaining. In the third, the friend said nothing, and in the fourth, there was no friend—you were at the restaurant alone. What do you do?

The clear response in this situation with simulated mavens was that the people who were urged to complain told researchers that they would be likely to do so, while those whose virtual maven was silent or advised against complaining were much less likely to do so. The people dining alone were somewhere in between.

• • • • • • • • • • • •

The case of Buick and the six-foot-tall bright yellow maven

Bill F. of Los Angeles invested $21,000 in a Buick from his local dealer. It was, by Bill's account, a real lemon, although not in the strict definition of California's "lemon law," which states that the same thing must go wrong four times for legal lemonhood. With Bill's car, it was one thing after another, once, twice, three times, but never four. The dealer was, of course, happy to keep repairing the car under warranty, but that was not good enough for Bill. He asked for his full payment back, plus an additional sum for his own expenses and irritation. The dealer, needless to say, refused. Bill was not a complainer by nature, so he turned to his friend Phil for advice, and soon after, the six-foot-tall lemon was born.

Every day, Phil bedecked himself in a bright yellow shirt and pants and yellow hard hat with green plastic leaves affixed. He politely walked back and forth in front of the dealership. He carefully and correctly did not attack either the dealer or Buick, but simply carried a sign saying that before anyone bought from this dealer, they might wish to hear his friend Bill's story.

Phil and Bill were in the catbird seat because the dealer had no idea how long this street theater would continue: an hour, a day, a month, forever? Only Phil knew, and he wasn't talking. And so, with a busy holiday weekend looming, the dealer offered a settlement: he would buy the car back for $22,000, $1,000 more than Bill had paid, if only the big yellow maven would pack up his lemon suit and go home. The deal was done.

• • • • • • • • • • • •

Pressure groups: complaints inspired by group action

A Gallup poll once determined that more than one-third of all complaint letters to politicians and to the mass media were written by someone who was asked to do so by a pressure group. They would not have written otherwise, they said. This is a hard thing to study, since many people who write at another's behest don't want to admit that they have done so. Indeed, they are often asked not to reveal this, so that the complaint letters will be seen (the pressure groups hope) as a spontaneous outpouring of individual opinion.

50,000 letters in the president's lap by Thursday

"Landing" a certain number of complaint letters in Washington within seventy-two hours seems to be an important criterion for the mail-lobbying power of a pressure group.

Many political action groups, whether related to matters of peace, civil rights, abortion, or Medicare, claim that in seventy-two hours they can "land 50,000 letters in the President's lap" in support of their cause. At least. An article in *Harper's* says that spokesmen for the National Rifle Association "claim privately that they can flood Congress with half a million pieces of mail in seventy-two hours."

How do pressure groups regard complaint letters?

One major study, by Lester Milbrath, found that big business and farm groups rank complaint letters very high as a useful tool, while educational groups and foreign government pressure groups rank them very low. "This suggests," Milbrath concludes, "that organizations with a mass membership enabling them to turn out thousands of [complaint] letters are more likely to believe that the tactic is effective."

But how effective is the tactic?

The very clear answer from all available research is that to the extent mail is identifiable as coming from a group, its value is negligible. In the words of one senator, "If the deluges of 'inspired' mail have any effect, it is to push me the other way."

Yet, despite general acceptance of the position that group action is unlikely to work, it is done all the time. One study found that about 25 percent of the thousands of letters received each week by the average member of Congress comes from pressure groups or as the result of a letter-writing campaign.

On individual issues, the number may be much higher. Another study found that when a bill that would have regulated cigarette advertising was being considered, 40 percent of the mail on that issue came from or was orchestrated by four tobacco companies who had much at stake in that issue.

The only thing less effective than a letter-writing campaign is a petition.

As Senator Estes Kefauver once wrote, "no one reads them.... Regardless of length or weight, petitions are of little value as a persuasive force [because] legislators know it is possible to get many people to sign a petition for almost any cause, worthy or not." In an experiment done in Portland, Oregon, people on street corners were asked to sign a petition to abolish "ten odious laws" (which were not identified as the Bill of Rights). More than half the people signed it.

Why, then, do people organize complaint-writing campaigns? The only logical answers can be that they do not know how ineffective they are and/or that it gives them and their constituents something to do—a feeling that at least they are doing *something*.

Harry and Bonaro Overstreet, writing about extremist behaviors, suggest that the purpose of many of the complaint behaviors are orchestrated simply to occupy people's time and minds: to give them busy work and an "exalted position."

Indeed, in Robert Welch's secret "Blue Book," the operating manual of his ultraconservative John Birch Society, he wrote that "letter-writing campaigns...would give the members of our local chapters and volunteer groups just one more activity, one more thing to do, by which they knew they were accomplishing something and being effective for the cause."

The right wing (and very likely the left, too) believes, along with Welch, that they should undertake "letter-writing of a different order of planned continuity and volume than anything attempted before...letter-writing of the kind that builds opinion exactly the way single grains of sand build a whole barricade...."

There are two interesting factors to look at here: how successful are the organizers of a complaint letter campaign in getting their constituents to write, and then how effective are those letters when they land at their destination?

In the course of my own doctoral research, I looked closely at a variety of complaint-letter-writing campaigns, in which one or more pressure groups had urged its members and supporters to write complaint letters to a specific company or organization. I then wrote to the same "targets" to ask, in effect, what happened.

Most of them responded by giving helpful information. One company (CBS) said they did not keep any record of their mail, and one (UniRoyal) said the information was available, but they chose not to share it with the likes of me. Here are five of the many stories.

◆ ◆ ◆ ◆ ◆ ◆ ◆ ◆ ◆ ◆ ◆

U.S. Chamber of Commerce: Communist front?

After a long period of strong anti-Communist sentiments, the U.S. Chamber of Commerce announced a policy change, suggesting that it might be all right to do business with Russia, China, and other such nations after all. Outraged patriotic groups such as the American Legion and the DAR were encouraged to flood the Chamber with complaints about this pro-Communist stance. During the duration of the letter-writing campaign, the Chamber logged in 1,611 cards and letters. After eliminating letters on other matters and support letters, about 1,500 items remained. "Obviously," the Chamber says, "it is not possible to know what caused [them] to be written, but the phraseology in most of them was quite similar."

◆ ◆ ◆ ◆ ◆ ◆ ◆ ◆ ◆ ◆ ◆

CASE STUDIES

"Don't fly that dreaded flag."

Chandler Pavilion, the Los Angeles Music Center, decided to fly the United Nations flag over the building, along with the American flag. Anti-UN forces were urged to write to the Chandler family and a dozen other people associated with the Center. A secretary to the Chandler family reported that "several thousand" pieces of mail were received, but, because they "all appeared to be form letters," no attention was paid to them.

◆ ◆ ◆ ◆ ◆ ◆ ◆ ◆ ◆ ◆ ◆

The un-American opera

People were encouraged to complain to the Metropolitan Opera when they announced their fall schedule would include Blitzstein's opera about Sacco and Vanzetti, which was perceived as an unpatriotic and anti-American opera. The Met didn't even notice that such a campaign had been launched.

◆ ◆ ◆ ◆ ◆ ◆ ◆ ◆ ◆ ◆ ◆

"Are the Boy Scouts going soft, too?"

The Boy Scouts of America scheduled the outspoken president of the National Council of Churches to speak at their national Jamboree. After a complaint-letter drive was launched with the goal of getting the Scouts to cancel the speech, the Scouts noted a few letters of objection, but nothing persuasive enough for them even to discuss, much less act on.

◆ ◆ ◆ ◆ ◆ ◆ ◆ ◆ ◆ ◆ ◆ ◆

CASE STUDIES

"United Nations Day is a terrible idea."

McDonnell Aircraft of St. Louis declared UN Day a company holiday. Several anti-UN groups launched a complaint campaign, urging people to send either a sarcastic postcard or a serious letter to let McDonnell know what they thought of this terrible idea. When I asked them, the reply was that about 1,000 postcards and letters were received over a three-month period. The sample they showed me was a standard preprinted one sold for a nickel each by the John Birch Society.

◆ ◆ ◆ ◆ ◆ ◆ ◆ ◆ ◆ ◆ ◆ ◆

What do we learn from these stories?

Remember the four factors that determine the response to a complaint: scope (is it a big deal?), commitment to the idea, quality of complaints, and quantity of complaints.

The outcome of these attempts to change the behavior of a company or organization perfectly fit the four factors. If the organization's commitment to an idea is strong, and if the idea is a big deal, then all the complaints on earth won't change their mind. And if the commitment is more modest, and the scope is smaller, then the quality of the complaints far overshadows the quantity.

Honesty: a relevant concept (especially if someone asks)

If one is presenting oneself as a certain kind of pressure group, there is a real temptation to fudge a bit on both the size of the group and the "important" people behind it because of the assumption that no one will check up on things. And generally they don't. But when they do, the facts do not always jibe with the claims. When there was an ongoing debate about whether China should be admitted to the United Nations, one of the pressure groups opposing admission called itself the Committee of One Million Against the Admission of China to the UN. Their literature listed 55 senators and 295 representatives as their supporters. When the *Charleston Gazette* received their complaints, they decided to check on the claims. Of the elected officials they contacted, only 8 percent said they had been consulted about the use of their name, and only 12 percent supported the position of the "Committee of One Million."

Is there any way to produce a secret mass complaint?

Is it really possible to devise a mass complaining campaign that doesn't look like one? Success and fortune may await the person who devises such a technology. Or perhaps they already have, since how would we know, if they have truly done it well? I'm a little uneasy addressing this matter, because if there is a solution, it inevitably will be used to complain about things I believe in. Ah, well. Such a solution would have to address these four matters:

1. The letters would have to look different from one another.

2. The content would have to be different.

3. They would have to come from a wide geographical area.

4. They would need not to flood in all at the same time.

But why bother, when the evidence is clear that one or two sincere statements can have more effect than a million letters? Compare the simple pleas of Sarah Brady with the avalanche of mail inspired by the National Rifle Association's opposition to the Brady Bill.

What People Complain About

ESSENTIALLY THERE ARE TWO MAJOR kinds of things to complain about: products and services. Very often, the first leads directly to the second: the new television is no good, *and* the repair service gave me a hassle over the warranty, and *then* they fixed it wrong three times in a row.

There's a real problem in trying to get accurate information about this sort of thing, in part because the vast majority of people don't complain, and in part because it is hard to define exactly what a complaint is: a phone call or a letter to the store; a direct complaint to the Better Business Bureau or other third-party agency; or just grousing to one's friends and family or walking around with some sense that things just aren't right.

Some kinds of problems are more likely to trigger an immediate complaint. If the washing machine is gushing water onto the floor, you are more likely to register a complaint than if the dishwasher doesn't get things quite as clean as you had expected.

One newspaper action line reports that the most common complaint they get, by far, is failure to receive mail-order items with appropriate speed. Defective products were a distant second, and home improvements (roofers, contractors, etc.) barely made the top ten.

But when the Better Business Bureau tabulated 250,000 complaints they received over a recent time period, retail sales topped the list, with home improvements a close second. At the BBB, the top four complaint categories (service firms and car repair were numbers three and four) accounted for more than half of all complaints, while the remaining twenty categories (mail-order sales to contests and sweepstakes) accounted for the other half.

How do we explain these differences? Clearly, people are more likely to complain about things that are more expensive, or more important to them, or both. A three dollar "spill proof" commuter coffee mug that spills just isn't worth the time, effort, and letter or phone call for most people; they just toss it out. But the three dollar defective roll of film that means we'll never have that picture of little Alexa taking her first steps—well, that clearly is worth complaining about.

From a variety of sources, including university research projects and lists kept by state and local consumer affairs agencies, I have put together these lists of those services and products that we complain about the most, and the least.

THE TOP TWENTY
MOST-COMPLAINED-ABOUT SERVICES

- Employment agencies (56 percent of people had complained)
- Computer dating (54 percent)
- Auto repair (49 percent)
- Nursing and rest homes (43 percent)
- Trains (41 percent)
- Architects (40 percent)
- Moving and storage (40 percent)
- Apartment rental (39 percent)
- Appliance repair (38 percent)
- Mail-order firms (34 percent)
- TV, radio, stereo repair (31 percent)
- Postal service (31 percent)
- Furniture and appliance rental (30 percent)
- Remodeling, decorating, landscaping (30 percent)
- Water softening (28 percent)
- Roofing, siding, painting (28 percent)
- Cable TV (27 percent)
- Plumbing, home repair, carpentry (25 percent)
- Taxis (25 percent)
- Doctors, nurses in hospitals (24 percent)

THE LEAST-COMPLAINED-ABOUT SERVICES

- Doctors, nurses in their office (19 percent of people had complained)
- Do-it-yourself laundry, dry cleaning (17 percent)
- Barbers, beauty shops (16 percent)
- Health insurance (16 percent)
- Stockbrokers (16 percent)
- Airlines (15 percent)
- Maid service (15 percent)
- Group insurance plans (15 percent)
- Auto insurance (14 percent)
- Parcel delivery (13 percent)
- Homeowner/renter insurance (13 percent)
- Septic tank service (13 percent)
- Tax preparers (12 percent)
- Life insurance (11 percent)
- Fire, theft insurance (10 percent)
- Water company (10 percent)
- Propane, fuel oil (9 percent)
- Credit unions (9 percent)
- Funeral homes (8 percent)
- Veterinarians (8 percent)

It is probably relevant to note that the two categories with the least percentage of complaints, funeral homes and veterinarians, are those whose clients are unable to complain.

THE PRODUCTS WE ARE MOST LIKELY TO COMPLAIN ABOUT

- Used cars (about 40 percent of people have complaints)
- Computers (36 percent)
- Cordless telephones (27 percent)
- Refrigerators with ice makers and dispensers (24 percent)
- Videocassette recorders (22 percent)
- Stereos (19 percent)
- New cars (18 percent)
- Washing machines (17 percent)
- Dishwashers (14 percent)
- Lawn mowers (13 percent)

THE PRODUCTS WE ARE LEAST LIKELY
TO COMPLAIN ABOUT

- Small televisions (6 percent are unhappy enough to complain)
- Food processors (6 percent)
- CD players (5 percent)
- Vacuum cleaners (5 percent)
- Coffee makers (4 percent)
- Air conditioners (4 percent)
- Irons (3 percent)
- Toasters (3 percent)
- Slow cookers (2 percent)
- Radios (1 percent)

"WAITER, I'D LIKE ANOTHER WAITER."
COMPLAINTS ABOUT SERVICE IN RESTAURANTS

Mass psychologist Barry Elkin points out: going to a restaurant is truly an act of faith. Putting your fate, your whole gastrointestinal system in some stranger's hands. And sometimes those hands are not so kind.

According to a report in the *Wall Street Journal,* not only are people growing more and more unhappy over the service in restaurants, but they are complaining about it more, often to the point of asking for a different waiter, and, if they don't get one, getting up and leaving. The four main kinds of complaints are that the waiter or waitress is

- Inept. Spilling food on people is a minor problem, and so is an incorrectly added-up bill (although some people suspect this would be a bigger problem if more people took the time to check the addition and the items listed). The complaints mostly deal with waiters who get the order wrong; who don't remember who gets what ("All right, who's the red snapper?"), who are not familiar with the items on the menu, and who fail to provide separate checks when asked to do so.
- Surly or otherwise unpleasant.
- Too slow, which may be a problem with the kitchen, but the waiter is on the front line when the kitchen fails.
- Too friendly. Yes, there really are lots and lots of people who don't want their waiter to introduce himself, and generally behave as if he were your long-lost brother from Cincinnati.

And so they complain about that, as well as the policy of reciting the day's specials instead of writing them down, and the matter of the waiter stopping by every few minutes to ask, "How's everything here?"

Do patrons really have the right to complain? Should restaurants really provide a new waiter? Well of course they do and of course they should. Unless the only waiter is the owner or a close relative, there is always another option for the restaurant. You were not forced to go there, and surely there are other places in town. So you're in charge and have every right to complain and to have your complaint dealt with. Still, a survey by MasterCard International found that only 48 percent of diners thought it was all right to request or demand a different waiter, no matter how unhappy they were.

The National Restaurant Association says that customer satisfaction in table service (that means non-fast-food) restaurants has risen substantially in recent years and stands at 69 percent. To me, however, the importance of this number is that 31 percent of the people are *not* satisfied, and yet more than half of them fail to complain. Most restaurants would much rather have you complain than silently sit there suffering as your new friend Bruce or Jason or Sally is saying, "Now, I'd like to tell you about my desserts this evening," and then leave, never to return (or, worse still, leave and tell everyone what a dismal time you had last night at the Leaf, Loaf, and Ladle).

But does the restaurant patron have the right to complain?

Alison Arnett of the *Boston Globe* put these four questions to an executive of the prestigious Culinary Institute of America and got these clear answers:

1. Is it ungracious to complain in a restaurant? No.

2. Should you complain when you are unhappy or pick at the food and mention it later? Now! Diners have the obligation to speak up at the time, so things can be fixed.

3. Should you suffer in silence, and simply never go back to that restaurant? No! (And if you decide not to leave a tip, be sure to make clear that is your way of complaining, or they will just assume you are a cheapskate.)

4. If you don't like the dish, should you be required to pay? No, but only within reason. If you eat it all and *then* say you didn't like it, you might be expected to pay at least part of the bill.

THE UNFRIENDLY SKIES

Every month, the Department of Transportation publishes figures on the volume of complaints received about airlines and their service. The complaints are not categorized, either by their content or their severity, so "They didn't have my favorite brand of beer" counts just the same as "I was stuck in the bathroom for two hours."

In a typical month, between 1,000 and 2,000 complaints will be received. In order to compare figures for the larger and the smaller airlines, the complaints are tallied by the total number of passengers flown. An airline with 1,000 passengers and 100 complaints is obviously much worse than one with a million passengers and 100 complaints.

In one recent month, the airline with the worst complaint record (MarkAir) had a complaint ratio twenty-five times higher than the best airline (Aloha). Interestingly, however, even the worst airlines (MarkAir, Hawaiian, Continental, Carnival, American TransAir) did not have such terrible records: no more than one in 10,000 passengers complained. (Of course for Aloha, it was about one in 400,000 who complained.)

Another way of looking at this is that even on the worst airline, if you took 10,000 flights, on only one would you have a problem sufficient to cause you to complain to the Department of Transportation (DOT).

Needless to say, here, as in every other area, most people don't complain, at least to the DOT. How do we know? In part because *Consumer Reports* magazine recently published survey data from 120,000 readers. Of these readers, 14 percent of those who checked baggage (more than 17,000 people) had problems and 28 percent (33,000) felt the plane was "very crowded." Yet at most, only a few hundred of these complained to the DOT.

The best news about airline complaints is that they may work quite well. At least we know that the two airlines that produced the most complaints to the Department of Transportation over the past decade have both gone out of business. Perhaps if Eastern and Pan American had heeded more of those complaints, they'd still be around. It is gratifying to note, however, that sometimes complaining really does seem to work, even on such a grand scale as bringing two huge airlines to earth.

◆ ◆ ◆ ◆ ◆ ◆ ◆ ◆ ◆ ◆ ◆

CASE STUDY

The case of the black sticky goo in the luggage

A family of three arrived home at Kennedy airport in New York after midnight. When their luggage arrived, they saw that one large suitcase appeared to be drenched with a black gooey substance, perhaps oil. When the man brought the case over to the Piedmont Airlines office, he was made to feel that the problem was his fault: that it must have been caused by something in the suitcase. He assured them that it could be no such thing, and anyway, how was it that the goo was all over the outside as well. Finally, somewhat belligerently, they searched his suitcase, but all they found was personal clothes and belongings, all saturated with black goo.

By now the man in charge was slightly apologetic. But, he explained, he was a low-level night supervisor (it was nearly 2 A.M. by this time), so he asked that the evidence be left behind for the day people to deal with. The luggage was returned the next day, with the suggestion that he wash the clothes. There was no hint of what the substance was, or what it might do to his washing machine, much less an apology or a refund offer.

Operating entirely by phone, the traveler called the airline headquarters, remaining calm but insistent, working his way up the chain of command. Finally he heard those words every complainer loves to hear, whether said in apology or, in this case, in exasperation: "What do you want me to do?" His answer was clearly in mind: "I want you to replace the suitcase and all the clothes in it, and to repay me for having to stay at the airport until 2 A.M. with my family. And, for suffering abuse from your personnel, I want three round-trip tickets from New York to California."

The airline representative said they would take that under consideration and be in touch within a week. A few days later came a letter that did not apologize and did not admit any wrongdoing, and did not identify the nature of the black goo, but said, nonetheless, that "as a customer relations gesture" they were issuing a check for the full refund requested, and enclosing three round-trip ticket vouchers—unaccountably not to California, but Florida instead. The complainer, who had been planning a trip to Disney World anyway, thought that was just fine.

◆ ◆ ◆ ◆ ◆ ◆ ◆ ◆ ◆ ◆ ◆ ◆

WHAT PEOPLE COMPLAIN ABOUT IN DEPARTMENT STORES

A graduate student analyzed over 1,000 complaints received by three large department stores. Over 90 percent of the complaints fit into the following five categories. The total adds up to more than 100 percent because many people complained about more than one thing.

Of those who complained,

67 percent could not find a salesperson.

62 percent said the store did not have an advertised item.

58 percent felt the salesperson was not polite or friendly.

40 percent said the salesperson was not helpful or knowledgeable.

38 percent said the price was not clearly marked or was wrong.

WHAT PEOPLE COMPLAIN ABOUT TO TRAVEL AGENTS

Travel agents are the subject of a great many complaints, the over-whelming majority of them for things that they did not personally do. To be sure, some of them make mistakes in their clients' travel arrangements, but in most cases, the problem lies with the providers for whom the travel agent is, well, an agent. Since a single trip can involve dozens of providers, from major airlines to rural Asian bus companies, the opportunities for problems are ample, and since no agents have time machines, the problem of a "ruined" trip produces a level of complaint more poignant than a faulty appliance. And because it is much easier to complain to a local company than a motel in Fiji, the agents bear the brunt of complaints, deserved or not. Courts and arbitrators commonly hold travel agents responsible on matters of interpretation (was it really an "ocean view" hotel if you could only see the ocean by leaning out the window?), but less often on matters clearly outside their influence.

◆ ◆ ◆ ◆ ◆ ◆ ◆ ◆ ◆ ◆ ◆

The case of the woman who wouldn't see the passion play without her priest

CASE STUDY

Annie Lucille Wheeler, a retired social worker in her seventies, read in her church's weekly newspaper that its editor, Monsignor John Foley, would be escorting a group on a three-country European tour, the highlight of which was to be the once-every-ten-years Passion Play at Oberammergau, Germany. Ms. Wheeler enthusiastically signed up and paid her $1,718.

When she got to Munich, she found that she had been assigned to a group with a different tour guide, not her priest. Old, confused, in a foreign land, she didn't squawk too loudly, and took the tour with another group. But immediately on her return, she filed a complaint with the travel agent. The agent sent her a letter of apology, and a refund check for $125 for her inconvenience. That was unacceptable to Ms. Wheeler, who promptly went to court.

In Philadelphia, many cases involving under $20,000 are heard by an arbitration panel. Mrs. Wheeler explained to the panel that she never would have gone if she had known that the Monsignor would not be her escort. "It's the principle of the thing, you understand," she said. "They shouldn't be able to do this to people." The travel agent pointed out that she had gone everywhere and done everything that the brochure promised, in the hands of a capable tour leader, who just didn't happen to be her priest. The travel agent further claimed that Ms. Wheeler had subjected him to undue harassment by getting a consumer protection activist group to picket the travel agency.

The arbitration panel decided she had indeed been wronged and awarded her $1,593 damages: the full cost of the trip less the $125 she had been offered. The newspaper reporter covering the event suggested that Ms. Wheeler was successful because she "possesses the tenacity of a bulldog worrying a trouser cuff."

◆ ◆ ◆ ◆ ◆ ◆ ◆ ◆ ◆ ◆ ◆

CHAPTER 5

How People Feel After the Complaint and What They Do Next

THERE WAS REASON TO COMPLAIN, so one of two things happened: you did something or you didn't. And then one of two things happened: things ended up OK, or they didn't. Of course there are lots of "in between" possibilities, but we can start by looking at things in a simple chart like this:

THERE WAS SOMETHING TO COMPLAIN ABOUT, AND		
	AND THINGS ENDED UP NOT OK	AND THINGS ENDED UP OK
ACTION WAS TAKEN	1	2
NO ACTION WAS TAKEN	3	4

Thus we have four "zones" to look at.

FOUR POSSIBLE COMPLAINT OUTCOMES

Zone 1: Action taken, but things didn't end up OK

This is where the dedicated consumer will go into action even more vigorously, with further complaining, going to third parties, boycotting, bad-mouthing, and the like.

Zone 2: Action taken, and things end up OK

This is the zone in which some complainers are so grateful, they pack away their pens, postage stamps, and telephone list, relax, and enjoy the fruits of their labors. But others are left with a sour taste in their mouths and will, at the very least, avoid further dealings with that company or service provider, and may continue the battle, either to secure justice for others down the road or simply to get even.

Zone 3: No action taken, and things did not end up OK

Well what did you expect? It is for a reason that some corporate complaint-handlers refer (privately, of course) to these people as the zombies. They just sit there watching Beavis and Butthead and take whatever is dealt out to them.

Zone 4: No action taken, but things ended up OK

Welcome to Shangri-La. This is the way it should be, of course: the consumer doesn't need to complain; the company notices the problem and makes everything right. Of course this happens in the real world, but when it does, it is often regarded as sufficiently rare to be newsworthy. The Saturn car company detected a serious, unfixable flaw in one batch of cars. Before a single buyer had time or cause to complain, they recalled more than 1,000 cars, physically destroyed them, then gave those startled owners a brand-new one.

DO DIFFERENT PRODUCTS OR SERVICES PRODUCE DIFFERENT KINDS OF COMPLAINT OUTCOMES?

In his massive compilation of complaint data, *When Consumers Complain,* Arthur Best has tabulated data from many researchers, and comes up with the following figures for some leading complaint-producing categories:

	% SATISFIED	% DISSATISFIED	DISSATISFIED AND...			
			DO NOTHING	WALK AWAY	COMPLAIN	GO TO 3RD PARTY
Appliances	35	44	42	1	51	2
Medical/dental	35	46	64	9	22	1
Carpets	47	37	68	0	30	2

	% SATISFIED	% DISSATISFIED	DISSATISFIED AND...			
			DO NOTHING	WALK AWAY	COMPLAIN	GO TO 3RD PARTY
Credit cards	49	29	55	7	34	1
Car repair	50	36	42	6	42	10
Home repair	53	30	37	4	46	6
Television	61	13	43	4	48	1
Mail order	68	19	41	1	55	2
Books	75	17	52	3	43	0
Clothing	75	19	66	7	26	0

What do we learn from all these numbers?

Here are five interesting things, for starters:

1. People are twice as satisfied with their televisions as with their doctors, dentists, or refrigerators.

2. Most dissatisfied people in most situations do nothing.

3. People who are unhappy about car repair are ten times more likely to go to a third party to complain than people who are unhappy about their doctor or dentist.

4. Nobody walks away from a problem with carpets; it's pretty hard, when they presumably are already on your floor.

5. A higher percentage of dissatisfied mail-order buyers complain than people in any other category, perhaps because so many mail-order sellers make it easy and straightforward for their customers to register their complaints.

SEVEN THINGS THAT AFFECT HOW COMPLAINERS FEEL THE NEXT MORNING, AND WHAT (IF ANYTHING) THEY DO NEXT

1. Was I treated fairly and justly?

There is a whole body of research that suggests that "perceived justice" is the biggie when it comes to deciding what to do after a complaint. This is, of course, an awfully subjective sort of thing, and each complainer would respond differently. If you feel that you are entitled to a $100 refund and you are offered $30, is that fair? $60? $90? $100 plus $20 more for your trouble? One study found that people who felt they were treated unfairly were likely to bad-mouth the store, and very much more likely never to go back there again. But another study found that the scope of the deal had nothing to do with the bad taste left. People who felt they were treated unfairly on a $3 purchase were just as resentful and just as likely to bad-mouth and boycott as those with a $300 purchase.

2. Was I treated with respect and courtesy?

One researcher looked at 149 cases where a consumer was genuinely unhappy with a major purchase of clothing, appliances, shoes, electronics, or watches: a $93 average purchase price. This was real unhappiness, not just the wrong size or color. Even though three-quarters of them bad-mouthed the store, their ultimate satisfaction level was very much dependent on whether they had been treated well.

In a survey of people who had complaints against three major service providers—an airline, a telephone company, and a hospital—the clear finding was that complainers who felt they had been treated respectfully were, in the long run, happier than those whose treatment had been impersonal or rude, *whether or not their complaint was satisfactorily resolved.* In other words, there are many people who, in the long run, would rather be told "no" politely than be told "yes" in a surly manner.

◆ ◆ ◆ ◆ ◆ ◆ ◆ ◆ ◆ ◆ ◆   *CASE STUDY*

Which is better: fair but nasty, or unfair but nice?

Two academic researchers, Jeffrey Blodgett and Stephen Tax, looked at the matter of fairness and courtesy as it affects a complainer's intentions of going back to the store, and his or her likeliness to bad-mouth the store. Being academics, they called their work "The effects of distributive and interactional justice on complainants' repatronage intentions and negative word-of-mouth intentions."

Research subjects were presented with one of four scenarios, and then asked whether they would go back to that store, and whether they would say unkind things to friends and family:

Nice and fair: You bought expensive tennis shoes, which turned out to be defective. You lost your receipt. The salesperson is polite (*nice*) and the manager lets you exchange them or offers store credit (*fair*).

Nice but unfair: Same story; the salesperson is polite, but the manager says no.

Nasty but fair: Same story; the salesperson is nasty and reluctantly calls the manager, who is fair and offers exchange or credit.

Nasty and unfair: Nasty salesperson, and the manager says no.

Results: It required both *nice* and *fair* for people to be willing to buy there again; either one alone was not enough. Also, either one alone was not enough to prevent bad-mouthing, but the two together resulted in no bad-mouthing.

The bottom line is that courtesy, kindness, and friendliness are not enough to overcome a negative experience.

How about the length of time it took to deal with the complaint? No big deal, according to the research of Julie Freeman at CSU Long Beach. She, too, found that niceness and fairness were the two main factors in satisfaction, when they were both present. And when they were both there, even complaints that took a long time to resolve left people feeling satisfied.

◆ ◆ ◆ ◆ ◆ ◆ ◆ ◆ ◆ ◆ ◆ ◆

3. Did the company or organization have control over the situation?

There are times when a person has a major complaint but recognizes that the company had little or no control over the situation, such as when an airline flight is canceled due to bad weather. There is often a gray area here. If a flight is canceled due to "mechanical problems," could the airline have fixed it sooner? They can't make it stop snowing in Denver, but if a plane had mechanical problems, they might have found a replacement.

The evidence is that the more you believe the company had control over the situation, the more likely you are to complain: writing, phoning, bad-mouthing, boycotting, and going to a third party.

Shirley Taylor demonstrated this in a simple but elegant experiment with 232 business school students who had an appointment with a career counseling service (and who did not know they were experimental subjects). Some of them were seen promptly, and some had to sit and wait for quite a while. Of this latter group, half were told that the problem was due to a scheduling error, the other half that the problem was due to a copier breakdown.

Taylor tossed in one more interesting factor. Half the people who had to wait sat in a bare, austere waiting room. The other half were in a friendlier waiting room with interesting literature to read.

Afterwards, the biggest complaints came from the people who felt the counseling center *did* have control (scheduling error), with many fewer complaints from those who felt the problem was outside their control (copier breakdown). And, as one might predict, those who were treated better had less to complain about than the others.

4. How did the outcome compare with promises made?

You're on an airplane waiting to take off. Would you be more likely to complain later if the pilot said, "We'll be taking off in ten minutes," but it turns out to be thirty minutes, or if the pilot said, "There is heavy traffic, and we won't be taking off for an hour," and the plane really does leave in an hour?

There is evidence that some ratio between what is promised and what is delivered affects the level of happiness or unhappiness after the complaint has been dealt with. When a plumber says, "I'll be there in an hour," or when a dentist says, "This won't hurt," and it takes three hours or it does hurt, there is a lot more unhappiness than if there was honesty at the start...but only up to a point. Many people have a preconceived notion of how things should be, in terms of time, money, service level, and so on, and even an honest answer that exceeds that will still produce dissatisfaction.

General Telephone surveyed some customers who had had problems with their phones. Even though the company standard for fixing a dead line was four hours, the company found that their customers were not happy even when honestly told the correct time, since they believed such an important thing should be fixed in two hours or less.

5. How important was the product or service, anyway?

As we might expect, the more important the product or service is to someone, the higher their expectations that their complaint will be dealt with promptly and well, and the greater their anguish if it is not.

6. How often have I been screwed by this or other companies?

Like Charlie Brown who tries unsuccessfully, year after year, to kick the football that Lucy is holding but jerks away at the last second, there are people who are unhappy with a company or organization but come back for a second try. In one survey, nearly half the people who had complained about a purchase from a television shopping channel continued to buy from that channel.

Some researchers have predicted that a person who complains and ends up satisfied is going to be an even *happier* customer than someone who was happy in the first place. But these predictions have not been borne out. For instance, one study looked at 404 people who purchased a major brand of carpet for their homes, half of whom had complained, the other half not.

Afterwards, the complainers who had been made happy were still not nearly as likely to deal with that company again or say good things about it, as those who were happy in the first place. The same thing happened with people who complained to Shell Oil about credit card billing or repair problems. A check of credit card purchases after the complaint showed that the satisfied complainers bought less from Shell, but the ones who felt their complaint had not been handled properly bought even less.

7. Am I ever likely to deal with this organization again?

There are certain situations in which a person is doing something probably for the only time in their life, and they have reason to complain. Whether it was a once-in-a-lifetime trip, major surgery, or buying an expensive wedding gown, does the consumer think, "This was a really big deal, and they blew it. I am tremendously unhappy, and I will let them know, most emphatically." Or does the consumer think, "Look, I'm probably never going to do this again, and there's no way to undo what has been done, so I'll just let go of it, and get on with my life."

The answer seems to be: some of each, depending on certain personality factors. There was, for instance, a study of people on an 89-day round-the-world cruise from hell. The ship's air conditioning broke, seas were rough, the chef jumped ship and the food was lousy, there were long delays in unpleasant ports, and more. The researcher who interviewed passengers afterwards found them in two separate camps, with almost no one in between. About 70 percent were outraged, livid, angry, and determined to see justice served, whatever it took. And the other 30 percent—including more than a few who would still complain about a faulty TV or a car repair problem—were pretty much ready to write it off. "These things happen." "All things considered, it wasn't that bad." "It was a real adventure, something to tell the grandchildren."

MAXIMUM AVOIDANCE: I HAVE COMPLAINTS ABOUT EVERYONE, SO THERE'S NOWHERE LEFT FOR ME TO GO.

What if one complains so often, and harbors enough grudges, there is nowhere left to go? Jonathan Huefner and H. Keith Hunt have written extensively about consumer dissatisfaction. They suggest that "by the time the consumer has eliminated all the stores being avoided there is a very limited set of reasonable alternatives remaining from which to choose."

Huefner and Hunt suggest these categories of reasons why unhappy consumers choose to avoid a particular brand, store, or service provider:

- poor quality of product
- unsatisfactory repairs
- unsatisfactory return or refund policy
- atmosphere of the place (dirty, dark, dingy, crowded, "wrong kind of people" as customers or clerks)
- rude, incompetent, pushy, or unfriendly personnel
- slow or poor service
- price/payment: too expensive; prices not marked, and so on
- miscellany: environmental concerns, parking, distance, stupid or misleading ads

When every option has one or more of these attributes, the consumer "is left with the difficult task of deciding which of the unacceptable alternatives is least unacceptable." The message here is that the more actively, effectively, and aggressively one complains, the fewer options there are left to deal with in the future. Like the elderly relative of mine who "went through" literally every single dentist within ten miles of her home, there was nothing left to do but either bite the bullet (but her false choppers didn't work well enough for that) or, as she did, move to another, larger town, and start all over. Or, presumably, one could focus one's complaints on those organizations that seem to have unlimited willingness to deal with difficult complainers.

◆ ◆ ◆ ◆ ◆ ◆ ◆ ◆ ◆ ◆ ◆ ◆

CASE STUDY

"And then would you like Mr. Bean to push a peanut up Fifth Avenue with his nose?" The case of L. L. Bean and the out-of-stock jacket

L. L. Bean is one of those companies with legendary customer service. Complaining customers are asked, "What will satisfy you?" Whatever it is, the company will do it, unless it is completely outrageous. And even then, only a director of the company can say "no" to a customer. The system was well-taxed by the caller who ordered a jacket that happened to be out of stock. That was totally unsatisfactory for the caller; she had a friend who was going into the hospital the next day, and she absolutely had to present her friend with that very jacket, or there would be hell to pay.

The Bean employee went into the mailing division, and searched through hundreds of boxes that had been returned as undeliverable or contained goods being sent back by customers. Against all odds, he found a return with the necessary jacket in the right size and color. Since it was by now too late for any normal delivery service, even the overnight ones, he hired a local taxi to drive the parcel from Maine to the Boston airport, where it was put on an express flight to New York, which was met by a hired limousine and delivered to the customer in the nick of time.

◆ ◆ ◆ ◆ ◆ ◆ ◆ ◆ ◆ ◆ ◆ ◆

CHAPTER 6

When Companies Complain about Other Companies

THE PICKLE WARS AND THE ICE CREAM SAGA

LET'S SAY THAT YOU ARE a pickle maker, and you pride yourself on the crunchiness of your pickles. Suddenly some new guy across town starts putting up signs saying that his pickles are the crunchiest pickles a person can buy. You write a stern letter, suggesting that your pickles are crunchier, but the other guy ignores you. Then what? How does one company complain about the marketing activities of another company?

Most companies deal with this matter by using the "truth and accuracy in advertising" service offered by the Council of Better Business Bureaus. And once in a while, a feisty company, like Ben and Jerry's Ice Cream, comes up with an innovative scheme to help them complain about a major competitor. Here's a quick look at the pickle wars and the ice cream saga.

Vlasic versus Claussen

Two of the most popular brands of pickles, Vlasic and Claussen, may once have been made by Mama Vlasic or Papa Claussen in their own kitchens, but now, as these things happen, they are each a division of a giant corporation, for whom the matter of crunchiness is of great importance.

So when the Claussen Pickle division of Oscar Meyer Foods started claiming, in their television commercials, that their pickles were crunchier than Vlasic's, the Vlasic Pickle division of Campbell (the soup people) felt they were out of bounds. Vlasic took their complaint to the National Advertising Division (NAD) of the Council of Better Business Bureaus, which was established in 1971 just for this sort of thing. The NAD is an investigative body. They check out the complaint by looking at the claims made, asking the companies for their rationale for making those claims (including research data, if any), and then they decide whether the complaint is valid or not.

If they find that it is, the company is asked (but not required) to make certain changes or to withdraw the offending ads entirely. If the company disagrees with the findings, they can appeal to a higher body, the National Advertising Review Board, comprised of 85 advertising professionals from companies, ad agencies, the academic world, and the general public. The Review Board's findings are not binding on the company either, but there is often a lot of pressure from within and without the advertising community to go along, and advertisers usually do.

In the matter of the pickle wars, the investigators learned that Claussen's pickles are refrigerated, while Vlasic's are boiled, which tends to cut down on crunchiness. And so they concluded that Claussen's ads did not overstate the superiority of refrigerated pickles over cooked pickles, at least crunchinesswise.

Because even a crunchy pickle can lose its crunchiness when left out of the fridge or when it grows older, Claussen, in a burst of honesty, did superimpose the words "as purchased" briefly in its television commercial. In response to a recommendation from the NAD, they agreed to make the words "as purchased" just a wee bit larger. Thus did peace descend upon the pickle battlefield.

Ben and Jerry versus Häagen-Dazs

In the mid 1980s, Ben and Jerry's was just beginning to have visions of going from a beloved regional ice cream in New England to becoming a bigger, nationally distributed brand. They found, however, that the major ice cream distributors were being told by the giant Häagen-Dazs division of Pillsbury that if the distributors took on Ben and Jerry's, they could no longer carry Häagen-Dazs.

Ben and Jerry devised a strategy that combined getting their customers to go to bat for them by complaining to Pillsbury, with a clear series of legal threats. They chose to go after Pillsbury directly, because it is, as the *New Yorker* report had it, "the sort of huge faceless corporation that makes a perfect foil for a company whose founders have their faces right on the pint container."

The complaint effort was launched with the theme "What's the Doughboy Afraid Of?" Ben and Jerry offered a free complaint kit, including a form letter to send to the chairman of Pillsbury (it suggested, "Why don't you pick on someone your own size?"), along with a bumper sticker, some promotional literature, and tips on complaining. People were urged to complain directly to Pillsbury, and many of them did. Some were quite straightforward ("I would admonish you to adopt a policy of fair play"), but many were either angry ("Quell your desire to use the corporate heel to stamp out your competition") or amusing ("May the bluebird of happiness poop into your vats if you do not lay off harassing Ben and Jerry").

Ben and Jerry backed up this campaign with letters from a hot-shot lawyer who was a specialist in restraint of trade matters and believed that Ben and Jerry would prevail in court, if the dispute ever got that far. But it didn't. The Doughboy may not have been afraid, but he was realistic, and in the end, Pillsbury agreed to an out-of-court settlement that helped propel Ben and Jerry into the popular and nationally distributed brand they are today.

MORE STORIES FROM THE COMPANY-VERSUS-COMPANY COMPLAINT ANNALS

CIBA Vision complains about Bausch & Lomb

The CIBA Vision Corporation, manufacturers of Vasocon-A® eye drops, challenged the truth and accuracy of two exclusivity claims, including "the only eye drop that relieves both redness and itching." During the course of an inquiry, Bausch & Lomb, Inc., voluntarily agreed to discontinue certain claims for its Opcon-A® eye drops appearing in print and broadcast advertising.

Castrol and Pennzoil complain about Quaker State

Following complaints by competitors Castrol and Pennzoil, the NAD recommended that Quaker State modify its advertising to avoid potential consumer confusion. Castrol, Inc., and Pennzoil Products Company challenged the truth and accuracy of Quaker State's ad claims appearing in print and broadcast commercials.

Land O' Lakes complains about Crisco

Land O' Lakes Inc., producers of butter and other dairy products, challenged the truth and accuracy of superiority claims in print advertising comparing cookies made with butter to cookies made with Procter & Gamble's Crisco. During the course of an inquiry by the National Advertising Division of the BBB, the Procter & Gamble Company voluntarily clarified its advertising for Crisco. Rather than disputing an alleged, unintended implied claim, P&G modified its current ads to communicate more clearly the intended message that it is comparing not the *products*, but *recipes* specifically designed for each respective product.

One Step Ahead complains about The Right Start

The manufacturer of One Step Ahead infant wear, toys, furniture, and carriages complained that its rival, The Right Start, was running inaccurate and untrue advertisements for its products. While the National Advertising Division was looking into the complaints, The Right Start agreed to modify claims of exclusive products appearing in their catalogue, as well as certain low price and shipping claims.

Liquid Plumr complains about Drano

Clorox, the manufacturer of Liquid Plumr, challenged Drano's claim that it goes to work faster. S. C. Johnson, the Drano manufacturer, supplied research evidence to the Council of Better Business Bureaus to show that Drano does begin working faster because of its high enzyme content.

Liquid Plumr complains about Drano again

Clorox, still as the manufacturer of Liquid Plumr, also complained about Drano's claim that its product can "Clear slow drains while you sleep! with the best build-up remover." This time, the Council of Better Business Bureaus sided with Liquid Plumr, and the S. C. Johnson company, manufacturers of Drano, agreed to modify its advertising to eliminate any implications that the product in question will remove build-up overnight.

And again: Liquid Plumr, this time complaining about Lysol

The Clorox Company, manufacturers of Professional Strength Liquid Plumr Build-Up Remover, challenged the truth and accuracy of print and television advertising for Professional Strength Lysol Drain Opener featuring the claim "It sends more power through standing water than other liquids." Following an investigation of the claim, the Lysol people agreed to take BBB's recommendations into consideration in future advertising.

Folgers complains about Maxwell House

The Folgers coffee division of Procter & Gamble complained to the National Advertising Division that the Maxwell House division of Kraft had exceeded standards of truth and accuracy when they said, in television advertising, that "the coffee perking in this pot is America's best-loved coffee." The investigators concluded that because the Maxwell House campaign was historical and nostalgic in nature, its claim was not intended to reflect actual research, and therefore "qualifies as puffery," and puffery in advertising is quite all right.

Clorox complains about Ultra Biz

The Clorox Company complained about the truth and accuracy of ads for Procter & Gamble's Ultra Biz Activated Color Safe Bleach, specifically the implication of the question "So who's better on tough stains? Biz or his?" and the summarizing claim that Biz is "the better stain getter." Based on research data submitted by P&G, the National Advertising Division of the Better Business Bureaus felt that the claims had been substantiated and could continue to be made.

Puffs complains about Kleenex

The Puffs folks at Procter & Gamble felt that the balloon-nosed stick figures used in Kleenex commercials to demonstrate the alleged superior softness of Kleenex Ultra Tissues were misleading. The investigators agreed with the softness claim, based on the research Kleenex submitted, but they were found to have overstated the advantages of that softness in their commercials. Kimberly-Clark, manufacturers of Kleenex, will modify its "visual depiction" in future commercials.

Peter Pan complains about Jif

Hunt-Wesson, manufacturers of Peter Pan peanut butter, complained that the Jif peanut butter division of Procter & Gamble was playing loose with truth and accuracy when they said in their ads that "Moms prefer the taste of Reduced Fat Jif over both the others" and that Jif had "more fresh-roasted peanut taste." The National Advertising Division looked into the peanut butter wars and concluded that Jif "has provided a reasonable basis to support its comparative superiority taste claim for Jif Reduced Fat Peanut Spread," and the ads can keep running.

BMW complains about Audi

The two German auto giants took their dispute to an American conference room. BMW maintained that in its advertising about the superior traction of the Audi Quattro, Audi did not make clear that the tests depicted did not make clear the exact test conditions, and that those conditions—the entire surface under the cars was slippery, not just a certain portion of it—brought into question the truth and accuracy of the claim. They insisted that the BMW 325i performance was not clearly depicted. Volkswagen, the manufacturer of Audi, agreed to modify the commercial following the recommendation of the National Advertising Division.

READ ALL ABOUT IT ON THE INTERNET

Whenever a company-versus-company complaint has been resolved by the National Advertising Division or the appeals board, the Better Business Bureau puts out a press release describing the matter. These press releases make fascinating reading, and they are available for inspection on the Council of Better Business Bureau's electronic home page on the Internet. With the appropriate computer link-up, you can find them at http://bbb.org/bbb.

CHAPTER 7

How to Complain

PEOPLE WHO ARE SUCCESSFUL at something, whether because of skill, dumb luck, or a combination of factors, nonetheless often become known as "experts" and thereupon write books and articles and go on talk shows to tell how they did it. If I win at the races by betting on jockeys with red hair, or if I achieve mail-order success by mailing things in green envelopes on Tuesdays, or if I succeed at the stock market by selecting stocks with a price-earnings ratio of exactly 14, then—whether there is madness in my method or not—if it works I am an expert (at least for a while).

So it is in the arena of successful complaining. My search turned up more than sixty books and five times that many newspaper and magazine articles by people who knew how to do it, because they had done (or perhaps fantasized doing) some things, which they said worked.

But their advice was often as different as day and night. Write first. Call first. Go straight to the person at the top. Start at the bottom. Sound threatening. Sound conciliatory. Write it by hand on folksy paper. Print it out with a laser printer on highest-quality bond. Hand address the envelope. Type the envelope. Don't use an envelope. Be wildly creative. Be very restrained.

The only conclusion, the only thing that it is safe to say with any certainty, is that there is no universal answer, no secret approach that will work all or most of the time.

But there is a lot of good advice in some of those books and articles. To spare you the need to go to them, I have chosen the nine best of the lot and have distilled the essence of them into a single paragraph or list. (Of course you may still consult them, and of course there is more to many of them than just this bit, but at least this is a good starting point.)

THE WISDOM OF NINE HELPFUL SOURCES

Fight Back and Don't Get Ripped Off by David Horowitz

America's most visible consumer advocate (he has been on network television for many years), David Horowitz suggests complaining through lower channels, but if that doesn't work, write the president of the organization and state that "if you don't hear in seven working days, you'll be forced to take 'appropriate action'."

In your complaint letter, Horowitz recommends:

1. Be firm and businesslike. Don't scream on paper.
2. Send it to someone with power. Don't mark it "personal, confidential."
3. Get to the point quickly.
4. Make a clear demand.
5. Show proof of your claim.
6. Set a time limit for a reply. Two weeks is fair.
7. Quote a law or statute.
8. Don't carbon the world; the company will be turned off because you didn't give them a chance.
9. Send everything by certified mail.
10. Don't mention or bring in third-party agencies until the second letter.

Getting What You Deserve: A Handbook for the Assertive Consumer by Stephen A. Newman and Nancy Kramer

The former head of the law enforcement division of the New York Department of Consumer Affairs and the senior attorney for the New York Public Interest Research Group offer these eleven guidelines:

1. Be sure you have your facts straight.
2. Be explicit about what you want.
3. Speak firmly.
4. Act as if your time were valuable. Give deadlines.

5. Never talk to anyone without authority or who won't give you their name and title.

6. Keep copies of all papers and take detailed phone notes.

7. Start the complaint process with a phone call.

8. Conclude each phone call with a restatement of what you believe to be promised: "So I can expect delivery on Tuesday."

9. When you write, choose the lowest-level person who seems authorized to help.

10. Escalate quickly. Set short deadlines for a response before you go to a higher level. Ten days is reasonable.

11. Indicate your intention of going to public agencies: government (even if you don't, the company may be impressed by your knowledge and intentions); small claims court; trade associations; action lines; newspaper or magazines where the seller advertises (because they may discontinue accepting ads if there are enough complaints).

How to Write Complaint Letters That Work
by Patricia H. Westheimer and Jim Mastro

This recent book has some good advice and a lot of sample letters for those who can benefit from that kind of help.

1. Secretaries wield enormous power. They control who and what gets through to the boss and when. Never get angry with a secretary because the problem is not his or her fault.

2. Try a "write, call, write" sequence. Wait ten days after the letter, then call. If you can't get through, write a stronger second letter, with a copy of the first one enclosed.

3. Write to the top: the owner, president, or chairperson. Send a copy to managers, who may be more responsible, and if they act quickly, they will look better to their bosses.

4. Address the letters to a real person. Actual names are essential. How do *you* like getting letters addressed to "Occupant" or "To whom it may concern"? If there is no name in your letter, there is no one to take responsibility.

5. Be creative with reference sources. Use the library. There are dozens of company and organization directories. Use the Internet, America OnLine, CompuServe, and Prodigy computer services.

6. If you have any doubts about a certain person, call the company to check. It's silly to write a blistering letter to someone who was fired or retired last month.

7. Many people become indignant and defensive when threatened. Companies are the same.

8. First impressions are important. Use good paper, and type or computer print the letter. Never use handwriting.

9. If the recipient company or person think they can outwait you and save themselves the trouble of addressing your problem, they will. Never give up.

Consumer's Guide to Fighting Back by Morris J. Bloomstein

1. Most of your complaints will be decided and settled at the very first stage—the one many people are afraid of—the direct confrontation between you and the store, manufacturer, or craftsman who has made such shoddiness your problem.

2. Therefore you must reach the right person at the very start. Phone first to determine who the right person is. "To speak to someone without authority is to waste your breath and beg for a brush-off."

3. Get everyone's name, and have them spell it, so they will know you're writing it down. "Pinned moths tend to worry."

4. Be subtle. Don't make threats, don't promise dire consequences or a lawsuit.

5. If you can't resolve the problem by telephone, then try to make a personal visit. Keep it short. Resist the common tendency to keep talking and talking. Stop and wait for an answer.

6. Only then should you write a letter. It should always be certified with a return receipt requested. "People have a tendency to treat mail they must sign for as much more important...almost a semi-official piece of correspondence...."

7. If the letter doesn't work, go right to the "blockbuster": a repeat of the last letter, with copies to the manufacturer, the Better Business Bureau, the Chamber of Commerce, your member of Congress, the Office of Consumer Affairs, Consumers Union, and a newspaper or radio action line.

How to Write a Wrong, Complain Effectively, and Get Results by the American Association of Retired Persons

The pamphlet is written for senior citizens (their definition is "over fifty") but is useful for anyone. Free from AARP, Box 2400, Long Beach, CA 90801.

1. Learn when to complain. When it is appropriate, then the sooner the better.

2. Be as specific as possible. For instance, people often forget that if a charge is to be removed, they should be paid the accumulated interest.

3. Always do things in writing. "More than any other reason, people are denied their consumer rights because they fail to write a record of their problem."

4. The tone of the letter is important. One should try to be "calm, but not apologetic...firm but not hostile."

5. Be brief but be thorough.

6. Send copies to consumer agencies, trade associations, state legislators, and the Federal Trade Commission.

"How to Write a Complaint Letter That Gets Results" by Joe Dziemianowicz (in *McCalls*)

This author is awfully optimistic when he reports that "experts say most businesses will bend over backward to appease a disappointed customer—if you know the right way to complain." Here are his main points:

1. Make it easy for the business to get in touch. Professional stationery may add clout.

2. Address your complaint to the president.

3. Be specific. Tell exactly what happened. If products are involved, give the model and serial number.

4. Enclose copies of your proof of purchase. Make it clear how the problem affected you.

5. Begin the letter with a genuine compliment if possible.

6. State clearly what you want the company to do, and set a deadline for them to do it.

7. Don't ramble. Never write more than one page.

8. Be firm but courteous.

9. If there is no response, send one more letter, with a clear deadline. If that doesn't work, go to third parties.

"It Pays to Complain" by Ruth Nauss Stingely (in *Reader's Digest*)

This author earned her wings on a day in which her watch broke, her insurance company rejected a major claim, and a clerk at a fast food restaurant was rude. After she sent off three good letters, she got a fixed watch, most of her claim paid, and some free meals.

1. Be sure your gripe is a valid, not a trivial, one.

2. Save everything: broken parts, letters, receipts.

3. A neat and tidy letter improves the chance of reply.

4. Write to the person in charge by name: either the president or someone lower with a copy to the president.

5. Establish rapport. Point out (if true) that you have been a loyal customer, that you admire the organization.

6. Don't write when you are angry.

7. Be short.

8. Say exactly what you want them to do.

9. End the letter positively. Invite them to phone you.

10. If there is no reply in four to six weeks, try again.

11. If there is no satisfaction then, go to third parties.

12. If you *do* get satisfactory results, send a thank-you letter.

"Contact the Right People" by Anthony Joseph (in the *Christian Science Monitor*)

This writer says that "the trick is knowing how to contact the right people. Contrary to general assumption, even large companies are usually willing to help you out....If you follow an efficient, intelligent approach, you should receive a successful resolution to your problem."

1. Be firm, but not angry.

2. Be businesslike. Don't use stationery with flowers or little animals in the corners.

3. Always write to the national headquarters, not to a local or regional office.

4. Always write to an officer, by name.

5. Consider writing to the consumer relations department first; save the president for a later offensive

6. Allow three to four weeks for response.

✦ ✦ ✦ ✦ ✦ ✦ ✦ ✦ ✦ ✦ ✦ ✦

"Sorry, I am not allowed to tell you my last name." The case of Safeway's Assistant Manager Bob

CASE STUDY

A few years ago, I purchased a dozen bottles of mineral water at my neighborhood Safeway supermarket. At the checkout counter, the automatic bar code reader decided that some of the bottles would cost 65 cents while others would cost 72 cents. The clerk said she could only charge what the bar code reader said. I didn't plan to make a federal case over 56 cents, but, since I have always been a bit distrustful of bar code readers, I decided to pursue matters a bit further, so I asked for the manager. When a person in charge arrived, I explained the situation to him. He said that there was nothing he could do; whatever the reader said was it. I asked for his name. Bob. Your last name? "We're not allowed to give them out," he said. I asked his title. It was Assistant Manager.

Time was of the essence, so I paid the inflated amount and the next day I wrote a letter to Safeway headquarters, explaining what Assistant Manager Bob said, and what I said to Assistant Manager Bob, and why I was annoyed at Assistant Manager Bob, and what I had hoped Assistant Manager Bob would have done, and so on. I didn't suggest that it was pretty silly to have to refer to the person in charge of this large retail enterprise as Assistant Manager Bob, but my letter may have made the point. I signed it "Customer John."

Safeway promptly mailed me a letter saying I could go in and get my 56¢ refund plus three free bottles of the mineral water. I presented the letter to a cashier, and within seconds, Assistant Manager Bob was on the scene. He expressed regret that I had gone and complained to headquarters; he would have helped me had he understood. I pointed out that he had understood and hadn't helped me. He smiled wanly and moved on.

◆ ◆ ◆ ◆ ◆ ◆ ◆ ◆ ◆ ◆ ◆

MORE TIPS AND HINTS FROM A VARIETY OF EXPERTS

Sounding like a lawyer

The matter of actually suing the company or organization that provoked your complaint is discussed later, in Chapter 11. But there are some law-related things that can be done in the process of making the initial complaints.

Consumer lawyer Richard Alexander suggests behaving as if there is going to be a lawsuit eventually, even if the chances are small. Document everything. Take photographs of relevant matters. Get notarized statements from witnesses and others with relevant information.

Various writers suggest using terminology that makes you sound as if you are acting with legal advice: "This is to advise you that I have waited more than 30 days for my mail-order merchandise. If you do not contact me by phone in five (5) days with an explanation, I will report this statutory violation of the U.S. Code to the postal inspector of your region for immediate action."

One travel article suggests that airline travelers carry a slip of paper in their wallets, to use as necessary: "Since the flight has been delayed/canceled, under CAB Tariff #142, Rule 380, I am entitled to meals, hotel room, transportation from the airport to the hotel or home, and a three-minute long-distance telephone call."

How do you know how to sound like a lawyer?

The flippant answer is, Does it really matter? If I tell the riding stable that would not make a refund when they only brought one pony instead of four to my daughter's party that their facility is "in violation of the National Humane Treatment of Animals Statute #6131.7," will they know that I just made this up, or possibly that it actually deals with keeping walruses in the bathtub? Well maybe. Better, probably, to follow the advice of Joyce Stewart of the *New York Times* Consumers World column: "Know your rights before calling. Call the state or federal agency that handles your type of complaint, and explain to the receptionist that your problem is very legalistic, and you wish to speak directly to on-staff counsel. Ask for copies of relevant laws. And get the name, to put as 'cc' in future letters to the company."

The preemptive first strike

Show up at the store or business with the small claims court papers filled out, but not yet submitted (or send copies of them with your letter) to show that you are serious and know what to do.

Be sensible

Legal threats may worry individuals or small companies, but the big companies have salaried lawyers in house, and rarely worry about fleas on their thick hide.

Don't expect General Motors to be more organized than you are

Many people seem to expect that when they call a large company, the first person they speak to should recognize their name and know all about their problem, or at least have immediate access to their complete file, including the exact status of their complaint, with the push of a button on the computer. Sometimes this happens, but more often, with the decentralization of records, poor filing systems, inexperienced staff and/or balky computers, the delay in helping you is unrelated to the fact that the company hates you. Being clear and pleasant with receptionists and assistants may well get you the best results.

Dress well

In one research study, people complaining in person at a major department store were videotaped, and analyzed for both appearance and style. Data from 112 sales clerks showed that the clerks were much more conciliatory with well-dressed complainers, but that style (friendly, hostile, jovial, etc.) was much less of a factor.

"Share my pain, IBM."

The popular psychiatrist Dr. David Viscott writes: "Business people don't care about your feelings unless they have reasons. For results, you must make the offender share your hurt. By establishing that they are at risk because of your hurt, you get their attention and some form of resolution."

Personal attacks make the reader defensive

And when the reader is on the defensive, then he or she becomes even more protective of colleagues and the rest of the company, even if there is a feeling that the company may have been wrong. One writer provides a charming example of an actual letter that probably didn't work too well: "What kind of filthy slobs work for you anyway? The interior of my car was ruined after one of your moronic mechanics tracked some of your slimy goo on my brand-new carpets. I'm going to sue the pants off you this time, meathead. You'll hear from my lawyers...."

Timing, timing, and timing

In her article "The Fine Art of Complaining," Betsy Wade of the *New York Times* says that with travel problems, "the three most important aspects of complaining are timing, timing, and timing." Her advice makes sense for other kinds of problems as well. Complain now, by telephone, since money can never buy back lost time, and at a later time it may be impossible to find the culprit who caused your problem. She says that if something is not right, don't eat it, sleep in it, or get on it. Separate emotion from reality, call your travel agent, tour operator, or the travel provider at once, and collect. Prepare your words carefully, say exactly what you require, and be firm.

◆ ◆ ◆ ◆ ◆ ◆ ◆ ◆ ◆ ◆ ◆ ◆

The case of the rip in Cousin Andy's pants

My cousin Andy is a firm believer in complaining at the very instant that a problem is happening. If his car broke down in the desert, he'd probably be on the car phone calling the president of General Motors before he called the auto club. I had the opportunity to see him in action when I picked him up at the San Francisco airport one day. As he bent over to jerk his suitcase off the conveyer belt, his wife Gloria noted a rip in the rear of his pants, caused, they were certain, by a less-than-comfortable, possibly defective seat on the plane.

Andy marched—well, no, he actually sort of sidestepped—over to the TWA baggage desk, displayed the problem, and asked for immediate settlement. They politely suggested that the problem might have been caused in some other fashion and handed him a form to fill out, suggesting that he give it to them, along with his pants, after which they would think it over and be in touch with him. He said no, he did not wish to remove his pants in the airport, but he did wish to head straight to a clothing store to buy a replacement pair, and he wished to do it with TWA money. When they declined, he asked to use their phone.

First he called directory assistance in St. Louis to get the number for TWA headquarters. Then he phoned and asked to speak to the president. Someone in the executive offices thereupon heard the tale of the ripped pants, and the need to do something instantly on this important business trip. The conversation went on for a while, and then the chap in St. Louis asked to speak to the TWA agent. After a moment, the agent hung up the phone, went to some secret source, extracted $50 in cash, and handed it over. Andy left the airport a little drafty, but a happier man.

◆ ◆ ◆ ◆ ◆ ◆ ◆ ◆ ◆ ◆ ◆ ◆

"No, I'm not a cheapskate, you're a bungler."

One of the most common forms of public complaining is leaving a small tip or no tip at all when the food or service is bad at a restaurant. Never do that without explaining why, or the staff will just assume you are a cheapskate.

"Well, what would *you* do in my situation?"

Whether on the phone or in person, if you're being stonewalled, it may help to try to get the person involved, by asking what he or she would do in your situation. Say, for instance, "I'm in business, too, and I would be upset to learn that one of my customers was being treated as poorly as your company is treating me."

"Excuse me, I've got *60 Minutes* on the other line."

When the local consumer affairs office can't resolve the complaint, says a Consumers Union spokesperson, "going to the media can grease negotiations. Sending the offender a 'copy' of a letter detailing the problem to *60 Minutes* has been known to get results. They may get right back to you and say 'Whoever said we can't fix this must have been a temp.' Companies don't like anyone looking over their shoulder."

Know your rights as a picketer

The fun of picketing is that it is *so* public and *so* immediate and *so* annoying to the store or business that caused your problem. And the beauty of picketing as a tactic is that the business has no way of knowing how long it will last. You may be there for half an hour, or you may have taken early retirement and plan to be there for the next twenty years. Stores and businesses are fond of claiming that picketing is illegal, but in almost every situation, it isn't, as long as you follow certain guidelines. Here are some common ones, but they are coming from a researcher, not a lawyer:

1. The picketer must have a genuine dispute.

2. What the picketer is seeking must be lawful.

3. The signs must be true.

4. No abusive language or violence.

5. Allow customers access to the store or business.

6. Picket the business itself, not the owner's home or other irrelevant site.

◆ ◆ ◆ ◆ ◆ ◆ ◆ ◆ ◆ ◆ ◆

CASE STUDY

The case of the lumpy furniture

The excellent book *Getting What You Deserve*, by two consumer lawyers, suggests that informational picketing is one of the tools in the arsenal of the wronged customer. They offer this example: Mr. and Mrs. B, a Wisconsin couple, took their sofa and two chairs to be reupholstered at a large furniture store. They prepaid the charges of $431. When the furniture was delivered, the B's were horrified to behold a great lumpy mess, indeed three of them: uneven stuffing, shredded cloth, and mismatched seams. The furniture store refused to talk to them, maintaining the job had been well done, and if there was a problem, it must be something that happened after the items had been delivered.

The B's approached a local consumer group, the Concerned Consumers League, which also tried to intervene but the seller wouldn't talk to them either. The CCL mustered its forces, and turned out the next Saturday to do informational picketing. Their leaflets were headlined:

SATISFACTION NOT GUARANTEED AT PARK FURNITURE

When Mr. and Mrs. B [their full name and address] took their furniture to be reupholstered at Park Furniture [address] they expected no less than an excellent job....They found the following things wrong:

[a list of 7 things]

Mr. Johnson, owner of Park Furniture, says he doesn't want to talk to Mr. and Mrs. B, because he feels they are unreasonable. We feel that the upholstering should be done to the B's satisfaction or that their money and furniture should be returned. What's your opinion?

Park Furniture's owners responded almost at once: they sued Concerned Consumers League, asking the court to order them to stop leafleting and picketing. Happily, the federal court upheld the right of customers to picket and publicly voice dissatisfaction. In fact, the court pointed out: "The method of expression used by the plaintiffs in this case is probably the most effective way, if not the only way, to inform unsophisticated consumers, i.e., by direct contact at the particular place of business."

After three weekends of picketing, with no end in sight, the furniture store finally agreed to make certain concessions acceptable to the B's.

◆ ◆ ◆ ◆ ◆ ◆ ◆ ◆ ◆ ◆ ◆ ◆

CHAPTER 8

Directing a Complaint

COMPLAINING IS CLEARLY AN ART, not a science, and that is nowhere more apparent than in the simple-sounding matter of deciding who should be the first recipient of your complaint. The experts in this field, both the academics and the people who write popular articles, are very much divided, and with good reason, because there clearly is no one approach that is best for all situations. Some people say, "Start at the very top: complain to the top officer of the company." Others suggest going back to the very clerk or underling who sold you the complaint-producing item or delivered the unsatisfactory service. Various other "experts" recommend virtually every possible step of the "chain of command" in between.

Let's look at one simple complaint-worthy matter, and see how complicated this issue becomes: the case of a woman who found a mysterious but regrettable-looking small dark object in her large taco at her neighborhood Taco Bell.[1] Being a squeamish sort of person, she did not actually examine this object too closely, but her companion did wrap it up in a napkin and put it in his pocket.

Let us freeze the action at this point, and identify all of the options available to this person at this time.

THE TEN AVAILABLE OPTIONS

1. Do nothing. Probably, regrettably, the most common response of all. Whether for lack of knowledge about what to do, fear of retaliation, mistrust of the system, indecision, or simply the feeling that it was "no big deal," a great many people would just walk away and forget it. From various research data, it would seem that a quarter to half of all people do absolutely nothing.

---

[1] Attention PepsiCo lawyers: This is a hypothetical example. I have never found anything untoward in a Taco Bell product, nor do I know anyone who has. But I did need a real company to illustrate my point.

2. Do nothing now, but bad-mouth later. "Honestly, Gloria, you wouldn't *believe* what I found in my taco last week." By the third or fourth telling, people may be wondering how that dead raccoon managed to fit inside the taco shell. From various surveys, it would appear to be common for anywhere from 8 percent to 20 percent of people to take this approach.

3. Complain in person at the lowest level: the seller of the taco or the shift supervisor. In a well-run organization, which has taken training seriously, there should be procedures in place to handle complaints. The main goal of the organization is to resolve the situation as quickly, unemotionally, and inexpensively as possible. In this instance, the seller of the taco, or her immediate superior (the shift supervisor), should have the authority to offer a replacement or a cash refund, without admitting any blame or possible corporate liability (which may be a bit much to expect of a sixteen-year-old part-time near-minimum-wage employee who may not speak English too well). It is when this level of personnel says something like "Oh, wow, look at that! Is it still moving?" that the wallets of trial lawyers begin vibrating expectantly.

4. Complain in person to the most authoritative person actually on the premises, probably an assistant manager. Such a person may have authority to do a little more, if the complaint is vigorous enough. There would rarely be a cash payment larger than the actual cost of the goods, but there is sometimes discretionary power to dispense coupons or gift certificates.

5. Complain by telephone or mail to the owner. Some fast-food establishments are owned by franchisees; others, directly by the main company. Some will have a notice posted identifying the owner or operator, others will not. It never hurts to ask, and if you are not given a clear answer ("It is not our policy to give out that information"), then the very fact of someone being evasive becomes a weapon in your arsenal of attack. This is the time to start writing things down.

6. Complain by telephone or mail to someone in the organization who may have influence with the owner. It may be library

research time. There is probably some association of franchisees and operators, which may have a local, a regional, and/or a national office.

7. Complain by telephone or mail to headquarters. Three minutes on the telephone to the reference desk at my public library yielded the knowledge that Taco Bell is a part of PepsiCo Restaurants International, a division of PepsiCo, the Pepsi-Cola Company. From standard reference sources, I was given the name and address of the president of Taco Bell, the president of PepsiCo, various other officers, and, for good measure, the names of their accountants and auditors, and their advertising agency.

At this level, there are six categories of complaint. You will find experts who support and challenge every one of these approaches (except for *f*, which is my very own invention and will be described shortly), and their logic is often impeccable.

One "expert" might say: "Write directly to the president first; you may as well go straight to the top, and he or she will certainly pass it along to the right person, and probably follow up to make sure something is done."

An equally expert "expert" might say, instead, "Don't *ever* write to the president first; people lower down will resent the fact that you went over their heads; besides, you can always write to the president later, if you are still dissatisfied."

The seven categories of complaint are:

a. The generic complaint, "to whom it may concern"

b. The "proper" complaint, to the "Consumer Affairs Depart ment" or the "Consumer Complaint Department"

c. The highest-level complaint, to the president of the company, by name

d. The "hardball" complaint, to the corporate counsel or chief lawyer

e. The "shotgun" complaint, to three or five or ten different people in the company, and perhaps to the accountants and the ad agency to boot

f. The crafty, guilrful, circuitous "proxy" complaint, to the president's husband or wife, at home.

◆ ◆ ◆ ◆ ◆ ◆ ◆ ◆ ◆ ◆ ◆

The case of the 100-letter barrage to the IRS   *CASE STUDY*

When our family moved from New York to California, the Internal Revenue Service computers found this situation impossible to deal with. Not only did we fail to receive the refund that we were due, but the IRS form letters were claiming that we had not paid our taxes at all for the previous year and that we were soon to be in big trouble.

We did all the things a responsible and polite citizen could be expected to do. We wrote letters to the New York and California IRS offices and sent them certified. We made long-distance phone calls and spent hours on hold, at our expense. We wrote and tried to phone supervisors. We drove up the value of Xerox stock with the number of copies we made of prior returns and letters. All to no avail. We didn't get our refund, and we kept being dunned.

Finally I fell back on the hypothesis that if you fire one bullet at a flock of birds, you might or might not hit one, but if you fire a million bullets all at once, the odds of bringing one down are pretty high. I did a couple of hours of research in the library and by telephone, and stopped when I had the names and addresses of 100 possibly relevant people, from the President of the United States to the Commissioner of Internal Revenue to dozens of underlings and regional officials in the IRS to all the members of the congressional committee that oversees the IRS to my own senators and congressman to other federal consumer and regulatory agencies to an IRS Assistant Commissioner at her home address (she fortuitously was listed in *Who's Who of American Women*).

I mailed all 100 letters at the same time. Three things happened. We got our refund check within five days. The IRS stopped dunning us for the taxes we'd already paid. And for the next two months, I got one or two letters a week from well-meaning underlings, saying things like "Don't worry; we're working on it; we should have your problem solved pretty soon now."

I wouldn't recommend doing this often (it is costly, time-consuming, and it does take up the time of some well-meaning people who might better be doing something useful), but there are times when the satisfaction of doing it outweighs the precautions, regardless of the consequences.

◆ ◆ ◆ ◆ ◆ ◆ ◆ ◆ ◆ ◆ ◆ ◆

◆ ◆ ◆ ◆ ◆ ◆ ◆ ◆ ◆ ◆ ◆

The case of the two John Bears and what the wife of the president of Amoco said when he got home that fateful day

In general, I do not endorse or recommend mischievous approaches to gaining satisfaction in a complaint matter. Since sticking to the tried and true methods of complaining is so often successful (a lot of sticking is sometimes required), why take the chance of unnecessarily aggravating, annoying, or provoking someone with an "off the wall" approach that may hurt your cause more than help it?

However, there are times when, either in desperation because nothing whatever is being done, or in indignation because something *was* done but it was the wrong thing, it is good to know about this particularly diabolical technique, which came to me during my everlasting battle with the American Oil Company.

When I lived in Chicago, I bought my gas at the neighborhood Amoco (American Oil) service station and charged purchases to my Amoco credit card. When the monthly bill came, I paid it, without scrutinizing every charge slip. Then suddenly one month, there was a bill for about ten times the usual amount because of a single big purchase of five tires. The copy of the charge slip was dutifully signed "John Bear" but *not* in my handwriting. And, curiously, there were two or three other charge slips, for modest gasoline purchases, also signed by the "other" John Bear.

I went back and looked at my bills for the past year, and discovered that nearly half of my receipts were signed by the "other" John Bear. But at the same time, I came to realize roughly half of my *own* gas purchases had never been billed to me.

The "other" John Bear's charge slips were all from a station in a nearby town. I checked the phone book and sure enough, there was a John Bear living there. In the course of a rather unusual telephone conversation, John Bear to John Bear, we discovered that we had been issued the same credit card number by Amoco, and that our individual charges were sort of randomly being distributed between us. For more than a year, I had been buying some of his gas and he had been buying some of mine, but neither of us noticed, until he went and bought tires, which the Amoco computer decided to assign to me.

The two John Bears found this all mildly amusing, but the Amoco company found it incomprehensible. They said that what happened was impossible, and therefore it could not have happened, and that was that.

We both wrote. We both phoned. We did all the things that an increasingly agitated complainer could be expected to do, and then some. We did this over a three-month period, with no results whatsoever.

I had, of course, written eventually to the president of Amoco, with no response. I was curious as to what sort of person this was, who could ignore the likes of me, so I went to the public library and looked him up in one of those "who's who in business and industry" directories. There he was, complete with photo, a bit of family history, and his home address in Indiana. That's when the inspiration hit me.

I wrote a very polite letter to the president's *wife* at home, apologizing profusely for bothering her, but telling briefly of the terrible problems I'd been having with her husband's company, and when he got home from work today, would she mind asking him if he could possibly look into the little matter, for this unhappy man.

Of course I don't know exactly what happened next, but I like to picture this poor guy, staggering into the palatial home, desperately eager to kick off his shoes, put his feet up, and have a stiff drink, when his wife comes over, waving a little white envelope, saying, "Dear, won't you see if you can do something about this."

Whatever the scenario, three days after I mailed that letter to Indiana, the other John Bear and I each got a telephone call from Amoco, assuring us that the problem had been solved, separate credit cards had been issued, and the billing had been sorted out. They claimed that I owed the company $187 for payments the other JB had made to my account, and as soon as I paid them, that would be the end of it.

A few days later, the bill for $187 arrived. I promptly made up my own bill to Amoco, charging them for my time, postage, certified-mail fees, and telephone charges. My total, amazingly, came to $187.05, so they owed me five cents. I returned their bill with my bill attached. I never heard from them again. They never even sent me the damn nickel.

◆ ◆ ◆ ◆ ◆ ◆ ◆ ◆ ◆ ◆ ◆ ◆

8. Complaining to one or more third party: government agency, newspaper or radio action line, the Better Business Bureau, the attorney general, and so on.

9. Engaging in creative complaining behaviors: picketing the company, trying to organize a boycott, running advertisements about your bad experience, and so on.

But "getting even" with one local restaurant, when there are more than 3,000 in the chain, would hardly cause a ripple at the corporate headquarters back in Purchase, New York.

10. Legal action, either in small claims court or in regular court. Can you imagine a high-powered theatrical lawyer, slowly and dramatically extracting that small black whatever-it-was from a taco, before the fascinated eyes of the jury?

A MILLION DIFFERENT APPROACHES— WHAT SHOULD I DO?

If we had a dozen comparable situations—a dozen identical taco chains with a dozen mysterious additives, then the chances are good that a dozen different approaches would result in a dozen different kinds of responses. There clearly is no one best answer for any one person in a given situation—or at least not one that can be known in advance—so it is a matter of what sort of thing you feel comfortable with, advice from others, and a dollop of creativity and instinct.

Here is what your fellow complainers do (and don't do). In one very large study of complaining behavior, the researchers found that

- 36 percent of the dissatisfied people did nothing (although 6 percent thought they might still do something, sometime, maybe, and 5 percent simply didn't know what to do, or they might have tried something)

- 25 percent complained in person to a clerk, manager, or someone else at the establishment in question

- 8 percent wrote a letter

- 8 percent complained to family, friends, and others

- 7 percent complained in person or by phone to a higher-up in the company or organization

- 6 percent simply stopped patronizing that establishment, but said nothing to anyone

- 3 percent complained to the Better Business Bureau, government agencies, a TV or radio or newspaper action line

- 3 percent returned a product for a refund
- 2 percent talked to a lawyer or went to small claims court
- 1 percent refused to pay a bill or credit card invoice or stopped payment on a check

The only thing that can be said with near certainty is that if you don't communicate with *someone*, then your complaint will go unresolved.

CHAPTER 9

Off-the-Wall Complaining and the Power of Creativity

A CANDID COMPLAINT HANDLER for a large corporation told me that her job was depressingly boring. Day after day, one dreary complaint letter or phone call after another. Some are well written, some are not; a few are mildly humorous, most are deadly serious. She handled them all, protecting the interests of her company while being as kind and reasonable as seemed appropriate to the complainers. I asked if her job had *any* bright spots at all. She smiled as she recounted several examples in which a bit of flamboyant creativity on the part of a complainer brought a reprieve to the tedium of her daily work and resulted in a more generous response to the complainer.

* * * * * * * * * * * *

CASE STUDY

The case of the gorilla who got the refund

One guest at her company's hotel spent a week in an executive suite, then felt he had been overcharged on checkout. He sent her a "gorilla-gram": one of those services one finds in the yellow pages, typically under "Telegrams: Singing and Entertaining." The person in the gorilla suit came to her office, sang a song, capered about, and delivered a message asking the hotel to "stop monkeying around with my bill." The $70 gorilla-gram got that particular customer a $400 reduction in his total bill.

* * * * * * * * * * * *

That man was rewarded in part because he may well have had a valid complaint, but mostly because he brought a moment of sunshine into her dreary day. A more modest creative effort had its good effect as well.

◆ ◆ ◆ ◆ ◆ ◆ ◆ ◆ ◆ ◆ ◆ ◆ ◆

CASE STUDY

The case of the 144-square-foot complaint letter

A family that had been forced to stay in a one-bedroom unit, when they had reserved a two-bedroom suite, sent her by United Parcel Service a fairly large cardboard carton. Inside, folded very neatly, was a single huge sheet of paper, made from white paper tablecloths taped together, perhaps twelve feet square. When she finally got it unfolded, her desk was completely covered with a huge, brightly colored message, complete with illustrations. The entire family had written an aggrieved letter about how the hotel foul-up had really put a damper on their otherwise lovely vacation. The result: she personally made sure they were sent a coupon good for a free three-night stay for the entire family in a two-bedroom suite.

◆ ◆ ◆ ◆ ◆ ◆ ◆ ◆ ◆ ◆ ◆ ◆ ◆

Of course creativity doesn't always work, and in these days of the madmen sending bombs through the mail, your creative complaint bundle might be hauled off in a bucket of water and exploded by the bomb squad.

The maverick president of Avis, Robert Townsend, whose fine book *Up the Organization* was once a number-one bestseller, writes that "the one thing the Establishment is prepared for is violent frontal attack. They may have pure lard inside but they've got twenty-four inches of armor plate in front." In other words, the "back door," or unusual, creative complaint may well be more likely to penetrate their defenses.

The head of a very large airline acknowledged this when he said, "You want results from an airline? Hand write your letter, stating your case succinctly. But write it on a competing airline's stationery while you're in flight. You will get immediate results, I promise you."

Unusual packaging, unusual contents, or an unusual public spectacle all can be successful...or can backfire, if the stodgy company is more determined than ever not to give in, especially to someone who shows up in a clown suit, or floods them with odd-shaped express mail bundles...especially if the media don't show up to cover your complaint spectacular.

CASE STUDY ◆ ◆ ◆ ◆ ◆ ◆ ◆ ◆ ◆ ◆ ◆

The case of the man who got arrested for selling the Bill of Rights, but not for giving away *Hustler* magazine

Our family once lived in a little art colony on the northern California coast, a place to which tourists came in large numbers on the weekend to enjoy the ocean and patronize the local galleries, gift shops, and boutiques. As happens in such places, various artists and craftspeople began selling their own works on the sidewalks, which alarmed some of the shop owners, who feared loss of business to these long-haired, disreputable-looking folk. The shop owners filed the appropriate complaint with the Board of Supervisors, which dutifully passed a law prohibiting the selling of any goods on the sidewalks of the town. To protect First Amendment rights, they allowed giving away free printed material.

The street artists complained to the supervisors and the press about this new law, but they were generally poor and young and the establishment did not pay them heed. I did not like the injustice of the situation and carefully considered my own complaint options. A well-crafted letter to the editor would be "preaching to the choir." The victims would love it, but no one in charge would pay attention. A legal countercomplaint would be costly and time-consuming. A petition, even with lots of signatures, would be easy to ignore.

And so, on a lovely Saturday morning at the height of the tourist season, I set up two card tables on Main Street. At one table, I was giving away free copies of *Hustler* magazine: perfectly legal under the new legislation. At the other table, I was selling copies of the Bill of Rights for five cents: clearly illegal under the new legislation. On cue, the local invited media people arrived, followed shortly after by the sheriff, who, in effect, read me my rights, and when I declined to stop the perfidious act of selling the Bill of Rights, dutifully arrested me.

The ensuing publicity and trial pointed out the folly of the new law as no formal method of complaining could have. The judge found the law to be unconstitutional, I do not have a criminal record, and the street artists returned to the streets of the town.

◆ ◆ ◆ ◆ ◆ ◆ ◆ ◆ ◆ ◆ ◆ ◆

When I was discussing the idea of flamboyant complaining once with a conservative businessman, he clearly was uncomfortable imagining what he might face in his own business if this sort of thing caught on.

"But, but, but what if *everyone* did this sort of thing?" he blustered. It was a pleasure to give him the simple and eloquent answer that Yossarian gave when challenged similarly in *Catch-22*: "Then I'd be crazy not to."

THE CREATIVE COMPLAINING HALL OF FAME

From all the wonderful and satisfying complaining stories that I have read or been told or participated in, I have chosen these five to nominate as the charter entries into the Creative Complaining Hall of Fame. Further nominations are most welcome, especially sent to me by mail in care of the publisher.

◆ ◆ ◆ ◆ ◆ ◆ ◆ ◆ ◆ ◆ ◆ ◆

CASE STUDY

The case of the forlorn veteran in the phony wheelchair

In his charming little book *Don't Get Mad, Get Even*, political prankster Alan Abel offers a superb example of creative complaining. A local garage advertised "$49.95 for a complete tune-up. Any foreign car. No kidding." Abel brought in his old Mark II Jaguar for a tune-up and a few minor (he thought) repairs. He said to do what was necessary, but not to exceed $200 for the tune-up plus any necessary repairs. Three weeks later, he got a phone call: "Your baby is purring nicely and you can pick her up."

At the garage he was presented with a bill for $1,700: $49.95 for the tune-up and $1,650.05 for various "minor" repairs. He was told that he must pay at once by certified check, or the garage would secure a mechanics' lien and sell the car to recover their costs. Abel phoned his attorney, who scolded him for not having a written agreement. "Pay the bill and take your lumps," he was advised. He considered making a complaint to a consumer agency or the Department of Motor Vehicles, but was worried that his car might be sold out from under him. That's when the idea came to him for a brilliant creative complaint.

"My strategy was to rent a wheelchair from a hospital supply company. Then I put on an old army uniform, and my wife took a Polaroid photo of me sitting in the chair looking ill and forlorn....The photo was reproduced on 100 circulars that read: ARMY VETERAN VICTIMIZED. "The Classical Car Repair Shop of Norwalk, CT, advertised a tune-up for $49.95 and I swallowed the bait. Without authorization they installed $1,700 in new parts and are now holding my car for ransom. Please join the boycott against this deceptive and dishonest business."

Circulars were posted at neighborhood gas stations, auto suppliers, and bars. Needless to say, Abel received an angry call from the garage's lawyer threatening a libel suit. He pointed out that his defense was that everything said was true, and by the way, he would be sending out thousands more flyers and would soon be picketing the garage in his wheelchair, wearing his uniform. The lawyer said, "Don't do anything; I'll call you back in an hour." When he did call, he attempted to negotiate a price, but Abel said that $200 was his bottom line. The lawyer agreed. Then Abel asked for written assurance that the garage had not tampered with his car to seek revenge, and that, too, was agreed, and the wheelchair was returned to the rental agency.

◆ ◆ ◆ ◆ ◆ ◆ ◆ ◆ ◆ ◆ ◆ ◆

CASE STUDY

"If you're black, we don't want your business."
The case of Mike Royko versus AT&T

Syndicated columnist Mike Royko was not being treated well by the giant AT&T. They announced a new 800 number, which happened to have the same seven digits as his office phone, so when people forgot to dial "1-800" first, as many do, they got his private line. Royko asked AT&T to change its number, but, needless to say, they declined and suggested that he change his. Instead, Royko came up with a masterful approach to creative complaining.

"When people called to complain about a defective phone—thinking they were talking to AT&T—I would give them technical advice, such as throwing the faulty phone out of the window, praying over it, or chanting a mantra. Sometimes I would express my sympathy for their problem by breaking into a fit of sobbing."

But the effect of this approach, Royko came to realize, was limited, because he was only dealing with one person at a time, and unlikely to attract the attention of AT&T. So he hit upon a new strategy, as demonstrated by this dialog he reported when he got a call that was clearly from an African-American:

Royko: "Tell me, are you of the black persuasion?"

Caller: "Yeah, what about it?"

Royko: "We are discontinuing service to all blacks."

Caller: "Say what?"

Royko: "Yes. You people use all that jivey language and, frankly, you laugh too much. And that causes a confusion in the electronic equipment. Our equipment is designed to handle traditional American speech, not all that jive talk."

Caller: "I don't believe this. How dare you."

Royko: "We dare because we are big and powerful. And you ain't. Goodbye."

Later, he told a Norwegian caller that she and all Norwegians were being cut off. "You Norwegians are just so dull, that we don't believe you have anything worthwhile to talk about on a phone anyway." An Italian caller was "struck speechless when I told him that we were refusing service to Italians because our technicians didn't like working on phones that were garlicky."

Royko concludes: "I don't know how much AT&T spends on public relations. I'm sure it is a considerable sum. But in the face of my campaign, it's going to be a big waste. So wise up, AT&T, and get a new number. Why I haven't even gotten around to the Hispanics, the Chinese, the Lithuanians, the..."

◆ ◆ ◆ ◆ ◆ ◆ ◆ ◆ ◆ ◆ ◆ ◆

CASE STUDY

The case of the animals in the furniture

Nancy Y. and her husband purchased a suite of fairly expensive living-room furniture from a local outlet. Eighteen months later, when any possible warranty had long expired, they began noticing little piles of sawdust on the floor, and tiny holes in the wooden parts of the furniture. Further research persuaded them that their lovely furniture was infested with termites. The store denied any responsibility, and various third-party agencies advised them that there was little hope of satisfaction after all this time.

Nancy brought some clear evidence to the local university entomology department and learned that the creatures in question were of a sort that would have been in the wood for two years before boring their way out. In other words, they were in the wood when the furniture arrived from the Philippines. Armed with this information, in a burst of creativity, Nancy went to the U.S. Customs Service, which was able to nail the furniture company for importing animals without a license! When the furniture was thus declared illegal, the manufacturer had no choice but to make a full refund.

◆ ◆ ◆ ◆ ◆ ◆ ◆ ◆ ◆ ◆ ◆ ◆

◆ ◆ ◆ ◆ ◆ ◆ ◆ ◆ ◆ ◆ ◆ ◆ ◆

CASE STUDY

The case of the dying child and the missing boom box

We purchased a portable Fisher tape player to use in the folk dance classes we teach. While the sound was adequate for an inexpensive unit, the search feature did not work properly. Under warranty, we returned it to the warranty repair center, a private electrical shop. A few weeks later, we were told that because they could not fix it, they had returned it to the Fisher company. We were told that the local repair depot would keep us apprised of the situation, that we were not to contact the company directly.

After another two weeks, I wrote a polite letter to the director of Consumer Services at Fisher. No reply. Two weeks later, I wrote to the president of Fisher: a polite, well-reasoned letter, explaining that our folk dance group was suffering because of low-quality music from a small portable, and the entire group knew that Fisher was to blame. No answer.

Around this time, our youngest daughter was in bed with a bad cold. With her reluctant permission, I wrote again to Fisher, explaining that my sick child (I did not explain how sick) was made cheerful by the joyous sounds of music from our Fisher tape player, and now, without her source of music, she was despondent and possibly growing sicker. No answer.

A couple of weeks later, I prepared a news release in the form of a newspaper story, and sent it by certified mail to the president of Fisher, hinting that copies might shortly be sent to all the major media. It began as follows:

GRAVELY ILL TOT ASKS: IS MY MUSIC BACK YET?
Fisher Company has taken months to repair the tape player that brought some joy into little Tanya Bear's life.
Berkeley, October 9

Distraught father John Bear left his daughter's bedside this afternoon to tell us about the dismal way the Fisher Company has been treating his gravely ill daughter, Tanya, age nine. "The sound of cheerful Greek and Russian music tapes, played on our modest Fisher tape player, was one of the few things that brought happiness into her gray days," Bear reported. But two months ago, the Fisher product was returned to the factory for repairs, and not only has it not been fixed, the company has failed to acknowledge Bear's increasingly desperate requests.

Every day, when little Tanya hears the letter carrier, she opens her eyes and asks, "Is my music back yet?" And every day, her sad parents must answer, "No, Tanya, Fisher hasn't sent you your music yet."

Two things happened. First, a brand new tape player arrived by overnight service three days later. No letter of apology, no letter at all, just the unit. And then, a couple of weeks later, the local repair depot called and said, "Good news. Your tape player has finally been fixed and returned." What the hell. We gave one to a local shelter for battered women and their children and kept the other. Fisher never did write, and years later, I still have a sour taste when I think of that episode. We have spent several thousand dollars on stereo equipment since then, none of it Fisher.

◆ ◆ ◆ ◆ ◆ ◆ ◆ ◆ ◆ ◆ ◆ ◆

CASE STUDY

The case of the iron that no got hot

When her out-of-warranty steam iron failed to heat up, a Marin County housewife wrote to General Electric to see if they might have suggestions before she sent it to a repair center. A GE engineer wrote back, offering some thoughts and suggestions. The woman tried them, they didn't work, but other possibilities came to her, so she wrote again. Once again, a prompt and thoughtful reply from GE. This exchange went on for a while, until it occurred to this woman that she didn't need a pen pal, she needed an iron. So she put the defective iron in a paper bag and, holding her broad tip marker in the opposite hand, scrawled "Iron, she no get hot" on the bag, and mailed it off to General Electric. Almost by return mail came a brand-new steam iron.

◆ ◆ ◆ ◆ ◆ ◆ ◆ ◆ ◆ ◆ ◆ ◆

THE POWER OF ONE

There are times when it seems inconceivable, unthinkable, impossible that one lone individual could take on a gigantic, monolithic, multi-billion-dollar international corporation. Someone once lamented to Mohandas Gandhi, "What can I do, I am just one person." The Mahatma replied, "But *everyone* is just one person." And so indeed, throughout history, from Moses to Joan of Arc to Gandhi himself, we have seen that "just one person" had a tremendous effect on others, on society, even on the course of history.

The lore of complaining has many heroes and heroines, some of whose stories are told in the case studies throughout this book. More than once, a single complaint has had quite a dramatic effect.

Dorothy Spielman of Norwalk, CT, complained about utility bills that seemed too high and questioned an unexplained 6 percent surcharge. After her state's Department of Consumer Protection and Department of Public Utilities Control did not help, she exercised her taxpayer's right to demand an audit of the utility's books. Soon the chief state's attorney became interested. The end result was that all three utility commissioners, a former commissioner, and three others were arrested for what Chief State's Attorney McGuigan called "wholesale debauchery" of the utility.

In some quarters, a lengthy published complaint from Jessica Mitford on the practices and performance of the Famous Writers School is given credit for bringing down that once large and famous institution.

This might be thought of as the brush-off that cost General Motors $20 million. Joe Siwek of Chicago took his Oldsmobile in for a checkup. That was when he discovered it had a Chevy engine in it. General Motors told him that the Olds engine is virtually identical to the Chevy, and he shouldn't worry his pretty little head over such matters. Incensed, Siwek went to the attorney general of Illinois. The end result of his visit was that the attorneys general of forty-seven states ended up suing General Motors for misleading advertising, and the company agreed to pay over $20 million in refunds to Oldsmobile owners.

Once in a while, a complainer goes off the deep end. He or she not only gets incensed, upset, or outraged, but also happens to have a rare combination of creativity, public relations skills, money, timing, showmanship, and a bit of luck, such that the complaint takes on a life of its own. Here are three such stories, culled from the pages of the *Wall Street Journal,* the *New York Times*, and (he said immodestly) my own archives.

David Merrick versus Chrysler Corporation

In 1967, the famous and flamboyant Broadway producer purchased a top-of-the-line, made-to-order Chrysler limousine for $14,000, a sum that at the time easily represented a year's salary for many white-collar workers, teachers, and professionals.

Before long, Merrick decided he had made a terrible mistake. As he tells it, one thing after another failed on this luxury car, and "I took it back 200 times—literally. In three or four years the repairs have cost $6,500."

Merrick attempted to return the car to Chrysler for a refund. After all, he reasoned, he had once closed one of his plays, *Breakfast at Tiffanys,* while still in rehearsal, because he felt it was awful, and refunded $1.5 million in advance ticket sales. Surely Chrysler could do the same for him. But they refused.

The *New York Times* sells small advertisements on page one of the newspaper. They are not inexpensive, and often hard to get, but Mr. Merrick bought one, on New Year's Eve. It read, in utter simplicity,

---

MY CHRYSLER IMPERIAL
IS A PIECE OF JUNK.
—*David Merrick*

In the ensuing furor, Merrick cheerfully gave out interviews and sent out press releases, describing almost gleefully his trials and tribulations. "They fixed the power steering at least 20 times. The transmission fell off of it. They were constantly having to fix...the alternator. The shock absorbers needed repair. And they always had some excuse why it wasn't covered by their guarantee."

Merrick claimed that the manager of Chrysler's repair center in New York, Hugo Percopo, admitted the car was a lemon. Percopo denies having said that. Percopo also denied that Merrick's problems were in any way unusual, and that it was repaired fewer than 100 times, not the 200 times Merrick claimed.

The manager of Chrysler's Manhattan dealership, Frank Suslavich, tells quite a different story from Merrick. He says Merrick wanted his money back, but instead he was offered the occasional use of a Chrysler in Hollywood. The manager went on to say that Merrick then asked for the use of a Chrysler in Washington as well, plus $25,000 in cash. Merrick absolutely denied this, saying, logically, "What would I want with another Chrysler?"

What Merrick *did* ask for, he says, was a free Mercedes-Benz, in return for which he would promise not to run any more ads. When Chrysler offered him, instead, a discount on a new Chrysler Imperial, Merrick went into overdrive. He produced an advertisement with a large cartoon drawing of a horse towing a Chrysler into a junkyard. The caption: "Good riddance! (signed) David Merrick."

While the *Miami Herald* and some other newspapers ran this new ad, at least ten, including the *New York Times* itself, rejected it. Merrick launched a new barrage of press releases. "If a corporation has the right to advertise its product, a consumer should have the right to answer that advertisement if he wants to pay for the space." For its part, the *Times* said that they never should have run Merrick's first ad, since they have a policy against such things, but it somehow slipped through during the Christmas rush.

Merrick's next salvo was a two-inch-by-four-inch ad reading

> CHRYSLER?
> Try it—you WON'T like it!
> (signed) David Merrick

Again, the ad was run in many papers, but some, including the *Wall Street Journal*, rejected it. "We just didn't think it was in good taste," said the *Journal*'s ad production manager. "We're not protecting Chrysler. It's just like we don't take ads for books on sex."

Merrick's final assault on Chrysler came by circumventing the problem of persuading a newspaper to run a hostile ad. He had thousands of posters printed up, recapping his story, and had them plastered on billboards, walls, and fences in New York and Los Angeles. And with that, he declared that his war was over, and clearly (he said) he had won, at least in terms of personal satisfaction. He had spent far more than the cost of his new Chrysler on his campaign, but "who knows how many other people bought a Cadillac or a Lincoln because of what I did. The company has to be hurting." And the *Wall Street Journal* referred to him as "the Ralph Nader of the limousine set," which he clearly enjoyed.

What of Merrick's car? Soon after Merrick moved on to other things in life, it was found, abandoned, without license plates, in upstate New York. For the rest of his days, Merrick rode around in taxis and never passed up an opportunity to bad-mouth Chrysler.

Jeremy Dorosin versus Starbucks Coffee

In the spring of 1995, Jeremy Dorosin, a thirty-seven-year-old owner of a scuba shop in a San Francisco suburb, purchased a $300 Italian espresso machine at the Berkeley branch of Starbucks, a $500-million-a-year national chain of coffee stores. When the steam pump broke soon after, he brought it back to the store, which cheerfully agreed to fix it and gave him a free loaner machine for the duration.

Dorosin liked the loaner machine so much that he decided to buy one as a wedding gift for a friend. He reports that he was concerned that the box looked a bit dog-eared, but he was reassured that European boxes often look that way. At the cashier, he asked for the free eight-ounce bag of coffee that Starbucks generally gives with the purchase of a machine and was told that he did not qualify. When he asked for at least a free cup of cappuccino, he says he was curtly told, "You get nothing." And furthermore, the gift machine turned out to be rusted, with a missing part, he said. (Starbucks acknowledged that he was not treated well, but denied the allegations about the machine.)

Dorosin now complained directly to Starbucks headquarters in Seattle, suggesting that it would be appropriate to send his friend their best espresso machine. (When he was told that their best machine sold for $2,500, he said that instead he would settle for their second best, at well under $1,000.) Starbucks declined, but did offer to replace both machines or to refund the purchase price.

Dorosin found this unacceptable and so, with his own savings, he purchased an ad in the Northern California edition of the *Wall Street Journal* (which clearly had overcome its shyness for accepting such ads, in the years since David Merrick):

> Had any problems at Starbucks Coffee?
> You're not alone.
> Interested? Let's talk.
> (800) 510-3483

While many people responded to the ad, Starbucks was not among them, and so a week later he ran it again, this time in an edition of the *Journal* covering fourteen western states. Shortly after the ad ran, Dorosin and his friend each received a bundle from Starbucks. Each was sent a new espresso machine (a $270 model), a pound of coffee, a steaming pitcher, a cup and saucer, salt and pepper shakers, a $30 refund, and a letter of profound apology.

Both packages were refused as "too little too late. The truth is that Starbucks did not take me seriously, and they did not send anything until after my second ad appeared."

Next, according to the *New York Times,* Dorosin demanded that Starbucks invest nearly a quarter of a million dollars in a national two-page ad in the *Wall Street Journal,* apologizing to him and admitting the error of its way. But he later suggested, instead, that the company underwrite a center for runaway children in San Francisco.

The battle goes on. Starbucks, which has prided itself on its level of customer service, seems baffled. "If we can't settle this, where are we as a nation?" asks Barbara Reed, the company's manager of customer relations. "I'm a lot poorer now but no more satisfied," said Mr. Dorosin, who reported that he had spent more than $10,000 on the ads and the 800 telephone service.

Customer service expert Ron Zemke, co-author of the popular book *Delivering Knock Your Socks Off Service*, points out that one irate consumer with deep pockets can have a real impact:

> Mr. Dorosin obviously feels he has not gotten any real
> sympathy for his situation from Starbucks, even though
> they have volunteered to rectify his material complaints.
> That lack of empathy, whether it's real or perceived, is
> what this case revolves on, and it's the point with which
> other consumers identify. The only way a company can get
> out of a hole like this is to make a dramatic gesture, and
> for a $500-million-a-year company, that would not be
> too painful. If I were Starbucks, I'd be in San Francisco
> right now with a shovel, digging the foundation for that
> runaway center.

John Bear versus Land-Rover

This is the story of how I fell in love with an automobile company, then fell out of love with them, and finally singlehandedly (well, I like to think so) put them out of business when they refused to respond to my complaints.

In the early 1960s, I bought a very used Land-Rover from Tom McCahill, then the automotive editor for a major magazine. "Old Hippo" was a fine vehicle, and I loved her, until one day, some vile thing happened to the transmission in the middle of nowhere, in downstate Illinois. The nearest Land-Rover dealership was more than 400 miles away. I telephoned the headquarters of the company in New Jersey, and there ensued that legendary kind of service scenario that I thought only happened to Rolls Royce owners, and even then, probably only in press agents' fantasies.

The company made a great many inquiries by phone, somehow located a retired British auto mechanic who lived not far from my disaster, made an arrangement with him, and air-freighted him the necessary parts and manuals that very day. They even made provision for me to stay at a pleasant local hotel. The next day, the parts arrived, the repairs were made, and I was on my way. They didn't know me from Adam, and they didn't charge me a penny.

We now skip forward a few years, when Old Hippo has been gracefully retired, and replaced with a brand new, bright red Land-Rover, purchased directly from the factory and delivered to the dock in San Francisco. We loved that car, which smoothly transported our family to Iowa City, where I was to take up a teaching post at the University of Iowa.

Only a few miles after the miserly 12,000-mile warranty expired, so did the engine. It quite literally exploded. A defective cylinder flew apart, with the ensuing shrapnel tearing parts of the engine to shreds. This time, the anguished phone call to New Jersey fell upon uncaring ears. "Bring the car into the dealer in Chicago," I was told. "They'll have a look at it." They didn't seem to appreciate that the vehicle was hundreds of miles away, and the engine was chopped liver.

The Iowa City towing service got its biggest job ever. And the Chicago dealer issued the standard refrain, "I've been working on these babies for twenty years and never seen anything like this." The quoted cost of replacing the engine was equivalent to two months' salary for an associate professor.

This did not seem right to me. I took an inner vow that either the company would make things right for me, or I would do my best to destroy the company. They didn't, so I did.

I began with all the polite and proper things one normally does. Letters to Land-Rover of North America. Letters to the main factory in Solihull, England. Certified, return receipt. Copies of all documentation. No replies, other than a few curt form letters.

Unlike Mr. Dorosin and Starbucks, I felt no need to get in touch with other unhappy Land-Rover owners. My wish was to get in touch with *potential* Land-Rover buyers and tell them my problems. I began by running the following ad in the classified sections of upscale yuppie political and social magazines:

THINKING OF BUYING A LAND-ROVER?
Let me tell you my sad story before you do.
[My name, address, and phone]

When people responded, and several hundred did, I sent them a detailed and documented write-up of my saga, complete with copies of repair bills and letters of opinion I had secured from three experienced British mechanics. I asked the recipients of this packet to write back and tell me what effect it had on them. It is important to note that at the time, the Land-Rover was quite a popular vehicle, riding the crest of a creative national advertising campaign.

One by one, just the sort of letters I had hoped for began to come in. "I was wavering between a Jeep and a Land-Rover, and your letter persuaded me to go for the Jeep." "I was going to sign the papers next week, but now I've put the deal on hold." I hit the jackpot with a long and thoughtful letter from a large New England surveying firm. Its senior partner explained how they had been researching the replacement of their entire fleet of vehicles, had narrowed their choice down to the Land-Rover or the Toyota Land Cruiser, and following my report and their subsequent investigation, they were now going to purchase twenty-eight Toyotas.

Now I had evidence that I was responsible, or partly responsible, for preventing the sale of more than fifty Land-Rovers, nearly half a million dollars' worth, and goodness knows how many others who didn't bother to write back to me.

Now I was ready for Phase II.

I prepared a thirty-two-page booklet, with the title *John Bear's War on British Leyland Motor Corporation.* British Leyland was the company that then made Rover and Land-Rover cars. The booklet contained the same case history and documentation that I had been sending to ad answerers, and copies of the many letters that I had received from would-be Land-Rover buyers who had bought something else.

I mailed a copy of my *John Bear's War* booklet to every Land-Rover dealer in the United States, along with a letter saying that I would continue until my demands were met. My demands were simple: a full refund of all my repair bills, and one of the new Range Rovers that the company had just introduced.

The really annoying thing here is that I could not be the fly on the wall, to see what those dealers thought and did and said to headquarters as they came to realize that some crazy man seemed to be dedicating his life to putting them out of business.

And the really satisfying thing is that right around this time, the company fell on really hard times and cut way back on its dealerships and activities in the United States, and worldwide. Although it was technically not a bankruptcy, a report by the National Audit Office in Britain revealed, to great public outrage, that the government had paid more than $6 billion to support the failing fortunes of British Leyland, which by then had been renamed BL Ltd., and later the Rover Group Plc. And even with that level of support, plus the sale of 20 percent of the company to Honda for another $2.5 billion, they went down and down. Finally, as *Automotive Industries* magazine reported a couple of years ago, "Automotive industry experts believe that Rover could not survive without a buyer." Sorry, I'm not interested.

Eight and a half billion dollars of needed support. I don't suppose I could have been responsible for *all* of that, but then, one never knows, does one?

There has been a long lull in my war. Even though I don't have a Range Rover (yet) I do have plenty of satisfaction. And I must confess that telling my story all over again in this book has set my militaristic juices flowing. So watch out, BMW (the new owner of that which once was Land-Rover), and hand me my musket, Ma, I am needed at the front!

CHAPTER 10

Avoiding the Need to Complain in the First Place

KEEPING YOUR PATIO FURNITURE DRY

THERE WAS ONCE A BOOK of handy home hints that actually contained the following handy home hint: "To keep your patio furniture from getting wet when it rains, bring the furniture inside." It is almost the same level of helpfulness to point out that the best way to deal with complaints is not having to complain in the first place.

It is not the province of this book to replace or even summarize the dozens of fine books and the hundreds of magazine articles that tell you how to be a wiser shopper and buyer, thereby reducing the need to complain later on.

I do not need to tell you to follow instructions, although I may make an exception for the woman who complained to Alberto-Culver that her hair was ruined when she washed it with a combination of Alberto VO-5 and Miracle Whip.

I do not need to tell you to comparison shop, to buy from known sellers, and to be very clear about the refund and exchange policy, not because this isn't useful information, which even you may benefit from, but because there is so much of it that it could easily fill this book and then some...and, thankfully, it is all available in other reasonably convenient places, including one quite wonderful free government source.

SOME REASONABLY CONVENIENT SOURCES OF CONSUMER INFORMATION

The only three phrases you need to be told, or reminded of, are public library, Better Business Bureau, and Internet.

The library

You built the public library, you taxpayer you, and you pay the salary of those generally very helpful reference librarians. Of course the library will have *Consumer Reports* magazine, and other consumer magazines, plus the *Reader's Guide* to direct you to magazine articles, and all of those books in the 380 section of the shelves, and whatever booklets and brochures may be lurking in those mysterious filing cabinets you've always wondered about. If they also have newspapers and magazines on microfilm or CD, or a connection to an on-line computer service, so much the better.

The Better Business Bureau

For all that is good and all that is bad about them, they do turn out an awful lot of booklets and brochures to help consumers avoid situations in which they will need to complain. When I checked just before publication, these were the booklets and brochures that were available without charge:

Scams

Yellow Pages Invoice Scams Proliferate
How the Faithful Can Avoid Investment Scams
How to Avoid Check Cashing Fraud
Boiler Room Schemes
Foreign Lottery Scams

Automotive

Filing an Auto Insurance Claim
Don't Get Soaked Buying a Flood-Damaged Car
Black Market Freon Could Damage Your Car
Auto Repair

Home

Buying an Unbuilt Home
Hiring a Home Improvement Contractor
Tips on Hiring a Snow Removal Contractor
Child Care Services

Money and Investments

Is the Scanned Price Always Right?
Refinancing Your Mortgage Loan

Money and Investments cont.
Going-Out-of-Business Sales
Tips on Shopping Overseas
What You Should Know about Pawn Shops
Buying Computers by Mail
Protecting Your Long Distance Service
Travel Packages
Planning a Cost-Effective Move
Tips on Tax Preparation
Living Trust
Certificates of Deposits
Child Care Services

Charity and Philanthropy
Charity Coin Collection Devices
Advertising in Charity Publications

Health
Home Health Care
Weight Loss Promotions
Ordering Medications from Abroad Is Risky

Jobs
Job Listing Services
Tips on Using a Temporary Services Agency

The Internet

Yes, I know that praising, much less talking about, the Internet for those 92 percent of you who wouldn't know what to do if it came up and bit you on the ankle, is as annoying as launching off into an essay on the pleasures of driving for people who don't own a car or who live on a tiny roadless island in the South Pacific.

So I won't belabor the point. I will simply suggest to those that have access, go without hesitation to the following address: http://seamless.com. There you will find immense amounts of valuable information on all legal matters, including consumerism and complaint avoidance. And, thanks to the effective and comprehensive efforts of the Alexander Law Firm, you will find the full text of more than one hundred consumer brochures culled from the offerings of many different government agencies.

THE BEST GOVERNMENT PUBLICATION OF ALL

In what may have been one of the best uses of taxpayers' dollars since the purchase of Alaska, our federal government has produced a truly remarkable little book that puts more valuable and specific complaining information in one place than anything else I have seen. It is called the *Consumer's Resource Handbook*.

Here, just read the introduction to get a quick overview of what this wonderful little book offers, before I tell you about its uncertain future and why you may not be able to get a copy.

> Dear Consumer:
>
> Given the appropriate tools and resources, every consumer can be empowered to be a consumer advocate. That is why the United States Office of Consumer Affairs is proud to introduce the eighth edition of the *Consumer's Resource Handbook*—a tool for consumers. This popular publication is one of our efforts to serve the public with useful consumer information.
>
> The *Consumer's Resource Handbook* is designed to help consumers make informed purchasing decisions and avoid problems in today's complex marketplace. When problems do occur, the *Handbook* is effective as a do-it-yourself manual for getting those problems resolved. Designed to be "user friendly," the *Handbook* helps consumers handle their complaints by listing contact names, addresses and phone numbers for corporations, non-profit organizations, and Federal, state and local government agencies. It advises readers about what to do before and after making a purchase, as well as how to handle problems with products or services. In addition, the *Handbook* includes valuable tips on a wide variety of specific and timely consumer topics, ranging from car repair to medical privacy. Many experts have given their time, talents and resources to make this *Handbook* the best ever. Please let us know if you find it helpful.

This splendid book is helpful. It's valuable. It is well designed and well written. It is on recycled paper. It is absolutely free. As I read through it, I marveled, over and over, how extraordinary it is for our very own government to have done this wonderful thing, to help untold thousands, perhaps millions, of citizens become more effective consumers. Here is our very own government, not only showing us how to get what we deserve from those huge corporations, agencies, car companies, and others, but even giving us the precise name and title of the very person we should complain to.

Surely, I thought, there must be immense pressure from all those politicians and bureaucrats in Washington, elected and supported with the help of money from these very plutocrats who must be suffering, at least a little bit, by the activities of the people who were sent this free book.

My worst fears were, I thought, confirmed when I called the Federal Information Center in Colorado in early 1995 and was told that the 1995 edition had been canceled. I was all set to go into high complaint mode myself. I started by calling the Department of Consumer Affairs in Washington, where the wonderful Estelle Rondelo defused my indignation even before I was able to shift into second gear. She told me that yes, the 1995 edition *had* been skipped, but the 1996 one was literally coming off the press that very day and would shortly be available to the waiting world. Good!

The bad news is that due to budget cuts, only a small fraction of the books needed to meet the expected demand were actually printed, and there is no assurance that there will ever be any more, either of the 1996 version, or ever again. Ms. Rondelo says gamely that "we'll do everything we can to ensure it stays in print."

Even if out of print, the book is available for inspection and downloading on the Information Center's computer bulletin board (accessible by computer at 202-208-7679), and also via their World Wide Web site on the Internet, which can be reached thus: http://gsa.gov/staff/pa/cic/cic.htm.

Because it's not copyrighted, here's what I've done.

Like most government publications, the *Consumer Resource Handbook* is not copyrighted because our government encourages wider distribution of its contents. Because there is so much good stuff in there, in the direction of heading off future complaints, I have extracted more than twenty pages of especially helpful information and deposited it in the back of this book as Chapter 18.

A FEW WORDS FOR COMPANIES

It is always sad, as a complaint-oriented consumer, to read about things like "Operation Freezer Burn," in which authorities in Jacksonville, Florida, installed a good used refrigerator in a home, had its perfect condition certified by two experts, then disconnected one obvious wire or simply turned down the thermostat, and called a repair service listed in the yellow pages, feigning ignorance of the problem. In fact, they called twenty-eight repair services, one after the other, and only eight did the "repair" promptly and correctly. Eight others took a long time but finally got it right, and twelve of the twenty-eight (43 percent) were so phony, claiming major repairs needed, with additional parts, that when the sting stung, they ended up pleading guilty to felonious fraud charges.

Ralph Nader has written about a comparable bit of depressing research done by some Washington, D.C., law students who removed a fuse from the back of a television set and found that most repair people wanted to replace the entire picture tube at a cost at least one hundred times higher than the cost of a fuse.

And I found more than a dozen articles in which newspapers and magazines, including the *Reader's Digest*, did the same sort of thing with car repairs and found an alarming number of service stations and repair people who did not behave as their Sunday School teacher might have wished, especially when the "victim's" car had out-of-state license plates.

So, while most sellers of goods and providers of services are undoubtedly honest and well intentioned, the ones who are not make knowledgeable and effective complaining a more important need and skill.

Even honest businesses can benefit considerably by monitoring, indeed *inviting* consumer complaints, as a means of identifying problems whose rectifying will head off more complaints in the future. Waiters who casually ask, as they whiz by, "How's everything here?" really don't expect a meaningful answer, but when Quality Inns calls each room half an hour after check-in to find out if everything is all right, they are genuinely concerned that their guest is pleased, or at least not likely to complain, and if there are complaints, they have learned about something to be changed in the way they do business.

CHAPTER 11

People Who Can Help

E VER SINCE THE ISRAELITES asked Moses to help them complain about higher taxes and government intervention in their lives, people with complaints have gone to third parties, in hopes of resolving their problems. Nowadays, we have a wide array of options, public and private, government and industry, helpful and unhelpful. Some do little more than send out form letters full of platitudes, while a few will (on occasion) marshal the troops and launch an all-out assault on your behalf.

But, as Arthur Best writes in his lengthy study of complaining,

> Almost all third parties handle complaints the same way. They attempt to mediate between the buyer and seller by reporting the buyer's complaint to the seller and the seller's answer, if any, to the buyer....In many instances, however, third parties create or acquiesce in consumers' unrealistic expectations of their role.

In other words: don't expect a lot. For many people, the main value of a third-party agency is being able to put "cc" or "copy to" at the bottom of your complaint letter. No offending company or service provider really believes that he or she will awake one morning to hear a bullhorn saying, "This is the Federal Trade Commission enforcement squad. Come out with your hands up." But the simple fact that you know enough to drop such a name identifies you as a more knowledgeable and thus perhaps more persistent and effective complainer.

GOVERNMENT AGENCIES

There are thousands of government agencies at the federal, state, county, and city level. The vast majority of them do not "accept" complaints from individuals and will, at best, send out a form letter suggesting some other agency. Some, like the Federal Trade Commission, will not intervene in an individual complaint matter, but they do keep track of complaints, and if there are enough of them, either about an individual, a company, or even an entire industry, they may initiate action.

Even worse, some of those that are mandated to deal with individual complaints really don't do so in any useful way, either because of being overwhelmed or disinterested or both.

For instance, for a long time, the president's consumer advisor's office had no power to do anything but reply in a friendly sympathetic way. "The letters we sent were horrendous," says one of the ghostwriters who wrote them. "It was a policy of the runaround," says another.

The way this office has responded to complaints is typical of what happens at many government agencies: the classic three-paragraph runaround.

The classic three-paragraph runaround

The first paragraph summarizes the complaint: "Thank you for your recent letter concerning your problem with the United Parcel truck that backed up into your mailbox and knocked it over." The second paragraph explains that this office is not the right one and/or is not able to intervene in individual complaints. And the third paragraph offers a few cliches, wishes them well, and quite possibly refers them to another agency.

An anonymous insider writes that when complaints come forwarded by members of Congress, they typically get a longer and more thorough response. From time to time, this particular office will pass letters along to companies, hoping that they will do something. It is certainly possible that something forwarded by the White House might carry a little weight, except with those receivers who know that no further actions will be taken and there is no enforcement procedure.

Is this really typical of how government agencies deal with complainers and complaints? In a word, yes. Of course there are many wonderful, conscientious people, ready and eager to help the public—probably some in almost every agency. But they are not in the majority, and with budgets being cut right and left for these "nonessential" matters, the situation is not getting any better.

One government complaint hotline, dealing with complaints about fifty-two different professions, from real estate agents to funeral directors to veterinarians, has twelve incoming lines, with three full-time and three part-time operators. They found that approximately 90 percent of calls produce a busy signal. Thus, on a typical day, 4,000 people call to complain, about 400 get through, and of those, about one-third "die" on hold.

Often, the telephone equipment cannot handle a sudden burst of calls, and as the calls start backing up, fewer and fewer people get through, even to be put on hold. On its busiest day, the agency just mentioned received 7,735 calls. Eighty-six people got through, and 7,649 got busy signals!

A study by the Pennsylvania state legislature found that when consumers telephone the complaint line at the Public Utilities Commission, 80 percent of all calls either produce a busy signal or are never answered. Of those that are answered, the average complaint required 56 days to be resolved (which, of course, doesn't mean *successfully* resolved), 35 percent longer than just two years earlier.

The most pervasive problem in the decline of government agency assistance to complainers is budget cuts. If, in the wake of cost-cutting mandates, a state is faced with canceling a proposed hiring of more prison guards, increasing tuition at the state university, or firing thirty people who deal with consumer complaints, it is the latter choice that will usually be made.

"There is a certain irony," says Randy Reid, a state consumer services executive. "Consumers are upset that there are not more of us here to help and not more incoming telephone lines, so they don't have to wait. The same person who is screaming, 'What do you mean you can't help me?' is, unfortunately, also the person who screams, 'Deregulation!' and wants to cut funding. If you want to have less government, that's exactly what you are going to have. You are going to have less services from the government agencies like ours. You can't have it both ways."

A law professor at Northwestern University attempted to get a handle on how all the major federal agencies deal with complaints.

Victor Rosenblum sent a lengthy questionnaire to eighty agencies. Sixteen of them never responded at all, despite several prompts and reminders. Some, such as Social Security and the Food and Drug Administration, took more than a year to respond. The average response time was about three months. And only thirteen of the sixty-four who responded had a clear office or unit or procedure in place specifically responsible for handling complaints. Only sixteen had any budget allocation specifically to deal with complaints. Fewer than half maintain any statistics on complaints received. Eighty percent say that complaints have not resulted in any changes in policy or behaviors. Indeed, the Environmental Protection Agency conveyed "the impression that citizen complaints have no relevance to protection of the environment."

The only thing that nearly all agencies had in common was the policy, whether written or otherwise, that when a complaint came in from the Office of the President, it was handled within twenty-four hours; from Congress, within seventy-two hours; and from the public "as soon as possible."

Things have clearly improved little, if at all, since one of the first occasions that the matter of consumer complaints was addressed by the Supreme Court. Justice William O. Douglas wrote, in the matter of *Johnson v. Avery*, 1969, that

> the increasing complexities of our governmental apparatus
> both at the local and federal levels have made it difficult for
> a person to...make a complaint. Social Security is a virtual
> maze; the hierarchy that governs urban housing is often so
> intricate that it takes an expert to know what agency has
> jurisdiction over a particular complaint....

For whatever it may be worth, a list of some of those federal agencies that have a complaint-receiving function, along with a list of each state's main state agency dealing with complaints, appears as Appendix C.

INDUSTRY-SPONSORED COMPLAINT AGENCIES

Companies that manufacture similar products or offer similar services often belong to industry associations. These associations help resolve problems between their member companies and consumers. Depending on the industry, you might have to contact an association, service council, or consumer action program. If you have a problem with a company and cannot get it resolved with the company, ask if the company is a member of an association. Many such associations are listed in Appendix E. If the name of the association is not included on that list, check with a local library. Generally, there are three types of programs to try to resolve complaints: arbitration, conciliation, and mediation. Usually, the decisions of the arbitrators are binding and must be accepted by both the customer and the business. In conciliation, sometimes only the business is required to accept the decision; the customer can either accept it or continue complaining. In some programs, decisions are not binding on either party.

RADIO AND TELEVISION ACTION LINES

Call for Action was a wonderful concept, started in 1963 by radio station WMCA in New York. It has grown into a national organization at radio stations with a staff, often mostly volunteer, available to help resolve complaints. Because the third-party complainer has the prestige and clout (or perceived clout) of the radio station, there may well be a greater likelihood of a successful resolution.

The national Call for Action office wrote to Ann Landers, inviting her to tell her readers that

> When you get ripped off, we help you get your money back. Our 650 volunteers nationwide are trained to follow each complaint until a resolution is found. If consumers contact our hot-line service, they can expect one of our experts to listen and take action. These scam artists are very good at what they do, but so are we. Consumers should write our national office with their full name, address and phone number, the name of the fraudulent company, how much money they lost and in what manner. We will put them in touch with the nearest CFA affiliate.

Their address is Call for Action, 3400 Idaho Ave. NW, Suite 101, Washington, DC 20016.

Not all radio and television action lines are a part of Call for Action. One of the most effective, an interesting hybrid, is the Consumer Help

Center of New York, a joint venture of the New York University Law School and the local PBS station.

They report that

> Intervention is successful in resolving seven disputes out of ten. Sometimes just the introduction of a third party into the dispute does the trick. Sometimes there has been a real misunderstanding and a neutral mediator can cut through this to hasten a settlement. More often, when intervention succeeds, it is a combination of persuasion and an explication of the consumer's legal rights to the vendor, coupled with the undoubted weight of the interview's identification with both a law school and a TV station.

NEWSPAPER ACTION LINES

Hundreds of newspapers have some form of an action line service, often connected with a daily or weekly column whose purpose, unabashedly, is to help sell more newspapers, hopefully while doing some good as well. But, as a study by Laura Nader found, over half the columns don't try to solve problems unlikely to be published. At best, they make routine and often unhelpful referrals to government or private agencies.

Still, as David Hapgood writes in *The Average Man Fights Back,* there is a new willingness among larger papers to disobey the wishes of government. Although the press ignores many of the "mundane daily screwings of the average citizen by, say, the health industry or a local bureaucracy, there is, however, one exception: the Action Lines...." Hapgood suggests that many of the columns "are occupied with fluff and trivia chosen to satisfy curiosity rather than need" and feature the "love of the cute item."

The *Detroit Free Press*, for instance, reports that

> [our] accomplishments have been both plentiful and unique. [We have] campaigned successfully on behalf of a woman reader who complained that D-cup bras unfairly cost more than smaller sizes; defeated a braggart bass fiddler who claimed he was the fastest plucker in town by arranging a contest with someone still faster; provided the proverbial two front teeth for Christmas for a boy who really needed them....

The *Baltimore Sun* claims a 70 percent "effective rate" for its action column, but, like the Better Business Bureau, they call "effective" those cases where the target says that nothing can be done.

Many of the action columns take some pains not to offend advertisers and other power-possessing beings. One survey found fewer than half the columns named names of offenders. The staff writers who turn out these columns sometimes try to evade this no-names policy. Trying to resolve a subscription dispute, one columnist wrote that he "called a famous men's magazine and spoke to a bunny there...."

Some newspaper columns are both militant, hard-hitting, and effective. Often cited as such is the *Rochester Democrat and Chronicle*. It named names, including, when relevant to the case, major advertisers in the newspaper. It enjoyed putting heat on slow-moving bureaucrats. One state official refused to send out scholarship moneys due. Columnist Jim Blakely promised to run his name every day in the paper, coupled with daily telegrams to the governor. After only a few days, "he became cooperative." Another time, there was an insurance company that caused many complaints. Blakely reports that "we just kept running the complaints until none of their insurance salesmen in a nine-county area was able to make a sale. People refused to deal with them. Finally the executives from the national office came down to straighten things out."

Mike Royko, Bob Greene, and other columnists

Some complaint stories are full of pathos, human interest, poignancy, and just make a darn good story. There are those syndicated and local newspaper columnists who, from time to time, take up a cause, write a column about it, and then, more often than not, write a second column to report on the effect of the first one.

◆ ◆ ◆ ◆ ◆ ◆ ◆ ◆ ◆ ◆ ◆   CASE STUDY

The case of AAMCO versus the eighty-three-year-old widow

An eighty-three-year-old Florida widow believed she had been fleeced when she brought her old but well-maintained car into an AAMCO shop for a checkup and wound up being charged $640 for a new transmission she didn't ask for and didn't think she needed.

Unable to gain satisfaction from AAMCO, she wrote to syndicated columnist Mike Royko, and here's what Royko did, and had to say about it, after he attempted to contact AAMCO on her behalf.

"What did they say? The owner of the AAMCO shop in Fort Lauderdale where the work was done said, in effect, that I could bug off. The people at the huge franchise chain's headquarters in Philadelphia said they had full confidence in the honesty of the wise guy in Fort Lauderdale.

"So I wrote a column about Mrs. Quinlan's experience and the response of the AAMCO people. And now I bring you the words of AAMCO's national director of consumer affairs: 'The facts were reviewed and brought to my attention. I decided that she would receive a full refund and may also keep the warranty.'

"That's nice of him. And had somebody at AAMCO decided to be nice—or practical—in the first place, we could have all saved ourselves a lot of bother."

◆ ◆ ◆ ◆ ◆ ◆ ◆ ◆ ◆ ◆ ◆

INDEPENDENT COMPLAINT-HANDLING AGENCIES

In addition to the governmental and the media-based complaint-handling agencies, there are some national, regional, and local consumer organizations, some of which deal with individual complaints, some of which tally them and lobby for changes within companies or industries, and some, like many government agencies, do some good and dispense many platitudes.

Often it is the small local or regional group, started or run by one or a few militant complainers, that have the most effect, such as TURN (Toward Utility Rate Normalization), which has had a dramatic effect on complaint issues with regard to public utilities in California, and CEPA (the Consumer Education and Protection Association of Philadelphia).

CEPA, the brainchild of longtime consumer advocate Max Weiner, has a simple three-point grievance procedure when a complaint is received: investigation, negotiation, demonstration.

After determining a complaint is valid (investigation), they will try to negotiate a settlement with the company. If that fails, CEPA members picket the business. They will start with the offending merchants or service providers. When relevant, they also demonstrate against the banks and other lending institutions that carry the loan paper on the complaint-worthy deals.

One of CEPA's first big successes followed demonstrations against banks and finance companies that would foreclose on mortgages and take over people's houses when only a small amount of money was owed. As Weiner exulted, "There were 50 or 60 lawyers representing those finance companies, trying to preserve that oppressive institution, and we beat them!"

A list of national private consumer organizations appears as Appendix B.

NOODGES AND KVETCHES

From time to time, the great idea occurs to people that there is a business in helping other people to complain. One such person is Beverly Sklover, the Noodge Lady. ("Noodge" is the Yiddish word for a relentless nag.) A former New York City planner and congressional aide with a law degree, the self-styled professional pain-in-the-neck takes on the battles of frustrated consumers who don't have the time, patience, tenacity, or other traits necessary to fight for what is rightfully theirs. She calls herself an intervener, conciliator, resolver of difficulties. She says most people don't know how to complain, and when they do, they often make matters worse.

One newspaper account of her skills tells the story of a woman whose remodeled kitchen was a disaster. The contractor knocked a hole in the wall, and the dishwasher leaked, ruining the carpet. Five months of complaining were to no avail, but when the Noodge Lady started noodging the contractor, a prompt settlement was reached. In such matters, she says problems occur long before they manifest themselves, usually by having a poor contract or none at all. There must be a penalty clause; there must be a statement that time is of the essence. "People don't realize how much leverage they have before they sign a contract. The contractor wants the job. There's not nearly as much leverage later."

My only complaint with the Noodge Lady is that, even though she is still in business and we had a very brief chat, she never returned my telephone calls. Maybe business is really good.

Or maybe it isn't. Three other such services that achieved a fair amount of publicity could not be found. Another person who achieved prominence in this profession, B. J. Ochman, the "Rent-a-Kvetch" ("kvetch" is the Yiddish word for someone who noodges a lot) could not be found. An ambitious new business called Customer Service USA, set up in Alabama to help people complain effectively, was not there three years later. And a "Special Forces Brigade" heavily promoted on the Internet as a service to help people complain electronically, never responded to my inquiries.

MEDIATION AND ARBITRATION

In these third-party services, one or more impartial people listen to both sides of a complaint, then offer their expertise in attempting to solve it. Mediation is a nonbinding activity. The mediator attempts to bring about a solution, but neither side is obligated to accept it. In binding arbitration, the two sides have agreed in advance that they will accept the decision of the arbitrator. If they cannot even agree on an arbitrator, often each side will choose one, and the two people thus chosen will jointly select a third person for the committee.

The American Arbitration Association (AAA) and comparable organizations in other countries offer professional arbitration services designed to be fast, affordable, and fair. The AAA makes use of a pool of more than 40,000 volunteer arbitrators, who don't have an easy job of it with many complaint situations. As the AAA says, "Consumer claims present a special challenge. Many disputes are between honest merchants and honest customers who disagree about the quality of the merchandise sold." Here is the "magic phrase" that, when inserted in any written contract, from the loan of a lawn mower to a neighbor, to the purchase of a skyscraper, will trigger binding arbitration, in lieu of endless complaints and, often, lawsuits: "Any controversy or claim arising out of or in relation to this contract or any breach thereof shall be settled in accordance with the rules of the AAA and judgment upon the award may be entered in any court having jurisdiction thereof."

Arbitration is not a panacea. One critic suggests that although it was designed as a simple, fair, low-cost alternative to litigation, it has become increasingly complex and increasingly like litigation itself. Nonetheless, one research study found that both parties are, if not thrilled, at least accepting of the arbitration decision 80 percent of the time, and more than 90 percent of the decisions are appropriately carried out.

Professional mediators can usually be found in the yellow pages under the heading of "Mediation Services." Many of them have been through training offered by some attorney general's offices or court systems, typically involving thirty hours of training, then a fairly long apprenticeship. In my part of the world, the phone book lists about thirty of them, ranging from private individuals (many of them attorneys) and businesses to city-run conflict resolution services, to a university-operated center for dispute resolution. Some are multipurpose mediators, while others specialize in a specific topic: divorce, business disputes, real estate, car problems, and even one dealing with trees that block other people's views.

THE COURTS

The courts are, in effect, the ultimate third party. When all else fails, the party with a complaint goes to court.

Small claims court

If the complaint involves money, and it is not too much money, then the small claims court is a reasonable alternative. The maximum dollar amounts vary from state to state, and range from $1,000 up to $10,000.

It can be simple, fast, and inexpensive. Most small claims courts don't allow lawyers; you and the other guy present your own cases, and a decision is rendered, sometimes on the spot, sometimes days or weeks later. And a study by Consumers Union found that in complaint actions, more than two-thirds are won by the consumer who complains.

Collection can be a real problem, whether you win a victory over the plumber who didn't fix your toilet properly or General Motors. The court may award you the money and order the other party to pay, but that doesn't mean they will without a fight or a chase. There do exist procedures in some jurisdictions whereby you can attach someone's bank account, salary, or car, but you often need the willing participation of a sheriff or other law enforcement officer who may be more concerned with catching brutal criminals than in helping you get a $75 refund from Macy's.

Be prepared. Many people "prepare" for small claims court by watching Judge Wapner dispense justice on the *People's Court*. It is probably better to read a good book on how to file and argue a case in small claims court, and there is none better than *The Small Claims Court Book* published by Nolo Press in Berkeley, California (800-992-6656).

Big claims court

If your complaint involves more money, or if doesn't involve simple money matters at all, or if it is sufficiently complex to require professional legal help, then you may wish to consider consultation with an attorney who specializes in your kind of complaint.

The following advice on this process comes from consumer lawyer Richard Alexander, whose most helpful Internet information area is described on page 111.

This is a big deal, and you must expect to spend a fair amount of time and energy, if not money, on initiating the process. Plan on devoting sixteen to twenty-four hours to finding the right lawyer. He or she should be a consumer specialist who will know many answers and thus not have to charge you for research. For instance, if your complaint is about a business in your area that gives off vile odors that make you sick, you will want a lawyer who already knows environmental law, so that you are not paying $150 an hour or more for them to hit the library and read up on these matters.

Where do you find the right lawyer? Not from the yellow pages or newspaper advertisements, please, although that can be one initial source. Here is how you will probably spend those sixteen to twenty-four hours: Almost every county has a county law library with available research materials. Every state has a state bar, the organization that licenses attorneys. Some state bars keep lists of attorneys by specialties, and if so, you can find some that specialize in your kind of problem. Call and ask for referrals.

Most states require Continuing Legal Education. Lawyers in charge of these programs are often good referral sources. The multivolume Martindale-Hubbell directory lists most of the lawyers in America, and many of the listings tell about specialties and qualifications. Some people ask judges of the general trial court in the county. The National Board of Trial Advocates (617-720-2032) and the National Association of Consumer Advocates (617-723-1239) make referrals of their members.

Alexander suggests that it is a good exercise to condense your entire complaint—why you think you need a lawyer—into twenty-five words or less. He offers these examples:

> "I worked with strong chemicals for years, and was just diagnosed with leukemia."

> "My mini van has been recalled three times and still overheats."

> "My contact lens company sells three different lenses that can be worn for different periods at different prices; they are all the same product."

Next, prepare a one-page typed summary of the complaint. When you telephone a possible law firm, offer to fax it or mail it to the paralegal who will be screening calls. You have every right to ask for a brochure describing the lawyer's services, fees, and professional resume. In addition, you should ask about the firm's track record in these kinds of cases. Ask for referrals to previous clients, and talk to them.

Many lawyers will not charge for their initial consultation, and some will not charge at all but offer, instead, to work on contingency. This means that if you win your case and collect money, the lawyer will take a percentage of the judgment. But if you are uncertain whether to initiate a lawsuit, it may be appropriate to hire a lawyer for an hour or two, as a paid consultant, to give you professional advice. If the lawyer says no, it isn't worth it, believe him or her (or seek a second opinion, and if it is the same, acknowledge that this is not necessarily a fair world, and some things are best walked away from).

◆ ◆ ◆ ◆ ◆ ◆ ◆ ◆ ◆ ◆ ◆ ◆ ◆ ◆

CASE STUDY **What Lana Turner's last husband did to me and what I didn't do back to him**

Her seventh and last was a man named Ronald Dante, a stage hypnotist who legally took the first name "Doctor," which was a lot cheaper than earning a degree. For years, using a whole Rolodex full of other names, Dante has operated a phony university, Columbia State University, from a mail-forwarding service in Louisiana. When I wrote about this operation in a book on earning degrees, Dante retaliated in a most ingenious way. He was able to trick the publisher of that book into renting him their mailing list of 18,000 people who had bought that book. Then he sent those 18,000 people a long "bulletin" purporting to come from some official agency in Washington, telling them what a reprehensible person I am, claiming I've been involved in dozens of phony ventures. This is, needless to say, absolutely and totally untrue.

I went immediately to a very good lawyer, who agreed that this was probably the clearest case of libel he had ever seen, but he strongly advised against suing, pointing out that to mount a really thorough suit could easily cost $50,000 or more, and in the United States, unlike England, the courts almost never require the losing party to pay the winning party's expenses. And, Sheldon Greene cautioned, even when we won, which we almost certainly would, the probability of collecting a dime from a man who, according to the Federal Trade Commission, has used more than forty aliases, is pretty slim. We did go through the exercise of using an assets-tracing service, and for a $400 investment, we learned about the location and contents of Doctor Dante's bank accounts and the size of the mortgage on his condo. If he is making big money selling phony degrees, then he is hiding it well. And so, with the greatest reluctance and considerable annoyance, I bit my lip, the bullet, and the dust, and let the matter drop.

◆ ◆ ◆ ◆ ◆ ◆ ◆ ◆ ◆ ◆ ◆ ◆ ◆

Consumer lawyer Richard Alexander points out that even when you find and hire a good lawyer, things will probably not move as smoothly as you might wish or expect from watching all those courtroom dramas on television. Good lawyers are very busy: in court, taking depositions, meeting other lawyers and clients, traveling, responding to motions. Do not expect your lawyer to be easily available when you call, or necessarily to initiate contact with you. He or she may have a hundred or more other clients at any one time, and some of them will fall through the cracks if they just sit back and wait for things to happen. Within reason, it is OK to be a bit of a noodge and a kvetch.

THE CLASS ACTION: PERHAPS THE ULTIMATE LEGAL COMPLAINT

The class action is a very special sort of complaint procedure, in which one person can bring a suit on behalf of himself or herself *and everybody else on Earth who might also have the same complaint.* The complaint can be initiated by an individual on behalf of all the others, whether they are known or not, and if successful, the offending company or organization must make amends to everyone who can be found and identified as a member of the group.

For instance, when a consumer believed that some airlines were illegally conspiring to fix prices, a class action suit was brought, resulting in tens of millions of dollars in refunds to anyone who could show that he or she had flown during a certain time period. Comparable class action suits have been victorious in matters relating to asbestos-related illnesses, long-distance telephone charges, silicone breast implants, overcharges on hotel bills, taxi fares, people denied employment for the wrong reasons at a department store, and the families of people killed by the Bhopal disaster in India.

For certain kinds of problems, affecting large numbers in similar ways, a single entity can bring a suit leading to the wrongdoer making amends to all consumers injured, plus judicial rulings requiring changes in future operations of businesses. Class actions can be initiated by one person; they do not require the participation or control of a third party. A single public-spirited citizen can accomplish much, to the benefit of all.

It is essential to find an attorney experienced in class action suits. Then the problem is often locating enough other members of the "class" to persuade the courts that there really is or was a serious complaint. That is why one increasingly sees big advertisements in national newspapers and magazines stating things like "If you worked at [such-and-such a store or company] between 1972 and 1979..." or

"If you flew on [such-and-such] airline between 1990 and 1994..." then get in touch with such-and-such a law firm regarding a possible class action suit.

◆ ◆ ◆ ◆ ◆ ◆ ◆ ◆ ◆ ◆ ◆

CASE STUDY

"You have what in your fan?"
The case of life and death in the Rising Sun

Dana Shilling, author of *Fighting Back: A Consumer's Guide for Getting Satisfaction*, lives in a New Jersey house she calls Rising Sun. ("It's been the ruin of many a poor girl, and I, oh Lord, am one.")

When she moved in, she discovered that the hot water heater had died; doors were hung at unusual angles; a sewer pipe fell out of the ceiling; and, the last straw, the out-of-warranty refrigerator had failed. Ms. Shilling telephoned the refrigerator manufacturer, whose customer service department gave her no hope of prompt service. She asked for a supervisor and was told that none was available.

After hanging up, she brooded a while, then redialed and this time asked for the legal department. When she got through to a staff member, she uttered what she believes were the three magic words: "class action suit." They asked if she would be home the next day. Yes, she said, writing letters to the editor.

A repair man arrived forty-five minutes later and removed two dead mice from the refrigerator fan at a cost to Shilling of $52 per mouse. The lesson she learned: "You must make the most dramatic threat you can short of threatening to blow up the plant; and...you must demand to speak to the highest possible officer."

◆ ◆ ◆ ◆ ◆ ◆ ◆ ◆ ◆ ◆ ◆

BUT WHAT IF YOUR EXPERT IS A CROOK?

Or not very bright, or not very caring, or on the payroll of the organization you're complaining about? It happens, but not often enough for one to grow too paranoid about it. There was one well-publicized case in which investigators for the New York City Consumer Affairs Department were indicted for accepting payoffs from managers of the very stores they were investigating. And the head of one of the large branches of the Better Business Bureau was similarly indicted for a wide range of offenses, including soliciting and accepting bribes from local businesses, in order to give them more favorable ratings.

But this is, thankfully, rare (as far as we know). Many of the complaints about the complaint process itself arise because consumers believe that a "third party" complaint handler is perhaps more of a "second party" one, in the employ of or influenced by the very entity being complained about. Sometimes this is obvious if you open both eyes. The Major Appliance Consumer Action Panel has been very helpful in resolving complaints, but it is financed by the appliance manufacturers themselves and may not always be as generous in their resolutions as, say, a small claims court judge or an independent arbitrator.

The most popular and most referred-to organization with regard to consumer complaints is in a complex sort of "gray area" and deserves looking at in some detail: the Better Business Bureau.

THE TRUTH ABOUT THE BETTER BUSINESS BUREAU

Is the BBB a "last best hope for the person with a complaint," or a "self-serving public relations agency"?

There are many "third party" organizations that you can turn to with a complaint, from federal agencies to Ralph Nader groups to the local newspaper action line. But no organization is turned to as often as the Better Business Bureau: well over ten million information requests each year. No organization is referred to as often by other agencies, consumer advisors, help lines, and well-meaning third parties.

And, it is safe to say, no other organization is as controversial as the BBB, in the sense that some critics find it a misleading, ineffective, untrustworthy, sometimes dishonest tool of business, while others see it as a serious force for good for consumers, and a provider of excellent and useful services for all. Where does the truth lie? As usual in such matters, somewhere in between, and the reason is a lack of understanding of what the BBB really is and really can (and cannot) do.

What the BBB says it is

There is no such thing as *the* Better Business Bureau. What we have is more than one hundred separate agencies, each with its own policies, rules, regulations, and mission. They are all members of a national trade association, the Council of Better Business Bureaus in Washington, but each one operates quite independently. Some offer free advice; some charge by the minute on a 900 telephone line; others sell annual memberships to consumers. Some offer arbitration and mediation services, some don't. Most are scrupulously honest, but then there was the disturbing case of the South Florida BBB, fifth largest in the country, whose president was imprisoned for, among other things, accepting bribes to make more favorable reports about certain companies.

The one thing that all BBBs have in common is that they are membership organizations, supported by local businesses, the very ones they are often asked to evaluate and make reports about. Can they truly be impartial? Stay tuned.

What the public thinks it is

As a result of all the publicity the BBB has gotten, both through its own public relations activities and the writings of many others, the public has come to think of it as a place to go to get honest, unbiased, objective information about a company or business, and a place to complain when one has a problem.

This alleged role is encouraged by many other agencies and organizations, either because they genuinely believe the BBB is going to help their client, or because they have nothing they can say or do, and so they are passing the buck, even if they know or strongly suspect that the BBB is inappropriate for receiving that particular buck. In other words, it gets those pesky, annoying consumers out of their hair (or office), and gives them someone else to complain to (and, in many cases, also complain about).

Such is the perceived power of the BBB that more than a few state, regional, or private consumer offices that went out of business due to loss of funding, have, as their official policy for those who approach them, a referral to the BBB. The no-longer-existent Alaska Department of Consumer Protection is one such example.

One study found that 90 percent of the people who complained to the BBB didn't know of any other way or place to complain.

What its worst critics say it is

In the delightfully titled book *Consumer Karate,* author Eric Reisfeld writes that the BBB is a

> self-serving public relations agency organized by local mer-
> chants for the primary purpose of deflecting the ire of their
> dissatisfied customers. Much like a lightning rod, they attract
> and direct complaints into a dead end, dissipating their force
> and thus protecting the local firm. The complaining customer
> rarely realizes that the person he is complaining to has his
> salary paid, in part, by the company he is complaining
> about....

In the hard-hitting book *Getting What You Deserve,* the authors (a former head of law enforcement for the New York Department of Consumer Affairs and the senior attorney for the New York Public Interest Research Group) say that the BBB is "often mistakenly believed to have some real power to resolve disputes. It doesn't, and is not a very aggressive pursuer of consumer rights—it is a business organization with a pro-industry stance."

In their 1994 book *How to Write Complaint Letters That Work,* Patricia H. Westheimer and Jim Mastro are quite blunt: "Better Business Bureaus are often included in a discussion of trade associa-tions....However we have excluded them here for a very simple reason: We have never been able to get through to the BBB for information or help."

A detailed report and analysis prepared by the staff of Congress-man Benjamin Rosenthal concluded that "it is a major conclusion of this study that the quality of information on firms communicated by BBB to consumers is extremely poor. With a few modest exceptions, it is misleading, inaccurate, and incomplete."

On what basis are these, and many more, criticisms based? There really is only one reason: a profound misunderstanding on the part of consumers, complainers, reporters, and indeed consumer-related agen-cies, of what the BBB really is and what it really does. Because of this, there are vast numbers of cases in which the consumer (and the press) feels that the BBB "didn't do its job," while the BBB would maintain that it was doing exactly what it should.

The misunderstanding is profound, and it is, in my opinion, a misunderstanding that is nurtured and fostered by the BBB itself, if only because of the misleading words that are used to describe their services and the outcomes thereof.

"The company said, 'Screw you.' Well, that's one more complaint resolved."

Various offices of the Better Business Bureau claim that upwards of 90 percent of all consumer complaints are "settled." For instance, the Philadelphia *Inquirer* newspaper was told by the second largest BBB that out of 20,000 complaints received in a recent year, there was a "dispute resolution rate of 91 percent on those complaints."

What exactly does "settled" mean? According to writer Joyce Munns, the BBB standard for "settled" is any one of these five results:

1. The company says it has corrected the problem.

2. The company says it plans to correct the problem.

3. The company offers a compromise that the BBB feels is reasonable.

4. The company offers a reasonable explanation for its position.

5. The company refuses to settle, saying the complaint is unjustified, and the BBB agrees.

"We have no negative information on Al Capone Industries." Does the BBB give out reliable information?

Often, to be sure. But not always, especially when you take into account the act of omission. If you call someone as you are checking up on an applicant for a job as a bank teller, and the person you call knows that this applicant just got out of prison for bank fraud, he may or may not choose to tell you this, depending on the exact question you ask and his relationship with the applicant.

The BBB rarely out-and-out lies (although that's what got the head of the south Florida branch sent to prison), but they don't always have the information you really want, or they choose their words very carefully in what they say, especially about their own members.

One researcher looked at twenty-eight companies that had been the subject of a complaint by the Federal Trade Commission. The FTC only files a formal complaint when there is clear evidence of violations of the laws against unfair or deceptive practices, typically following a long and thorough investigation. Indeed, more than 95 percent of FTC complaints result in formal "cease and desist" orders by the courts.

These twenty-eight companies were all local ones (the local BBBs might not keep information on the local branch of a national chain), and the complaints all involved matters of direct interest to consumers, not more complex matters like restraint of trade.

The BBB is supposed to report on negative government actions. Joyce Munns called the appropriate local BBB to ask what they could tell her about each of those twenty-eight companies. There was no report available on two, but on fifteen of the remaining twenty-six (58 percent), the BBB either had nothing negative to say (eleven cases) or only a hint of something possibly negative (four cases).

Of the completely misleading reports, 46 percent (and possibly as many as 63 percent) were on members of the BBB, while of the accurate or suspicious reports (telling or hinting about the FTC action), only one out of eleven was definitely a BBB member, seven were not, and seven were probably not, but accurate information was not available.

More depressing results from two other studies

Congressman Rosenthal's office asked the appropriate local BBB about twenty-five firms in which various law enforcement authorities had taken disciplinary action. Only one BBB report mentioned that fact, and only three of the twenty-five were negative at all.

And Joyce Munns learned about seventeen cases in which unhappy consumers had complained to the BBB and later said they were not satisfied with the outcome of their case. Munns phoned the relevant BBBs and asked, "Have you ever had complaints about such-and-such company?" In twelve of the seventeen cases, the BBB report "was clearly inadequate." For six cases, they said there had been no complaints, and for six more, they said the complaint had been "satisfactorily resolved." Here are some of those "satisfactory resolutions."

◆ ◆ ◆ ◆ ◆ ◆ ◆ ◆ ◆ ◆ ◆ ◆

"Wait a minute, I know they're here somewhere."
The case of the plumber who lost his tools

A Buffalo, New York, woman complained to the BBB about a plumber who billed her for 3½ hours of time while he was searching for his tools and certain parts, and 4 additional hours for the actual work done. The plumber replied to the BBB inquiry, "I feel we have been fair and there is no more credit due." The BBB, maintaining that they cannot resolve "factual disputes," closed this case and marked it "satisfactorily resolved."

◆ ◆ ◆ ◆ ◆ ◆ ◆ ◆ ◆ ◆ ◆ ◆

CASE STUDIES

The case of the FBI agent and the $30 tune-up
that cost $188: Chapter 1

Retired FBI agent Conrad Banner drove his old sedan to the Precision Tune Service Center, which was advertising a $29.90 tune-up special, 8 cyl. slightly higher. The "slightly" was $20 more, or 67 percent, but he bit his lip and told them to go ahead. Thirty-five minutes into the tune-up, Banner was called into the work bay. Much of his engine had been dismantled. He was told that one of his eight spark plug wires was defective. How much could that cost? Well, it turned out that Precision Tune had an unposted and unadvertised policy: they won't replace one wire, it has to be all eight or none at all. As Banner saw it, if he said, "None," he would have paid full price for an incomplete tune-up and would have to go elsewhere to replace the one wire and complete the tune-up. So he agreed to an $87 charge for the eight wires, seven of which he didn't want or need.

Next he was told the price did not include the distributor cap or rotor. So he ended up paying $188.45 for his $29.90 tune-up. He went home and wrote the local franchise and the parent corporation, Precision Tune Inc. "They stonewalled my complaints," he says. Then he wrote to the FTC complaining about deceptive advertising. The FTC referred him to a local consumer protection agency, which in turn referred him to the BBB, and then the fun really began.

◆ ◆ ◆ ◆ ◆ ◆ ◆ ◆ ◆ ◆ ◆ ◆

◆ ◆ ◆ ◆ ◆ ◆ ◆ ◆ ◆ ◆ ◆

The case of the FBI agent and the $30 tune-up that cost $188: Chapter 2

The BBB wrote to Precision Tune, asking for an explanation. The parent corporation responded, condoning its franchisee's actions. The BBB wrote to Banner that there was nothing further they could do because "under our economic system...companies can establish their own policies." Case closed, and marked "satisfactorily resolved."

◆ ◆ ◆ ◆ ◆ ◆ ◆ ◆ ◆ ◆ ◆

CASE STUDIES

And Chapter 3

Banner now filed a complaint against the local BBB, to the national Council of BBBs. Five months later, they replied, saying that the local BBB had behaved appropriately. Case closed, complaint resolved "satisfactorily."

◆ ◆ ◆ ◆ ◆ ◆ ◆ ◆ ◆ ◆ ◆

Finally, Chapter 4

Banner now went to his local Citizen Assistance Office. They went to bat for him aggressively and got Precision to modify its advertising, publicly post its "all wires or none" policy, instruct its people to explain policies to customers before dismantling their engines, and they refunded $78 to Mr. Banner for those seven unnecessary wires. Case well and truly closed.

◆ ◆ ◆ ◆ ◆ ◆ ◆ ◆ ◆ ◆ ◆

"Five tons of what?"

A West Virginia senior citizen ordered five tons of coal, to get him through the winter. What he got was about two tons of coal thoroughly mixed up with an additional three tons of rocks, dirt, and unmentionable substances. Following a complaint, the coal company assured the BBB that they had delivered just what the customer ordered. Case closed, satisfactorily resolved. The man went to a local senior citizens' program, which in turn threatened legal action, and, three months later, the proper coal was delivered to a now nearly frozen consumer.

◆ ◆ ◆ ◆ ◆ ◆ ◆ ◆ ◆ ◆ ◆

"Oh did I say days? Surely I meant months."

A woman in California brought her television into a local shop for repairs. She was promised her set back in two or three days. After more than two months of frequent phone calls and complaints, she brought her complaint to the BBB. Before the BBB even had a chance to send out its routine inquiry, the set was finally returned. The woman notified the BBB, which was able to record another "satisfactory" resolution, although the TV owner suggested the BBB should still have worried about the long delay and the failure to communicate.

◆ ◆ ◆ ◆ ◆ ◆ ◆ ◆ ◆ ◆ ◆ ◆

What then do we make of the BBB?

For all the nasty comments made about the BBB over the years, more than a few of them in the preceding pages, they do enough useful things to warrant paying attention to them, and even seeking their help, as long as you are very clear on the parameters under which they operate.

They are one of many places to start, either for checking up on a firm before you deal with them or for making a complaint about something a firm did to you.

In the former matter, don't expect full disclosure. The BBB may not know about certain problems, or they may not regard them as seriously as you would, or they may believe that the company has satisfactorily reformed and changed its policies. The one thing that is pretty certain is that if the BBB is worried about a company, then you should be. And if they aren't, maybe you *still* should be.

As for complaining yourself, be clear about just what your local BBB (or the one in the company's area) will and won't do. If the problem company is a member, and if the BBB offers arbitration, that may be a useful solution—but it also could mean you'll have to travel a great distance to take part, since such things usually happen in the company's own region, not yours.

But, like retired FBI agent Banner, more than a few people have ended up being more annoyed with the BBB than they were about the company that produced the original complaint.

The BBB on-line: a genuinely helpful outreach

The BBB has well and truly joined the twentieth century with its Internet outreach. When you sign on to their home page at http://bbb.org/bbb, you find a wide array of useful information, including their press releases and consumer alerts, the doings of their advertising review boards, a list of all of their 180 or so offices in the United States and Canada (although, in early 1996, only a small handful of those were also available on-line), and, most conveniently, a long and detailed complaint form, which consumers can fill out on-line and then transmit electronically to the BBB, which presumably passes it along to the relevant office.

The only problem with all of this is that this convenient way of getting information and interacting with the BBB is only available to that tiny percentage of consumers who know how to use the Internet and have ready access to it through their home or office computer, or a publicly available library computer.

CHAPTER 12

Revenge: When All Else Fails, There's Always This

SOME PEOPLE THRIVE ON REVENGE. It gets their juices flowing, and they savor the experience. Others find the concept repulsive, or alien to their way of thinking and acting, or karmically inappropriate. (More often than not, these two kinds of people are married to each other.)

No book on complaining would be complete without at least acknowledging that fact that when all else has failed—when it is unlikely that a complaint will ever be resolved in any satisfactory manner—there are some people for whom "getting even" is the way they close their file on the matter.

In his book *Techniques of Harassment,* Victor Santoro points out that "you can't go around indiscriminately harassing anyone who rubs you the wrong way. You'd spend your entire life settling grudges and this is a pretty negative way to live." Well said. However, Santoro goes on to suggest a wide array of unkind, unpleasant, perhaps illegal things to do, of which the least offensive may be taking out a subscription to a certain carefully chosen kind of magazine (nudist, Nazi, etc.) in the name of your "victim" but sent to his or her next-door neighbor's address, so everyone will be sure to know.

If you must consider something in this direction, please be gentle. Be *creative*. You can make your point, annoy people or organizations, and feel some measure of satisfaction, without causing real harm. Consider the family whose morning newspaper was regularly tossed into a puddle or their fish pond. When complaints failed, they paid their bill with currency floating in a jar of water.

There are far too many books out there on nasty revenge: the sort that could really cause lasting physical or emotional harm or that could have dire financial consequences for the victim. They have titles like *Get Even* and *Poor Man's Justice* and *The Complete Book of*

Dirty Tricks and *Your Revenge Is in the Mail*—you're going to have to find them on your own because I don't want to make it easier for you. Just don't do anything with Crazy Glue or fake letterheads. Moths and chickens? Well that might be another matter entirely, at least given certain circumstances.

◆ ◆ ◆ ◆ ◆ ◆ ◆ ◆ ◆ ◆ ◆ *CASE STUDY*

Revenge by moths

A man was at a movie in one of those twelve-theater complexes when nature called. On his way back from the men's room, he headed into the wrong theater. An usher intercepted him and accused him of trying to sneak from one theater into another. His explanation fell on deaf ears. When he asked for the manager, he was told the manager was not available, and he was firmly escorted from the building. No refund was offered. A few days later, early on a busy Saturday evening, he returned to the theater and bought a ticket for the most popular show. No one saw the large glass jar beneath his coat. At a crucial moment in the movie, he removed the lid from the jar, and the dozen large moths inside immediately flew into the beam of light from the projector, where they stayed, and stayed, and stayed.

◆ ◆ ◆ ◆ ◆ ◆ ◆ ◆ ◆ ◆ ◆

The days are past when one could get even on a nasty bank by renting a safety deposit box under an assumed name and storing a lovely fresh fish inside. However, one revenge book suggests that a chicken (packaged, from the supermarket) can be considered an inexpensive little time bomb, which can go undetected if left somewhere for a few days, but as time passes, its vapors will surely be noted, often long before the offending bird can be discovered.

◆ ◆ ◆ ◆ ◆ ◆ ◆ ◆ ◆ ◆ ◆ *CASE STUDY*

Revenge by chicken

One story tells of the young couple who bought a king-size bed at one of those huge sprawling discount furniture marts. But what the store delivered was a pair of twin beds. The salesman had written up the order wrong, and the couple had signed it without reading it. "Too bad," said the store. "You signed it. Your problem, not ours." After the couple complained, the store "graciously" agreed to take the twin beds back less a 20 percent "restocking fee." The couple reluctantly agreed. A few weeks later, they returned on a busy weekend afternoon, and when they left, miscellaneous chicken parts had been secreted in half a dozen locations around the store, under cushions, stuffed down into hide-a-beds, and so forth. Like many revenge-seekers, they were not present to witness the results, and the stories their imagination told them may well have been better than real life.

◆ ◆ ◆ ◆ ◆ ◆ ◆ ◆ ◆ ◆ ◆

I would like to think that it is just as satisfying, perhaps more so, to be creative and clever rather than out-and-out nasty when "getting even."

◆ ◆ ◆ ◆ ◆ ◆ ◆ ◆ ◆ ◆ ◆

CASE STUDY

Press here for a message

Jerry and LaDonna had a less-than-wonderful experience in a major chain hotel. Their room was not ready when they arrived, and it was not as clean as they might have wished. The air conditioner was noisy, there were not enough hangers in the closet, their room service breakfast was cold, and they were charged for an in-room movie they did not watch. And when they attempted to complain, they were told that the assistant manager was busy with a problem and could not talk to them. Their complaint letter produced a mild apology, but no offer of recompense. Back home, they noted that their local branch of this chain was headquarters for a regional political convention. LaDonna produced some very official-looking labels on her office computer, and just before the convention, she and Jerry installed them in a dozen locations in all of the hotel's public restrooms. And so every single one of the hot-air-blasting hand dryers had, affixed with strong glue, next to the "on" button, a rather official-looking sign that said, "Press here for a message from Bill Clinton."

◆ ◆ ◆ ◆ ◆ ◆ ◆ ◆ ◆ ◆ ◆

Elsewhere, I have discussed the matter of complaining as therapy. For some people in some situations, the act of complaining is the important thing, to get it out of your system. The result is less important. This is especially true of many of the revenge-based complaints. The ones that are especially elaborate or risky or both can take on a life of their own, such that it is hardly necessary to know whether it had its desired effect.

◆ ◆ ◆ ◆ ◆ ◆ ◆ ◆ ◆ ◆ ◆ ◆ ◆   *CASE STUDY*

The flowers that bloom in the spring, uh-oh

Ole and Lars, two brothers who live in a rural Minnesota town, applied for a business expansion loan at the only bank in town. They were turned down by the bank president not, they were quite sure, because they were unqualified, but because twenty years earlier, Lars had married Karen, a woman in whom the bank president also had a serious interest. They felt he was finally getting his revenge. The bank president lived on a large parcel of land, with rolling green hills, on the main highway just outside of town. Ole and Lars drove to the city one weekend, where they made certain purchases at a nursery, paying by cash. Working with military precision, they implemented their battle plan at dusk on a November evening when they knew the bank president would be attending a Rotary Club dinner. Time passed. Winter came, followed as usual by spring, and with spring, the daffodils Ole and Lars had planted came into full bloom on the hillside by the highway, spelling out a very rude seven-letter noun, plus an arrow pointing to the banker's home.

◆ ◆ ◆ ◆ ◆ ◆ ◆ ◆ ◆ ◆ ◆ ◆ ◆

From a research standpoint, not very much is reliably known about complaining through revenge and retaliation, in part because it is such an uncivilized or undignified sort of thing to study, and in part because it is almost impossible to get reliable data. People who actually do these things, many of them borderline or very illegal, are reluctant to talk about them, and those who do talk about them are quite likely to be lying through their teeth for the sake of telling a good story.

Some people researching complaint behaviors at Brigham Young University did acknowledge the role of retaliation, which they suggested was often illegal, and "most were outside the bounds of social propriety," especially, we must assume, in Utah society. The kinds of retaliation fit into one of six categories:

- destruction of property
- theft
- frivolous legal action

- spreading rumors and lies (the person who started the stories that McDonalds puts horse meat in its hamburgers and Bubble Yum contains spider eggs—Paul Krassner has claimed responsibility for both—probably had a pretty good reason to complain)

- physical disruption, such as switching dog food and stew labels on cans in a market, putting syrup into insect repellent sprays

- psychological hassling (threats, phone messages) and individual harassment (for example, having thirty-six pizzas delivered to the home of the manager of an offending company)

◆ ◆ ◆ ◆ ◆ ◆ ◆ ◆ ◆ ◆ ◆ ◆

CASE STUDY

The stubborn bank and the even more stubborn customer

Dr. Stuart Johnson was doing a real estate deal in Hilo, Hawaii. He needed to extract $25,000 from his account at the Bank of Hawaii and deliver it to the escrow company a few blocks away. When he asked for a cashier's check in this amount, he was told there would be a $10 fee. He marched over to the manager's desk to complain that it was inappropriate to charge him anything to remove money from his own account. The manager shrugged his shoulders and said, sorry, that is their policy.

Johnson then asked if he would be charged to be given cash from his account. "Of course not," he was told. "Fine," he said, "I'd like $25,000 in cash."

That simple request occupied the time of two tellers plus the supervision of the manager for more than an hour: bringing the cash out of the vault, counting it, recounting it, counting it a third time when the first two counts didn't match, then a fourth for good measure, then rebundling the bills in a tidy package. Dr. J never believed that the bank would respond to his complaint in this way, but what the heck, he had the time, and besides it made a good story to tell his friends when they were looking for a bank to do business with.

◆ ◆ ◆ ◆ ◆ ◆ ◆ ◆ ◆ ◆ ◆ ◆

Cathy Goodwin, in her doctoral work at U.C. Berkeley, looked at role relationships as they relate to various modes of complaining, including retaliation. When the consumer feels that he or she is in an ineffective or impotent position, up against a person or a company or an agency with considerable power and commitment, there is an increased likelihood of resorting to thoughts of getting even.

But then again, there are those times, those many times, when the gentle, creative revenge, designed to make a point without actually causing lasting harm, can really be the most satisfying of all. I do speak from experience.

◆ ◆ ◆ ◆ ◆ ◆ ◆ ◆ ◆ ◆ ◆

CASE STUDY

"Jacob, my son, I hear you are telling people that I don't exist, that you made me up."

I really enjoyed the book *Lost Christianity*, a purported nonfiction account of the author's, Jacob Needleman's, encounter with a "mysterious" Middle-Eastern holy man, Father Sylvan, and the manuscript (comprising the bulk of the book) that Sylvan's brotherhood delivered to Needleman after Sylvan's death. I liked this Sylvan fellow, and so I was really very annoyed when I learned, several years later, that Needleman was telling his students that Sylvan did not exist; he was a "literary creation." Annoyance produces complaining behavior, at least in my life, but who was there to complain to? Surely not the author, who knew just what he was doing. Friends? Colleagues? Bookstores? How about the publisher? As it happened, I was to be in Jerusalem in a few weeks. So I bought a large old book at a used bookstore and removed several of the blank pages, to secure sheets of old and weathered paper. I had a print shop turn those sheets into two letterheads of an obscure monastery in Palestine, and on those sheets, using an old typewriter at the public library, I wrote two letters from Father Sylvan. One was to the publisher of *Lost Christianity*, complaining that his manuscript had been printed in Needleman's book, and even worse, Needleman was now claiming he didn't exist. The other was a fatherly letter to Needleman, saying, in effect, "Jacob, Jacob, my son, have you truly forgotten that I am real, and that we met in that airport in Bangkok all those years ago. I hear you are telling people that I do not exist...." Both letters were duly mailed from Jerusalem. And that's the end of my story. Maybe those letters were dismissed as bad jokes or crackpot schemes. Maybe they caused a few moments of concern or amusement or wonder. I was so pleased, at the time, with the nature of my complaint that maybe I don't *want* to know what happened. (Well, maybe just a little.)

◆ ◆ ◆ ◆ ◆ ◆ ◆ ◆ ◆ ◆ ◆

CHAPTER 13

Complaints and the Media

THERE ARE TWO WAYS in which the media (newspapers, magazines, radio, and television) are relevant to complaining: complaints
about the media themselves, and using the media (most typically a letter to the editor or an article) to complain about a third party.

It is wonderful to think that in our great democracies, the right
of the people to complain, whether about their leaders, their country's
politics, or the local plumber who gave them bad service, is well established and defended. "I detest what you write," Voltaire said, "but I
would give my life to make it possible for you to continue to write."
This is often cited as the more eloquent if less accurate "I disapprove
of what you say, but I will defend to the death your right to say it."
The editors of *America* magazine wrote: "The mightiest man-made
force in human affairs is neither the H-bomb nor dictatorship, but
public opinion. This is a responsibility which no individual past child-
hood can escape."

But most people do indeed escape the responsibility. There is much
research that shows that fewer than 10 percent of people ever complain to or about a print or broadcast medium (6 percent is a commonly used figure), and even that tiny number is further divided into
those few who communicate regularly and the many who may only
communicate once in their lives.

Research on the people who write letters to the editor, or send letters or faxes to complain about radio or television programming, typically find a very small number of people account for a high percentage
of the messages. In one survey, 3 percent of the people wrote 67 percent of the letters; in another, 20 percent of all the mail received by
a television network—thousands of letters—came from the same forty-
four people.

THE PRINT MEDIA VERSUS THE BROADCAST MEDIA

Complaint letters to newspapers and magazines are both written and received with entirely different expectations from letters written to television and radio networks. Letters to the print media are primarily written to express the opinions of the writer: his or her complaints (most common reason), opposition to someone else's complaints (next most common reason), or to praise someone or something.

No one who writes to the *New York Times* to say, "Your sports coverage stinks," or to *USA Today* to protest their running Larry King's column has even the remotest expectation that the *Times* will cancel its sports section, or that *USA Today* will fire King.

But when the same writer writes to NBC to say that *"Roseanne* stinks," he or she often has some real expectation, based on many previously publicized instances, that if enough people write comparable letters, the program will indeed be canceled.

COMPLAINING TO THE MASS MEDIA

Do complaints actually have an effect on network programming? It seems certain that they do have *some* effect on decisions made by the broadcast industry, although there is much contradictory evidence as to just what that effect may be.

To be sure, people within the industry, as well as its critics, have often gone on record to urge the public to complain—to write not just fan letters but letters and phone calls designed to change the networks' minds.

At the peak of his popularity as a variety show host, for instance, Ed Sullivan said that the ratings system may be valuable but "your letters are tremendously important in shaping television. They are important in shaping anything. Any merchant stocks what the people want...."

In a series on the future of television, the *Christian Science Monitor*'s John Cuno writes that one of the questions most often asked by the suffering viewing public is "What can we do?" His answer: "We can get busy writing letters, organizing groups, and making our viewpoints felt. [Complaint] letters to networks are read and often answered. Broadcasters are very sensitive to what people who watch their programs are thinking." The author provided the names and addresses of the presidents of the three largest networks, and urged his readers to voice their complaints to those three gentlemen.

Let's look at some typical cases, and see if there are any common lessons to be learned.

There have been a great many instances, regularly reported by television columnists, in which so many thousands of letters are reported to have been received, almost always in support of a popular program whose cancellation is either rumored or has already been announced, or when, as in the case of *Murder, She Wrote* in 1995, there is a change to a different day and time slot. Sometimes the letters are reported to have an effect, sometimes not.

Often the networks themselves will cite the effect of the mail if they renew a program that may have been in jeopardy or, in rare instances, had already been canceled and has now been brought back from the dead. But whether the mail had any effect on the decision or was simply mentioned to reassure viewers that they really do pay attention (even if they don't) remains to be seen.

ABC reportedly uncanceled and rescheduled the *Jimmy Dean Show* after "thousands of letters" were received protesting the announced cancellation. Similarly, NBC restored one of its Sunday morning religious programs, *Frontiers of Faith*, following receipt of "more than 15,000" letters of protest.

On the other hand, even though "hundreds of thousands" of complaint letters may have had some effect in extending the original *Star Trek* for a third year, "millions" (by some accounts) of letters could not fly the Enterprise into the fourth year of its five-year mission. And when one of the most popular family programs ever, *I Remember Mama*, was canceled, a genuine outpouring of spontaneous annoyance, coupled with some well-organized campaigns, resulted in more than 750,000 complaint letters sent directly to the star, Peggy Wood, who passed them along to an uncaring network. The show stayed canceled. A few years later, a comparably well-orchestrated campaign produced hundreds of thousands of letters complaining about the cancellation of *Star Man*, but to no avail.

NAFBRAT, the National Association for Better Radio and Television, believes that complaint letters to networks are usually fruitless.

"Letters may flood network offices, but they are ordinarily handled with polite 'we're sorry' form letters regretting the necessity for the network's decision."

As NAFBRAT puts it, the essence of the problem is that there is "little opportunity for any organized expression of public attitude. There is no way for one [complaint] letter-writer to know if his effort is joined by others, and the publicity which is a necessary part of any organized effort is controlled or submerged by the network which is itself the target of the campaign."

In other words, they believe that the networks, like the politicians, typically release the figures on mail received only when it suits their purposes. And when the mail genuinely comes from thousands (or even millions) of individuals, with no organized campaign and no publicity, there is literally no way of knowing how much mail was sent, unless the receiver chooses to tell. (The *Star Trek* and *I Remember Mama* figures were known because most of the mail was sent directly to the producer, Gene Roddenberry, and the star, Peggy Wood.)

THE ONE THING COMPLAINING MIGHT DO

The evidence suggests that once a decision has been made by a network, it is virtually inflexible. Even 750,000 complaint letters can't change it. A million complaint letters can't change it. But *while* the decision process is under way, the fear of what the public response *might* be may have a definite effect in shaping that decision.

The important point here is that it is only the fear of a large unorganized or spontaneous protest that is likely to have an effect. Or, significantly, one that is seen as spontaneous.

Networks fully expect protests from various predictable special interest groups and pressure groups, to whom they will often pretend to throw a sop. "Oh, yes, League to Encourage Ladies to Wear Underwear, because of your earnest efforts, we have canceled *Charlie's Angels*." And while Charlie and his jiggling brood are leaving through the front door, look, there come the plans for *Bay Watch* sneaking in the side entrance.

The chief censor at NBC has said that he can almost always predict just who will be affronted and write in to complain about just about any program, theme, word, or skit, and it isn't just the National

Rifle Association and the National Organization for Women. There are, for instance:

- hat makers, when a hero doesn't wear a hat in an appropriate scene
- dental organizations, whenever people are shown being afraid of going to the dentist
- plumbers, when comedians make plumber jokes
- wine makers, if the word "wino" is ever used
- antismoking groups, if anyone in any scene lights up a cigarette, cigar, or pipe
- language and education groups, when actors say "ain't" and newscasters say "nu-kew-lar" and sportscasters say "ath-a-lete" and *everybody* says "Feb-yew-ary"

and so on.

The NBC censor says, "If we paid attention to all the complaints, our villains would be faceless and formless, with no background and with no visible means of support."

◆ ◆ ◆ ◆ ◆ ◆ ◆ ◆ ◆ ◆ ◆

CASE STUDY

How Captain Kangaroo's life was saved

For many years, the National Association for Better Radio and Television (NAFBRAT) lobbied for improved children's programming. When the immensely popular Captain Kangaroo children's program was relatively new, CBS officials seriously suggested that his time slot might better be filled with yet another Saturday-morning-type cartoon show.

NAFBRAT came up with a complaint scheme of great complexity, skill, and subtlety, based on the fact that television networks only release complaint figures when it suits their purposes.

In order to try to save the Captain, NAFBRAT sent out more than 300 press releases discussing the merits of Captain Kangaroo. These went mostly to television columnists and to parents' groups such as PTAs. Individuals were urged to write directly to NAFBRAT, not to CBS, to complain. When the first sixty complaint letters were received, copies of those were made and sent to more than 800 sources: the original 300, plus 500 additional newspapers and parents groups, and, for the first time, directly to CBS executives. This second wave generated still more letters and, significantly, many more editorials.

While the third wave of reprinting and recirculating was being planned, CBS reversed its decision and announced that Captain Kangaroo was saved for, as it turned out, another two decades. The fly on the wall might well have learned that CBS believed that untold thousands, perhaps millions, of complaining letters, press releases, and editorials were floating around out there, but NAFBRAT revealed later that the total number of complaint letters received was only "several hundred."

◆ ◆ ◆ ◆ ◆ ◆ ◆ ◆ ◆ ◆ ◆

HOW TO HAVE A CHANCE OF HAVING AN EFFECT

The broadcast media have behaved quite schizophrenically with regard to complaints. On the one hand, they have *received* untold millions of complaint letters and done nothing. On the other hand, the *fear* of getting huge numbers of complaints has driven more than a few decisions, including the almost charming example of the case that Dr. Kildare couldn't cure.

◆ ◆ ◆ ◆ ◆ ◆ ◆ ◆ ◆ ◆ ◆   *CASE STUDY*

The case that Doctor Kildare couldn't cure

NBC announced that a unique television event was in the offing: the first-ever continuation of a plot from one highly rated program into another. In brief, a young high school student was going to contract syphilis on the extremely popular *Mr. Novak* program on Tuesday evening, and then be treated by the equally popular *Dr. Kildare* on Thursday evening.

Because of the controversial nature of the subject matter, NBC went all out to be sure that no one could possibly be offended. The scripts for the two programs were written and then gone over with a fine-toothed comb by representatives of the American Medical Association and the National Education Association. Both approved.

Finally, NBC Standards and Practices Division, which tries to anticipate all possible objections to all NBC programming, approved. That should have been the last hurdle.

Nevertheless, just before the programs were to air, a junior executive of NBC New York telephoned NBC Los Angeles to say that an unsigned memo from a high source had instructed him to cancel both programs.

Rather extensive detective work by author Jessica Mitford unearthed the reasons for the decision. Although no one person would ever take responsibility, a group of scared executives apparently had a secret meeting, where the prevailing feeling was that there would be a deluge of complaint letters if the programs were shown. Since both programs were already popular, there could be little advantage in taking this risk.

A few months later, rival ABC showed a prime-time documentary on venereal disease, and not only was the audience three times larger than had been anticipated, but not one single complaint letter was received.

◆ ◆ ◆ ◆ ◆ ◆ ◆ ◆ ◆ ◆ ◆ ◆

CAN YOU COMPLAIN EFFECTIVELY TO THE BROADCAST MEDIA?

Unlike corporate or political situations, where a single sincere, well-written complaint can have an effect, there has probably never been an instance in which a single complaint to the broadcast media has had a noticeable effect ("Here's a guy who wants us to move *Monday Night Football* to Tuesday, because Monday is his bowling night. Hey that's a great idea. Let's do it.").

The only complaints that have had a prompt and dramatic effect are those that are backed up by an organization with considerable legal clout, financial clout, or *the appearance of either.*

Legal clout

This is not really a topic for this book, since the only legal threats that seem to have a chance of getting through to the media are those that come from organizations so huge and wealthy that there is real fear about the size and duration of a possible suit. When, for instance, in late 1995, CBS canceled a *60 Minutes* interview with a former research executive for a major tobacco company, there was apparently genuine concern that the determination of Brown & Williamson to inflict heavy damage on CBS was so strong, and so well-funded, it was not worth the risk. This sort of thing is, thankfully, rare.

Financial clout

In those countries of the world that have commercial television, nearly all sell air time to sponsors, but not sponsorship of a specific program. Thus if an advertiser buys a minute of time on a British television channel, the ad will appear on a particular day and time, but the actual program that surrounds, precedes, or succeeds it is not chosen by the advertiser. It might be a Princess Di tell-all interview, or it might be a dry lecture on the migration habits of the African kudzu. However, in the United States and a few other places, advertisers choose to sponsor a given program, often paying vastly different prices depending on whether it is half-time at the Super Bowl or a third-rate situation comedy. And so, instead of complaining directly to the networks, creative complainers often go directly to the advertisers, or use the threat of an advertiser complaint or boycott as the basis for their threat to the networks. And they have had their successes. Television's biggest advertiser, Procter & Gamble, has pulled its advertising spots from dozens and dozens of episodes of situation comedies, adventure, or crime shows because of complaints they received about sponsoring examples of violence, profanity, or sexual dalliance.

The appearance of clout

The beauty of the NAFBRAT campaign to save *Captain Kangaroo* is that they did not let on how many complaint letters they were getting, and fostered the image that it might have been in the millions, when it was, in fact, well under one thousand. It was also a very smart move to imply that the campaign would just keep growing and mushrooming outward, and that the instigators were prepared to stay with it forever. This is the exact equivalent of the complaint technique of picketing an offending store: the proprietor cannot know if you will be there for an hour or a year, or how many others may join you.

THE SPECIAL ROLE OF THE RELIGIOUS RIGHT

Media analyst Todd Gitlin suggests that while many of the preceding observations and rules are still operative, there is another force out there that parlays certain religious viewpoints into considerable effect on network programming. Gitlin's title nearly says it all: *Inside Prime*

Time: Why Hill Street Blues *Succeeded,* Lou Grant *Was Axed,* M*A*S*H *Soared,* Today's FBI *Fizzled, and How the Networks Decide about the Shows That Rise and Fall in the Rough and Tumble Real World behind the TV Screen.*

He suggests that in the early 1980s, a new force, the fundamentalist right, arose to challenge the prevailing view that "whatever the vagaries of the marketplace, the essence of network cultural power was that no one else could tell them how to manage the national airwaves."

Until then, network decisions were loosely based on a sense of the wishes of their affiliate stations, and the relevant federal regulations were a "vague, distant, minor concern." But then there arose a lobby that challenged the networks' very ability to program as they saw fit.

> The fundamentalist right...recognized a national target of opportunity. The assemblage of groups that the Hollywood writer Larry Gelbart calls "the far righteous" had a keen sense of how to play the press, and eventually got a huge boost from panicky advertisers. When the dust cleared, the networks, sensing no real audience counter pressure, had retreated from their high-water mark of sexual titillation, indeed from controversy in general. The pivotal figure in this successful surge was the Rev. Donald Wildmon, a Methodist minister straight out of a bicoastal network executive's grim dream of a benighted Middle America....

When ABC scheduled *Soap*, a farcical send-up of sexually indulgent soap operas, it got 32,000 letters of protest, many mobilized by Wildmon. A few years later, when ABC announced a plan to make a movie of Marilyn French's feminist novel *The Women's Room*, letters flooded in again as Wildmon denounced, sight unseen, this "antifamily" project. Wildmon got through to the major advertisers, and ABC lost 10 of 14 minutes of spot ads before the air date, arguably a bad business decision since the program had an extremely high rating. Significantly, there were only a few letters of protest after the show.

Wildmon subsequently teamed up with Jerry Falwell and Phyllis Schlafly to organize monitoring groups to scrutinize network schedules for signs of obscenity ("skin scenes, sexual innuendo, implied intercourse"), profanity, and violence.

The Wildmon approach also extends to companies, urging them

not to place ads on certain programs (ranging from *Married...with Children* to specials by Madonna and Michael Jackson) or to avoid commercial tie-ins with certain reprehensible television characters, such as McDonalds and the caped crusader. Holy hamburgers, Batman.

In their sensible book *Changing Channels: Living (Sensibly) with Television*, Peggy Charren and Martin Sandler suggest that "you'll be amazed at how seriously your letter is taken by people in influential positions." And especially, suggests an editorial in the *International Magazine of Religious Radio and Television*, if the complaint is on religious grounds. "The eloquent pen of the righteously indignant availeth much. If you don't believe it, ask any owner of a television or radio station." And especially one on Mr. Wildmon's list.

COMPLAINING TO NEWSPAPERS

The only effect that complaint letters have on newspapers appears to be either bringing about certain minor changes (replacement of a comic strip, adding a bridge column), or confirmation of the view held privately by more than a few editors that most people don't read much of the paper anyway.

◆ ◆ ◆ ◆ ◆ ◆ ◆ ◆ ◆ ◆ ◆ ◆   *CASE STUDY*

"What, *another* dratted African drought?"

One major metropolitan daily carried out a rather depressing experiment, in association with researchers at a nearby journalism school. The plan was to print the same news story at the bottom of page one day after day for a week, to see how many people noticed and complained. The story was on one of those very important matters that affects the lives of many, but is of little personal interest to most Americans: something relating to a devastating drought in an African nation. After the same story ran in the same place for a week, the total number of complaints, or even inquiries, received was zero.

Then the newspaper planned to repeat the experiment by reprinting the same popular comic strip every day for a week. But when "Peanuts" was repeated for the first time, the volume of complaints was so high, the experiment was terminated at once, lest the number of threatened subscriber cancellations put the paper into jeopardy.

◆ ◆ ◆ ◆ ◆ ◆ ◆ ◆ ◆ ◆ ◆ ◆

Just as politicians do, newspaper and magazine editors use the mail to support their own positions in making points with staff and management. And, just as other complaint-getters may well be truly moved by a single poignant lament, there have been cases where a newspaper made a modest change in policy because of one objection. One paper, for instance, stopped printing the names of rape victims. A few others added a "consumer warning" notice at the top of their astrology column, suggesting that it was not science, but for fun only.

How to complain to a newspaper or magazine

The only two pieces of advice that are heard over and over again in this regard are (1) make it legible, and (2) keep it short. Beyond that, almost anything goes. How legible? More than a few complaint-receivers simply do not read handwritten communications, no matter how good the penmanship may be. One might do well to follow the advice of the editor of *America,* the Catholic weekly:

> First set your [margins] at 40 characters to the line. That is
> the approximate length of the line in our correspondence
> section. When you have completed 60 lines you have taken
> up a full column of type. So tear up your 60 lines and throw
> them away. They were only a warm-up anyhow. You are now
> ready to say what you really wanted to say. When you have
> finished, cross out all unnecessary adjectives and adverbs and
> all repetitive phrases. You will probably find whole sentences
> that you can eliminate with no great loss. If you don't, we'll
> have to do it for you. And it will break our heart.

One magazine editor divides his complaint letters into four categories:

- The Twitting. Helpful, if annoying letters, generally pointing out typographical errors, complaining about grammar, grumbling about the illustrations or typography, griping about one thing or another.

- The Caustic. Sometimes just two words, "Drop dead," and sometimes essentially the same message, but taking sixteen pages of single-space typing or closely bunched handwriting to say.

- The Rambling. The long, generally friendly letter, written by people with too much time on their hands, commenting on the weather, sports, politics, and then, "Oh, by the way," and then comes the complaint.

- The Careful. The kind that editors love: short, to the point, complaining gently but firmly, clarifying issues, calling attention to lapses, and often furnishing additional information to support the position taken.

Like those company complaint managers who receive so few clever and well-executed complaints that they rejoice when something unusual happens, many newspaper and magazine editors and owners have written about the importance of the *good* complaint, a rare commodity among the annoying ones and the repetitive ones.

As James Fixx once wrote,

> each letter, wise or witty, critical or complimentary, is studied with care and respect; and each one, whether published or not, has a potential impact on the world the magazine and its ideas reach. In a world in which the carrying power of the individual voice sometimes seems to be growing weaker and more insignificant, the man at his typewriter or with pen in hand can still have his innings.

Longtime *Saturday Review* editor Norman Cousins echoed those sentiments, and particularly addressed the complaint letters: "While letters commending us for a job well done are gratifying, those that disagree with the views of our writers and editors have a greater influence. Critical letters, even a vitriolic one now and then...are no doubt good for us."

Complaints may even have an effect on editorial policy, although this is rare. William Buckley once wrote a delightful article for *Esquire* magazine, on "why we don't complain any more." He said that he was told "by the editor of a national news magazine" that "as few as a dozen letters of protest against an editorial stance is enough to convene a plenipotentiary meeting of the board of editors to review policy." It was generally assumed at the time, although not confirmed, that the magazine to which Buckley was referring was his own, *National Review*.

Much more common is the response of the editor of the *Kansas City Star*, when they hired a controversial new cartoonist, whose work seemed to offend many readers. But the paper had made a firm commitment, both ideological and financial, to hiring Bill Sanders, and so, as the editor wrote, "Even though we got complaint letters from all over the country, we paid no attention to them. As a matter of fact, I felt kind of bad about ignoring them, after they'd gone to all that trouble. But the only thing you can do is ignore them."

Fixx suggests that

> many newspapermen admit, usually privately...that they have no real solution to the problem of extremist [complaints].... Nonetheless there does seem to be one basic rule that has so far not failed: don't give ground. In virtually every case on record, when the John Birch Society or any similar group has been faced squarely and identified for what it is, the community has benefited and the extremists, who are not noted for any extraordinary staying power, have shriveled into obscurity.

CHAPTER 14

Complaining to Politicians

PRESIDENTIAL MAIL THROUGH THE AGES

POLITICIANS HAVE BEEN RECEIVING complaint letters, designed to influence or affect their decisions and their opinions, ever since the postal service began more than two hundred years ago.

In revolutionary times, the Committee of Correspondence did indeed correspond. They set a precedent by conducting letter-writing for political purposes.

In the post–Revolutionary War days, with Ben Franklin's post office system running relatively smoothly, there were many people who believed that the United States should have a king, just like England. People who opposed this notion began writing to George Washington, urging him to take a stand against being king, most of them suggesting that instead he become president, or possibly prime minister, chancellor, or some other less royal title. Washington apparently received as many as a hundred letters—enough for him to record in his journal that he was "troubled and embarrassed by a sudden deluge of letters. That I am to be the first president is apparently taken for granted."

Thomas Jefferson received as many as a thousand letters in one year. He wrote to his predecessor, John Adams, in some distress that "every mail brings a fresh load...from persons whose names are unknown to me."

Half a century later, by Lincoln's time, presidential mail had increased to more than 200 letters a day. The numbers grew quite slowly over the next three-quarters of a century, rising to a level of 400 to 600 a day in Hoover's time. The quantum leap, the discovery of mail by the common man, came with the election and inauguration of Franklin D. Roosevelt. He received 450,000 letters during his first week in office—more mail than all the presidents before him had gotten in total. Many were expressing either joy or hatred over his election, but untold thousands of those, and a high percentage of the 8,000 letters a day that FDR averaged thereafter, were letters of complaint, urging him to solve a problem, whether with a closed bank, a local pharmacy that was overcharging, or even a no-good brother-in-law who wouldn't repay a debt.

After Roosevelt, mail to people in Washington continued at a high level, both to the president and to senators and congressmen. One long-time senator reported that his mail had grown from 50 pieces a day in the 1930s to more than 5,000 pieces a day, in times of crisis, during the 1950s.

During the 1980s, Ronald Reagan received about 32 million letters during his eight years as president, an average of 4 million a year, or more than 12,000 a day: 7,000 during his less controversial years, and more than 20,000 during the Iran-Contra episode and other more lively moments.

George Bush received, on the average, about three-fourths as much mail as Reagan—about three million letters a year—plus a separate burst of two million letters and cards, many of them nearly identical, received as the result of organized opposition to possible cuts in Social Security payments.

With Bill Clinton, there was another quantum leap, both in terms of the volume of mail and in the style in which people wrote.

In his first five months in office, Bill Clinton (and his family) got more mail than any other first family in history: 3.5 million pieces, or an average of more than 30,000 letters a day. Of course, they weren't just complaint letters. Indeed, the Clinton mail typically included

- thousands of coupons good for a Big Mac (they were donated to charity)

- hundreds of pairs of jogging shorts, plus caps and even shoes

- recipes, weight loss schemes, allergy potions

- medical bills (typically to Mrs. Clinton with messages such as "Can you believe this?")

- medals: Gay soldiers mailed them in to complain about Clinton's policy on gays in the military, and Vietnam era vets sent them in to complain about Clinton not having joined the military at that time

- lots of one-of-a-kind items, including a kitty litter box inside a model White House.

Lillie Bell, who has been director of White House Mail Analysis for twenty-four years says that the tone of the Clinton mail is different. "In the old days, people who wrote the President wrote to him as a figure way up above them. But most people write to this President the way you would write a friend. He's not way up there. There is no awe in the letters."

The Clinton mail is testimony to the unusual personal relationship between the president and the people. Some love him, some hate him, all write him. And many do so as "Dear Bill," when the great majority would never have considered writing "Dear Ron," "Dear George," "Dear Gerald," or even "Dear Jimmy." Indeed, letters with personal salutations used to be set aside for special handling, since they almost certainly came from friends; who else would write to the president by first name? Now nearly everyone does.

Incidentally, there is a paid staff of just over a hundred employees, plus dozens of summer interns and several hundred volunteers who sort and answer presidential mail. As with all his recent predecessors, the current president is given a sample of praise and complaint letters ever week. A few are personally answered. Mail to Socks, the first cat, gets a form postcard (unsigned).

HOW POLITICIANS DEAL WITH COMPLAINT LETTERS

There are two very different schools of thought. The politicians themselves suggest that letters of all kinds are immensely important to them because, as one senator wrote, "If I do not know the needs, problems, complaints, and opinions of my constituents, I cannot speak for them; I cannot vote in their interest; I cannot protect them; I cannot counsel them. In short I no longer represent them."

The other school of thought, supported by a good deal of research, suggests that letters in general, and complaint letters in particular, fall very much into the same model as all other complaint letters. That is to say, the four crucial factors, in this order, are commitment to an idea, the scope or importance of that idea, followed at a distance by the quality of the complaint, and at a very great distance by the quantity of complaints received.

Let's look at these two schools of thought and their proponents, and then see what conclusions can be drawn when it comes to complaining to politicians.

WHY YOU *SHOULD* COMPLAIN TO POLITICIANS

Many elected politicians, in their articles, speeches, and letters home, have stressed the importance of learning what's on the minds of the American people in general, and their constituents in particular. Former majority leader Jim Wright wrote that "with exceptions so rare they are hardly worth mentioning, members of the national Congress positively do read their mail....The mood and tenor of the daily mail from home is a recurring topic of conversation in the rear of the house and senate chambers or around the coffee cups in the dining rooms of the Capitol." When he was a Montana congressman, Lee Metcalf wrote that "of all the means of communication between the people and their elected representatives, mail is the most important. Every day of the year, I receive a bushel of mail. I scan it all...and I read and answer [most of the] first class letters."

THE VERY SUBTLE AND HARD-TO-MEASURE ROLE OF COMPLAINT LETTERS TO POLITICIANS

There have some well-documented and well-publicized cases where a single letter, or a small group of them, has had an important effect on changing the mind of a politician. For instance, Congressman Morris Udall of Arizona wrote that "as for impact, there have been instances where a well-worded and persuasive letter either changed my mind or caused me to review my opinion."

But in private, it is safe to say that most politicians would agree with the candor expressed by the young senator John Kennedy when he wrote that mail is "only rarely interpreted as accurate barometers of public opinion and used as guideposts on pending decisions."

The real role of complaint letters to politicians may well hinge on one of the intriguing findings in communication research on how opinions are formed. In a nutshell, there is persuasive evidence that people remember the *content* of a message long after they have forgotten the *source* of the message.

In one experiment, subjects were given what looked like real newspaper stories, attributing a certain opinion to a certain person, either respected or reviled. One article, for instance, might say that Albert Einstein had believed that eating too many green vegetables caused children to become belligerent or quarrelsome. Another group of people would read the identical article, except instead of Einstein, it would say "Adolf Hitler" or "Saddam Hussein." Some months later, in an opinion survey, those subjects were more likely to believe the "fact" about green vegetables than the control subjects who had not read the phony articles, no matter which "source" the first group had read, and indeed the great majority had no idea where they got that information—they "just knew it."

In this respect, at least, politicians are quite possibly no different from the rest of us. Thus the real value of complaint letters could be expressed in these two words: planting seeds.

If we accept even the possibility of this phenomenon, then there may well be merit to the views of the League of Women Voters, which says that "constituents are the most important people in a representative's or senator's life. Their very existence as members of Congress rests upon their ability to take the pulse back home."

It is hard to imagine any politician opening a single letter and saying, "Gee, here's someone who says that those nasty Chinese are not treating the people of Tibet well. I guess I'll change my vote on 'most favored nation' status for China." But if there have been a few, or a few dozen, or a few hundred complaints about a certain stance he or she has taken or should be taking, there could well be enough of an adjustment of the neurons in some part of that political organ called the brain, so that the politician might think, "I have the feeling, somehow, that common sense might dictate that I vote 'no' on this bill." In the unlikely event of being pressed on the issue, the only response might be, "It made sense to me; it seemed the appropriate thing to do."

If this is so, then things are *really* unequal

If the notion of planting seeds through complaint letters has merit, then it is very clear that the seeds are being planted very unequally and inequitably by the members of the public. To begin with, according to a Gallup poll, fewer than 10 percent of the adults in America have *ever* written, phoned, wired, or otherwise communicated with an elected politician, even once in their entire lives. And the people who do communicate are by no means typical of the population as a whole. They are, in fact, far, far wealthier than those who don't communicate. In one large national survey, the Roper organization found that 9 percent of the complainers were poor, 20 percent middle class, 34 percent prosperous, and 37 percent wealthy.

It is data like these that cause Verba and Nie, in their book *Participation in America,* to write that citizen participation through complaints is a "potent force" in setting governmental agendas and priorities. Put simply, government leaders "respond more to the participants than to those who do not participate," and this unequal complaining results "in an overrepresentation of upper-status groups in the participant population." (Well, we *knew* that, but here it is in black and white, with research data to back it up.)

A Minnesota congressman wrote that "it is commonly said that in a democracy, decisions are made by a majority of the people. Of course that is not true. Decisions are made by a majority of those who make themselves heard."

And that, it seems, is the important thing. Congressman Jim Wright said it best: "If you are wondering whether or not it is really worthwhile to communicate your views...consider this fact: others who disagree with you are doing so constantly...." As Congressman Udall points out, "Your ballot box isn't far away. It's painted red, white and blue and 'U.S. Mail' is written on it. Use it."

But wait a minute, perhaps it's not the complaints but how they are used

What is the effect of the more-than-a-billion letters sent every year to elected and appointed government officials in Washington, other than the $400 million "bonus" to the Postal Service for all those stamps?

In a nutshell, it is that most elected officials, whether they will admit it or not, typically treat their complaint and protest letters in two totally different and opposite ways *at the same time*. On the one hand, they will privately admit that they are rarely personally affected or influenced by their mail. But on the other hand, many of them use "how my mail is running" as a factor in justifying their own opinions or trying to win the support of other politicians, the media, and the public.

In other words, if they agree with the letters they get, they will wave them around during photo opportunities and sound bites, and say, "The public clearly stands behind me on this vital issue." And if the mail disagrees with them, they rarely comment, and probably dismiss it as the misguided letter-writing drive of some muddy-thinking opponents.

In one of the few comprehensive studies of the way congressmen and -women make up their minds on a key issue (this one involved repeal of an arms embargo), researchers discovered that the great majority of elected officials make up their own minds, based on their personal convictions, regardless of how their mail runs. But if their mail supports the position they have already chosen, they will use the mail count to attempt to gain support.

It wasn't the message on the postcards, it was the number of postcards

Boris Joffe reports one occasion when the administration wanted to cut back a particular program to help the unemployed. A group of workers launched a postcard-writing campaign, which caught on and snowballed. They had carefully targeted a small group of congressmen who were believed to be undecided on this issue and complained to them that passage of this bill would worsen their already-difficult plight. Hundreds of thousands of cards were received, and when organizers of the campaign went to Washington, they found that every one of the congressmen who had received the cards had piled them up in his office as visible justification for his decision. And every one of them voted against the bill, which was defeated in a close vote. Did the cards really have an effect? To the extent the politicians believed that the cards represented the will of the people, or at least of the voters in their district, it is safe to suggest that they did.

This, then, becomes an interesting argument for political complaining. If only one senator is truly undecided, and if that one senator is nudged just a tiny bit, just enough to become slightly on your side, and if that senator casts the deciding vote in a one-vote victory, then of course it was worth the letter-writing effort, even if it was wasted on the other ninety-nine senators. But this would seem to be a rare event, if indeed it happens at all. The available evidence does not seem to support the League of Women Voters' view that "the amount of mail on a particular piece of legislation frequently helps determine the representative's approach to an issue. In fact, some members use their mail count on a bill as the sole determinant when voting." Well, they might *say* so, but it is hard to believe they really do it. It may well be that the time and energy spent trying to create a snowball could be better spent in other ways.

Newspapers perpetuate the myths

Newspapers often pay lip service to the so-called importance of complaint and protest mail to Congress by reporting regularly "how the mail is running" on key issues, either because the politicians themselves regularly report it or because they see it as a news story in and of itself. Nixon justified his overtures to China, at least in part, by reporting that his mail was running heavily in favor of recognizing the mainland nation. A few newspapers at the time even kept a daily box score of public response, and urged readers to "cast their vote" by writing, especially if their side was "losing."

WELL, WHAT *DOES* WORK THEN?

Despite the skepticism regarding the effect of complaining to politicians *in general,* there is still ample evidence that suggests complaining can and does have an effect—especially in those matters of lower commitment and lower scope of project.

A survey by American University of the staff in 123 political offices found that "spontaneous individually composed letters from constituents are the most effective way of communicating with congressional decision makers. These letters receive more attention than any other form of written communication."

But it is surely the quality, not the quantity. A senator from Montana put it this way: "Letters that count come from people who count....One penciled page from a respected farmer or businessman will outweigh in influence a hundred form letters inspired by a pressure drive."

Perhaps an even more influential kind of letter is the one that politicians find hard to categorize, other than to identify them as outpourings of utter sincerity. The example is frequently given of a letter written in a crude hand on a page torn from a notebook, or even on a piece of wrapping paper. Senator Javits of New York spoke eloquently about such a letter, literally tear-stained, complaining about the treatment the writer had received from the Immigration and Naturalization Service. Javits was so moved that he introduced a bill that had a small but significant effect on immigration laws in the United States as well as a private bill to address the specific situation of the letter-writer and her family.

ADVICE FROM POLITICIANS AND INSIDERS

Let's start with things that *don't* work. Addressing this issue, Walter Judd, then a powerful senior congressman from Minnesota, issued a list called "things your congressman does not like."

1. Letters that demand or insist, without telling why.

2. Threats of defeat at the next election.

3. How influential the writer is back home.

4. Being asked to commit himself on a bill, if it is still in committee and there are hearings to be held.

5. Form letters, or letters that quote other letters.

6. Letters from people outside his district, except when dealing with the work of a committee of which he is a member.

7. Being deluged by letters on the same subject from the same person. Quality, not quantity, is what counts. Congressman Udall adds that "people who write often are called 'pen pals' and are consigned to the bottom of the mail priority list."

A lot of people sound very negative when they complain, and that really turns off politicians (and their staffs). And since few if any politicians actually rip open the envelopes, it is a staff member who will make the first decision about how to deal with any given complaint, which can range from putting it on the boss's desk at once, to letting it slide to the bottom of the pile or even into the circular file.

Here is some additional wisdom, from people who deal with complaints reaching politicians, and the politicians themselves.

- Don't threaten. "A writer has the right to make [threatening] assertions in a letter, but they rarely result in successful intimidation, and more often result in an adverse reaction to a point of view."

- Be specific. With tens of thousands of bills introduced each year, the complainer must identify a bill by name and number, while recognizing that the original number may have changed as the bill moves through its process. It is useless to say, "I don't like that bill dealing with fouling the environment." There might be 500 of them.

- Don't assume the politician or his or her staff are stupid. They might be, but it is unlikely. Letters are actually written starting, "This is too complicated for me to explain or for you to understand..." or "Of course you don't know anything about this, but...."

- All letters asking for action should contain "a concise statement of the reasons for your position, particularly if you are writing about a field in which you have specialized knowledge. [The politician] has to vote on many matters with which he has had little or no firsthand experience. Some of the most valuable help he gets in making up his own mind comes from facts presented in letters from persons who really know what they are talking about."

- Be concise.

- Relate national legislation to your local needs.

- Show familiarity with the politicians' prior actions on an issue, especially if you disagree with him or her.

- Enclose pertinent editorials or articles from local (not national) papers.

- Never start "As a citizen and a taxpayer...." They know this.

- Never say, "I hope this gets past your staff." This irritates the staff, and as a result it might not.

- Say something positive, even if most of the letter is a complaint. "I appreciated your vote on the off-shore drilling ban, but I think you're wrong about the sale of timber in national forests." An Iowa senator was delighted by a letter that read, in its entirety, "My dear Senator: We extend to you the season's greetings. Merry Christmas. Happy New Year. Hark the herald angels sing. Peace on earth, good will to men. Give your support to the removal of restrictions on the sale of margarine."

- Although threats of "I won't vote for you if you..." hold little water, a complaint suggesting that *many* votes could be involved will get attention. Some complainers achieve this by working with organizations, others try to achieve it by having a letterhead printed reading "Citizens United for..." (whatever).

- Say thank you if they do what you wanted (whether or not you had an effect). Then, if you do need to complain later, a staff may remember you as "that nice person who wrote us that thank you letter."

In the best of worlds, every politician would share the views of the honorable Francis J. Myers of Pennsylvania, who had this advice for complainers when they write:

> Was it a complete letter—did it, for instance, translate the national issue you were writing about into terms of your own locality, your own business or job, your own neighborhood. I'll tell you that letters that do those things are effective letters. They are read and read carefully. Whether such a letter coincides with my point of view or not, whether it supports or opposes a point of view to which I may feel committed, it may do much more than merely notify me of

your own belief—it may change my belief and my vote—it
may open up to me an altogether new course of action
which had not previously occurred to me.

WHEN PRESSURE GROUPS TRY TO GET YOU TO COMPLAIN

Because corporations, organizations, and political action groups know
that a "grassroots" flood of complaint or protest letters can have an
effect politically, they spend, according to one congressional estimate,
"hundreds of millions of dollars" organizing such campaigns, presumably in the hope either that the politicians will believe they are
spontaneous, or that they will still be awed and influenced by the sheer
numbers of items received.

When the Business Roundtable, a coalition of two hundred businesses, took a four-page ad in the *Readers' Digest*, they were able to
get over one million people to send a prepaid postcard to Washington, urging the president to reduce the federal deficit. A public relations person at the magazine said, "They want this to serve as a public
mandate. They want to create such an incredible reaction that the government cannot ignore." And did it work? Did that expenditure of
millions of dollars have anything to do with the deficit crisis that shut
the government down for a week in late 1995? Surely no politician
would ever say, "Because one million postcards were sent, I voted for
a balanced budget."

Politicians are, by and large, not stupid. "If," as one western congressman pointed out, "surveys show that people in my district are
divided 50-50 on gun control, but my mail is running 100 to 1 against
gun control, I know something funny is going on."

PETITIONS ARE USUALLY EVEN WORSE

When petitions are submitted, they tend to be either ignored entirely,
or worse, carefully checked. One congressman writes that his constituents regularly send in petitions.

In general, a petition is not the best way to communicate
with your congressman. Too frequently, after I have sent a
letter to each signer of a petition, I receive replies indicating
that many either didn't know what the petition said or that

they do not agree with [it]. Some say they signed the petition
to get rid of the person circulating it, or they were in a
group who signed and did not wish to become conspicuous
by refusing to do so.

Congressman Lee Metcalf of Montana wrote that "I was once handed a petition with 50 signatures, allegedly representing every teacher in my district. I checked, and only one signer was a registered voter. Thus it was the way of one person to try to seem more important."

TWO-STEP AND THREE-STEP COMPLAINT LETTERS

When he left office, Idaho congressman Orval Hansen assumed the presidency of the Columbia Institute for Political Research, an organization that has used modern computer technology to zero in on individuals sympathetic to a given cause and write them, encouraging them, in turn, to write letters of complaint, protest, or support to key politicians. The two-step complaint process is now often used, and occasionally even a three-step process has worked. When the federal government was considering legislation requiring banks to withhold for taxes a portion of interest on deposits, the American Bankers Association wrote to all its member banks (step one) urging them to organize their customers (step two) so that the customers would write to Washington to complain (step three). Millions of complaint letters were written, and the proposed law took another and less odious form entirely. Did the mail have an effect? Given that it was a large volume on a matter of small importance to most legislators, the chances are pretty good that it did.

A few years ago, legislation was proposed that would have deferred certain long-distance access charges. *Direct Marketing News* reported on a campaign by AT&T against this legislation. Clearly, AT&T wished the charges to begin sooner. The corporate giant presumably felt that a great surge of letters from the public would have more effect than whatever other lobbying they might be able to do. Since there was no clear profile of the kind of person who either supported or opposed access charges, if indeed many people had views on that at all, a research group conducted surveys to learn more about such people. Were they Protestant or Jewish, old or young, rich or poor, and so on. At a cost of several million dollars, large numbers of people who, the research suggested, would agree with AT&T were given form letters and encouraged to use them, rewrite them, or (what a novelty) telephone. The research group claimed credit when the legislation was defeated, even though many politicians claimed to be unaware that there had even been a protest campaign (which may, come to think of it, mean that the campaign was effective but invisible, perhaps the most effective kind of all).

That's the way the big boys plan. At the other end of the scale, the tiny local level, a rural religious group that leased land for a retreat in a national park was alarmed that proposed legislation would revoke this privilege and close them down. They set up shop in a shopping mall, not just passing out literature, but making available writing paper and prestamped envelopes in a wide variety of sizes, shapes, and colors, plus pens of various colors, and urging people to sit down and write a complaint letter there and then. They knew that if they asked people to do it later, most would not do so. In one weekend, they collected more than 200 letters, which was a lot for a tiny matter in a tiny place. Their congressman agreed, and the proposed law was modified to assure the group's continued existence.

A FEW MISGUIDED EFFORTS

Usually the way it happens is that a group or organization that has had little or no cause to complain politically suddenly finds itself faced with a threat and responds in the worst possible way: demanding that an avalanche of mail descend upon Washington in order to persuade lawmakers of the importance of their cause and their complaint.

When the powerboating world was faced with federal legislation to create "no wake" zones near harbors and marinas, motorboat owners were exhorted, through direct mail and articles in their magazines, to "flood those fud-headed lawmakers with an avalanche of outrage, to show them that we mean business." Even if the flood descended, it is hard to imagine many members of Congress reacting to a threat from someone who declares, "I drive a powerboat, and I vote." The failure of their campaign may have been related as much to the approach as to the, uh, fud-headed content of the complaint letters.

In another comparable crisis matter, the people who fly radio-controlled model airplanes became concerned that some of the frequencies used for model plane control would be taken away and assigned to other users of the airwaves. Urgent editorials in *Model Airplane News* suggested that "an overwhelming avalanche of letters from modelers to Congress and to the FCC can...exert tremendous influence...A draft letter is reprinted (below)." Readers were told to "personalize your concerns: I am retired and derive many hours of pleasure from operating radio-controlled models....As a student, I learn valuable lessons from building and operating models." A case where a few sincere non–form letters could have gotten attention, but a modest avalanche of form letters did not attract any sympathy for that cause.

A GOOD RESOURCE FOR LOCATING POLITICIANS

Many almanacs and other annuals available in bookstores and libraries offer lists of elected officials at the local, state, and national level. In addition, the Voters Education Fund of the League of Women Voters puts out a very helpful manual called *Tell It to Washington: A Guide for Citizen Action*. It includes a complete directory of members of Congress and lists all the congressional committees and who serves on them. The guide sells for $3.75 (1996 price), including postage, from the League of Women Voters, 1730 M St. N.W., Washington, DC 20036, phone (202) 429-1965.

THREE COMPUTER PACKAGES JUST FOR POLITICAL COMPLAINERS

Your local software dealer or mail-order house can get you three different products that will, the purveyors say, facilitate your political protesting.

Contact Software International sells a database called "Write Your Congressman." This $40 package contains profiles of all senators and House members and the justices of the Supreme Court, along with their addresses, telephone numbers, fax numbers, and committee assignments. The software contains a letter-writing feature to facilitate producing letters, memos, or faxes, and a "contact manager" feature keeps track of to whom you have written and whether you've heard back.

"Political Action" is a comparable package from Political Systems, selling for $70. It does not have the contact log, but it does have names and addresses of important business persons and members of the press. It can also be used to send messages to bulletin board services and via a fax modem.

Soap Box Software sells "Federal SoapBox" for $129. It appears to have similar features. Further, it shows the chain of command within committees and organizations, and it includes a guide to lobbying and a copy of the Freedom of Information Act.

POLITICAL COMPLAINING ON THE INTERNET

The President of the United States is available on the Internet (president@whitehouse.gov), as are an ever-increasing (but still small) number of senators and members of Congress, and governmental agencies. Whether an electronic complaint is more or less likely to achieve a satisfactory result than a written one remains to be seen. On the one hand, the younger and more electronically sophisticated staff members who handle complaints may relate more to on-line complaining. On the other hand, electronic complaints lack many of the trappings that have helped separate the "important" ones (engraved stationery, colorful enclosures, certified mail) from the others (bad handwriting, pencil-stubbed laments, yellow lined paper). No research has yet been done on these matters, but common sense dictates that the same four key factors—commitment, scope, quality, and quantity—will come into play, whether the complaint arrives in the mailbox or directly onto the computer disk drive.

FIGHTING CITY HALL

For serious matters that go beyond the scope of ordinary complaining, Thomas Pezzuti has written a useful guide entitled *You Can Fight City Hall and Win,* which covers "practiced and proven techniques you can use to combat political or bureaucratic waste, inefficiency or malfeasance at the local, state or Federal level." It is published by Sherbourne Press, Los Angeles, but is apparently out of print, so good luck at the library.

CHAPTER 15

What Companies Need to Know about Complainers

THERE IS A NATIONAL ORGANIZATION of people who deal with consumer complaints: the Society of Consumer Affairs Professionals in Business. Their promotional literature sounds the appropriate warning: "The company that doesn't pay attention to what its consumer affairs staff is saying won't be around long."

IT ISN'T SOME LITTLE THING THAT WILL GO AWAY

Despite the apparent wishes or beliefs of some companies and government agencies, complaining is not an inconsequential little matter that requires minimal attention. When Arthur Best reviewed immense amounts of research on complaining for his excellent book *When Consumers Complain,* he found that one out of every six purchases leads to an ultimately unresolved consumer problem. That represents an awful lot of unhappy people.

This dismal figure is supported by the research of Hiram Barksdale and his colleagues, who found that 60 percent of consumers agreed with the statement "It is hard to get complaints resolved." Only 1 percent strongly disagreed. When Barksdale asked for a response to the assertion that "most businesses make sincere efforts to adjust complaints fairly," only about half the people agreed, while many were uncertain. Finally, in the matter of fairness of dealing with complaints, 61 percent of consumers felt that complaint-handling was *not* fair, while only 22 percent felt it was, the rest being uncertain.

In his 1970 book *Exit, Voice and Loyalty,* A. O. Hirschman used the vocabulary that has become pretty standard in university research on complaining. "Exit" refers to a person with a complaint who simply walks away and doesn't buy the product or use the service again; "voice" refers to the act of complaining, whether to the culprit, an outside agency, or friends and relatives; and "loyalty" is what satisfied customers (and even some satisfied former complainers) demonstrate.

There is ample evidence, both from the academic and the business world, that unresolved complaints can dramatically affect the well-being of an organization. In a study entitled *Customer Satisfaction, Market Share and Profitability,* Eugene Anderson of the University of Michigan and his colleagues found a high correlation between happy customers and a happy bottom line on the balance sheet. Other research suggests that poor service and an unsatisfactory system of dealing with complaints can cost a business 10 to 15 percent of its annual volume. That can be enough to bring about failure. Can it be entirely coincidental that the two biggest airline failures in recent years, Eastern and Pan Am, were among the airlines with the worst complaint records of all?

But still, many companies don't really seem to believe this. John Tschohl's company, Service Quality Institute, advises companies on customer service. As Tschohl writes in his recent book *The Customer Is Boss,* "What I find is most businesses and government agencies believe they're already perfect in service. The reason is most [unhappy] customers don't do or say anything."

IF ONLY DEMING HAD BEEN *OUR* NATIONAL TREASURE

One of the most famous men in Japan over the last four decades has been the American W. Edwards Deming, whose writings and lectures on total quality management (TQM) were virtually ignored in the West, but taken to heart in the power centers of Sony, Toyota, Panasonic, Nissan, and the like. Indeed, Deming was declared a National Treasure by the government of Japan.

Deming taught that company planning, strategy, and operations, at the highest levels, all begin with the voice of the customer. Before Deming, quality management used to mean little more than inspecting the final product. TQM expands this concept to include all aspects of the production process and, after the sale, all business functions associated with the product: its packaging, delivery, maintenance, exchange, and repair.

Importantly, Deming regarded service as a commodity: the only commodity that is produced and consumed simultaneously. He taught that the use of service is inseparable from the process by which it is generated.

In the years just after World War II, "Made in Japan" (or even "Made in Occupied Japan") was a sure sign of shoddy goods and miserable service. How did that country get from there to the Lexus and the Acura? For many Japanese there is a one-word answer: Deming.

The encouraging news is that the Western world did finally discover Deming—about forty years after the Japanese did—and in the final years of his life (he died at ninety-three in 1994), he was very much in demand in the boardrooms of America.

MOST PEOPLE NEVER COMPLAIN

In *Dear Miss Afflerbach,* his book about advertising, subtitled *The Postman Hardly Ever Rings 11,342 Times,* Howard Gossage writes that "we generally figure that 1 percent of the people who think about writing in will actually do so. God knows where we get this figure, since how could anyone possibly tell."

How indeed? Everyone concerned with complaining would seem to agree with research at the State University of New York, suggesting that "a large majority of dissatisfied consumers do not complain publicly. But undetected complaints may have a far more serious consequence to marketers" as customers quietly exit and switch their loyalty, often bad-mouthing the product or service. In the words of Marjorie Wall at a Canadian university, these unresolved complaints "may continue to exist and slowly erode markets. Active consumer complaints may often represent only the tip of an iceberg."

How big an iceberg? Gossage's guess of a 99 percent "silent majority" may well be high, but a Nielsen study did find that only 2 percent of consumers who had complaints about various packaged goods actually passed those complaints onto the manufacturer. (Others complained to the retail store, but such complaints rarely are passed on to the source.)

Consumer advocate James Beltran writes that "if you have one customer who complains, you can figure there are ten or fifteen others out there who are dissatisfied but who aren't bothering to complain."

The Conference Board, in a report on how to operate a consumer affairs department, says that

> consumer affairs specialists acknowledge that the number of complaints received by a company is seldom an accurate barometer of the total number of unhappy customers it may have. Studies conducted by one airline showed that there were usually an additional 25 dissatisfied customers for every [registered] formal service complaint. Other firms report comparable ratios of "silent complainants...."

Whether it is Gossage's 99 percent, Nielsen's 98 percent, the airline's 96 percent or "only" Beltran's 90 percent, the message is abundantly clear: most people *don't* complain, and those unhappy noncomplainers can make or break a business.

UNHAPPY COMPLAINERS CAN DO REAL DAMAGE

It is generally agreed that unhappy customers are much more likely to tell other people about their unhappiness than happy customers are to report their satisfaction. As Susan Greco phrased the cliche in her *Inc.* article on customer service, "You're lucky if a satisfied customer mentions your company to a few friends, but you'd better believe that unhappy customers complain to everyone they know."

The basic rule of thumb, based both on hunch and on research, is that a customer with complaints will tell about twice as many people as one with high satisfaction, although the actual numbers told vary considerably from case to case. General Motors found that satisfied customers tell eight to ten others about their positive experience; dissatisfied customers share their complaints with sixteen to twenty others. MCI found that telephone customers with complaints told six people, while the happy ones told three.

BUT HAPPY FORMER COMPLAINERS
ARE WORTH CULTIVATING

For years, there was an assumption that a complainer who was well treated was even happier than someone who liked the company in the first place. One article on complaint resolution suggested that "once pacified, a disgruntled customer emerges as your best publicist: 'Remember that time I bought a fuchsia that died and you replaced it? Well I told 100 people about that.'"

There is, however, evidence that even though former complainers *do* have positive things to say, they don't say it nearly as often as people who are happy in the first place. One university study found that people who complain and then become satisfied tell two or three others, while those who are happy in the first place tell four or five others.

John Goodman, president of Technical Assistance Research Programs, a research firm that tracks customer service trends, says that "people who are satisfied with the way their gripe is resolved tell five people about it, whereas those who are dissatisfied tell ten."

General Motors learned that out of every hundred customers with complaints, sixty never tell the company or a dealer. And 90 percent of those sixty people will never buy a GM product again. But of the 40 percent who do complain to the company, as many as 80 percent will buy another GM product, even if they are not happy with the resolution of their complaint. Just the act of complaining seems to have the effect of making about 16 percent of the unsuccessful complainers feel better about GM.

There seems to be at least one arena in which satisfied complainers are even happier than noncomplainers. One researcher looked at patients who either were or were not happy with their doctor, and either did or did not complain. Patients who complained and had a satisfactory resolution now liked their doctors even more than those who had no reason for complaining. Perhaps they really enjoyed having a doctor over whom they felt they could exert just a little power or influence.

IT'S NOT THE COMPLAINT, IT'S THE WAY IT WAS HANDLED

Two doctoral dissertations on complaining offer clear evidence that what goes on during the complaining process itself can affect the way people end up feeling about the complaint. Even when the original complaint is resolved in the very way the customer hoped it would be, suggests Diane Halstead at Michigan State University, customer perception of the way they were treated as a complainer will predict their overall satisfaction level. In other words, the way they were treated may be at least as important as the outcome.

And Mary Gilly at the University of Houston compared the monetary size of the amount being complained about with the consumer's ultimate satisfaction. She found that the size of the settlement was a factor, but the intangibles related to the complaint process were really important.

Although being treated politely is not, in and of itself, enough to overcome a major complaint, the absence of courtesy or friendliness from the company may well result in a sour taste in the mouth, even if there is an appropriate settlement made.

How far can this notion be carried? In an article called "Real World Customer Service," Susan Greco writes in *Inc. Magazine* about one chief executive officer on the lecture circuit who says that complaining customers are the only kind that help a company grow. He insists that he purposely and regularly ships mildly faulty products just for the chance to demonstrate his company's responsiveness in dealing with the complaints they generate.

YOUR BEST NEW CUSTOMERS ARE YOUR OLD CUSTOMERS

People who write about marketing seem quite confident that it costs a lot more money to find a new customer for one's product or service than it does to keep an existing customer. There is an often-quoted rule of thumb that suggests, as Chester Wolford writes in *Business Communication*, "It costs a lot more—five to ten times more in advertising dollars—to replace a customer than it does to keep one." In *Managing to Keep the Customer*, R. L. Desanick writes that "it costs five times as much to attract a new customer as it does to retain an old one." Even General Motors researchers have written that "it costs five times as much to gain one conquest (customer) as it does to retain an existing one."

Even if there is no clear research that produces this five-to-one rule, there are probably few people in the business world who would disagree with marketing guru Jay Abraham that "your best new customers are your old customers."

Abraham specializes in helping companies in deep trouble survive. Very often he does this by discovering that the company has a great many former customers who were just a *bit* unhappy with the product or service, but *very* unhappy when their complaint was not dealt with to their satisfaction. Abraham goes to the customer records and picks out the names of people who had once bought the product, stayed at the hotel, eaten at the restaurant, rented the car, and so on, but haven't been heard from for a few years.

Time after time, he demonstrates that an outreach to these people—a friendly letter and a special offer—will bring many of them back into the fold, and at a much lower cost than the amount of advertising it would take to acquire totally new customers. (A restaurant wrote to former charge-account customers, offering a free bottle of good wine with their next dinner, and 23 percent of those contacted took them up on it.)

In this regard, Jeffrey Blodgett at the University of Mississippi looked at some actual numbers at a retail store whose average customer spent $542 a year, of which $190 was profit to the store. In a typical complaint, a customer wished to return a product for which he or she paid $93. The store would "lose" $28 by taking this item back—a small price to pay, compared with that $190 in profit *every year* from that customer, not to mention the bad-mouthing the customer might do if left unsatisfied.

"You're a good customer, so I don't have to be nice to you."

There is one small body of evidence that suggests that if customers are loyal, they do not have to be treated as well. A Vanderbilt University researcher and his colleague surveyed season ticket holders to a series of plays at the Tennessee Performing Arts Center. People were asked if they had any complaints and if they would be buying a season ticket again next year.

Among the subscribers with complaints, the ones who had been subscribers for the longest time were the least likely to walk away from the series. They were more forgiving of the causes of dissatisfaction than newer subscribers, leading to the unsettling conclusion that it may be more important to take care of your newer customers than your older ones.

WHETHER YOU WANT THEM OR NOT, COMPLAINERS CAN BE OF REAL VALUE

Alan Resnik and his colleagues at Portland State University point out that from the management perspective, complaints not only provide an opportunity to increase customer satisfaction, but valuable information for the organization's decision makers.

Indeed Ko DeRuyter wrote his doctoral dissertation in 1993 on *Dissatisfaction Management: A Study into the Use of Consumer Dissatisfaction as a Source of Management Information by Organizations.* Based on a detailed study of seven U.S. and seven Dutch companies, DeRuyter suggests that dissatisfaction data offer a rich source for strategic planners and for operational decision making.

An extreme and almost instantaneous example of making use of complaints occurred when the Coca-Cola Company introduced "New Coke" in 1985. The flood of complaint calls to their "1-800-GET COKE" toll-free phone line, plus their mail, persuaded them that a disaster was in the making, which they were able to head off by renaming the original product "Classic Coke" and continuing to sell it, "due to popular demand."

For her Harvard Ph.D., Betty Diener studied *Information and Redress: Consumer Needs and Corporate Responses: The Case of the Personal Care Industry.* She concluded that a careful audit of complaints serves much the same function as extensive customer research, but at a much lower cost. For instance, the complaint letters about allergic reactions received by Mennen after they introduced their new "Mennen E" antiperspirant gave them prompt and valuable data. The product was removed from the market within a year.

There are more than a few examples of cases where complaints led to new products and new packaging. As result of complaints about fabric stains, Right Guard introduced a new nonstaining formula. Hand pumps replaced aerosol sprays on many products. The metal box containing first aid bandages was redesigned to prevent causing further injuries while trying to extract a bandage. New Lego products were created. And Polaroid found a modest but worthy new direction for the company.

◆ ◆ ◆ ◆ ◆ ◆ ◆ ◆ ◆ ◆ ◆

The case of the one-armed photographer

CASE STUDY

June L. saw a Polaroid commercial on television and decided to buy the instant camera featured for her daughter. But in the store, she was dismayed to see that the camera in question had its shutter button in a place where it could not be operated by her daughter, who did not have the use of her right arm.

June was one of the 10,000 or more people who telephoned Polaroid's toll-free number that week. The customer service representative listened to the complaint, then went into the factory to talk it over with some of the engineers in the design department. The first outcome was that the customer rep and a couple of technicians were able to design a jury-rigged system with a pistol-grip shutter release on the left-hand side. The one-of-a-kind camera was sent to the customer free of charge.

And, significantly, as an outgrowth of this complaint, the company formed a unit called Special Needs Adapted Photography, designed to make special adaptations of their equipment, working with occupational therapists and special education teachers. With more than thirty million disabled people in the United States alone, this was a good business move, as well as a highly ethical one.

◆ ◆ ◆ ◆ ◆ ◆ ◆ ◆ ◆ ◆ ◆ ◆

ON THE OTHER HAND, SOME COMPLAINERS MAY NOT BE SO GOOD FOR YOUR COMPANY

Michael Schrage is the "innovation columnist" for the *Los Angeles Times*. In a *Wall Street Journal* article entitled "Fire Your Customers," he writes about how customer service has become the "quality mantra" of the 1990s.

> The business press and battalions of management seminars
> are filled with inspirational sagas of service to customers that
> go far beyond the call of duty—like the one where the Nord-
> strom salesperson lets someone return a set of tires, even
> though Nordstrom doesn't sell tires.

Schrage acknowledges that most companies do need to upgrade their customer service, but he calls for a reality check.

> The smartest thing most customer service–oriented companies could do today is lay off about 10 percent to 15 percent of their customers....The real corporate craziness is acquiring or keeping customers and clients who end up costing more than they are worth. Banks learn this the hard way. Having the courage to identify, and then fire, low-value customers is a healthy first step.

He finds it unfortunate that "today's trendy customer satisfaction ethic asks organizations to view the customer as a child to be indulged rather than as a peer or a colleague." He sees the Nordstrom tires story as a sad one, in which customer service is taken into realms where it might better be excluded.

Schrage does not suggest the ways and means of choosing which 10 percent to 15 percent of the customers should be fired. While the idea of firing some customers of my mail-order business is appealing, I find myself thinking of those many times when for instance,

- an annoying seven-phone-call potential customer, or
- a man who seemed so dim he could only communicate with pencil-stubbed postcards, or
- a woman who read off a list of the authorities she would complain to if her order were delayed, even before she placed it

all came through with huge multi-thousand-dollar and essentially trouble-free orders. I am reminded of John Wanamaker's marketing lament: "I know that half my advertising dollars are wasted; the problem is, I don't know which half." I suspect that I could benefit from "firing" 15 percent of my customers, but I don't know which ones they should be.

MISS MANNERS ON HOW A BUSINESS SHOULD DEAL WITH COMPLAINTS

Judith Martin, "Miss Manners," had a complaint that her morning newspaper was unaccountably missing from her front porch. She decided to "use the opportunity to expand on the question of how complaints should be politely handled...by...businesses that serve the public and are subject to periodic failures, which is to say all businesses that promise service."

She proposed three steps: (1) An apology. (2) A promise to do something. (3) Acknowledgement that mistakes should not happen. ("Skip (4) Bitter laughter. That is best done privately.")

Miss Manners suggests that when a complaint-taker is surly, or says, "That's not my department,"

> as a result the customer's original dissatisfaction with the service is compounded by the feeling that the company doesn't care that it hasn't delivered what it promised....Employees don't think of this themselves, because they are thinking of themselves. They know that they are not at fault, they know that there is no such thing as perfect service, and they also know that customers are equally likely to commit faults...exceeding the bounds of politeness when making their complaints.
>
> But where, then, may a customer direct his dissatisfaction? Who is qualified to answer for the company? A proper employee should be taught not to think of himself, or herself, when on the job, as an innocent individual under attack, but as the voice of the company, who is therefore able to accept the company's responsibility, express its regret, and pledge its renewed effort. As an impersonal spokesman, the employee could state official shock that less-than-perfect service ever occurs, accept any auxiliary comments to be passed on to those responsible, and even tolerate anger, knowing that it is directed toward the business, not himself.

Music on hold compounds the problem because of

> sound reproduction techniques that make all telephoned music irritating. Instead of attempting to entertain them with music, why not play a recording of the day's headlines? This is only a modest suggestion, intended to illustrate that one diffuses a complaint first by sympathizing with the complainer and then by considering his needs rather than one's own. It does not hurt the company to pretend that it is upset at mistakes, nor does it compromise the individual employee to assume the role of spokesperson rather than attempt to defend himself as an individual from what was never directed at him.

HOWARD GOSSAGE ON WHY COMPANIES
WANT TO HEAR FROM YOU

Gossage, the first inductee into the Advertising Hall of Fame, encouraged people to write to his advertising clients, whether with complaints, praise, comments, or even to enter silly contests. The important thing was that they write.

> There is no great mystery as to why advertisers want people to write in. A client leads a lonely life, isolated from his ultimate customers. He knows them not as men and women, but as neck sizes and sleeve lengths. For him to receive [any kind of] letters from them as real, live human beings, and to find out that they regard him likewise...is a delicious experience. It transforms him. He smiles at himself while shaving. He becomes unbearable around his club. He becomes an expert on advertising. He writes a book about it.

CHAPTER 16

How Companies Deal with Complaints

IT'S REALLY HARD TO FIND OUT

DESPITE THE BEST EFFORTS of academic researchers and popular writers to learn more about the ways in which companies deal with complaints, the information we have is largely superficial and anecdotal.

Many companies just don't to reveal all that much about the way they do business, believing it might benefit their competitors.

Some companies don't want to encourage complaining, especially when there have been situations in which they may have "given in" to a complainer, and they might worry that if the news gets out, large numbers of people will attempt the same action.

Some companies, including some very large ones, have such a disjointed, erratic, inconsistent complaint-handling process that they really wouldn't know how to respond even if they wanted to.

Of course, just about every company pays lip service to the importance of dealing responsibly with complaints. When a Heinz spokesman says, "If our customers have any problems with any of our products, we really do want to hear from them. We investigate and evaluate their complaints; we respond to all of them," there is no reason to doubt the sincerity and dedication here. When a manager at Ralston Purina says, "We work hard on complaints because it's still easier to keep old customers than to get new ones," he is no doubt reflecting company policy and intentions.

I wrote to a great many major corporations, asking about their complaint-handing policy. When my questions were general, I received a polite generic answer: "Chrysler is always responsive to the needs and concerns of the public...." When my questions were very specific, such as my letter to Crown-Zellerbach asking for more information on a rumor that they had changed their hiring practices for blacks in the South as a result of complaint letters, either I got no answer at all or, after a bit of persistence, a polite but firm rejection: "After careful thought," the public relations department replied, "we decided the best course to follow was...not to comment (about our mail) and I regret to tell you that we do not wish to supply the information you request."

And when Congressman Benjamin Rosenthal attempted to study complaint-handling, he found that most companies are willing to talk freely, but they are "not willing to release current statistics on categories and dispositions of complaints."

THE STRUCTURE OF COMPLAINT-HANDLING WITHIN COMPANIES

Fortunately I didn't have to do much research here, because E. Laird Landon Jr. did it for me, in his doctoral dissertation at the University of Houston, *Responding to Consumer Complaints: Organizational Considerations*. Landon points out that

> It was not too long ago that a generally held opinion in
> business was that "consumers who write complaint letters are
> cranks and weirdoes." The fact that very few letters were
> received was *prima facie* evidence that these consumers were
> atypical. But as the number of letters grew, it became more
> and more difficult to dismiss them. Some response became
> imperative.

But the idea of a "complaint department" or "complaint desk" within a big company or agency was a new one in many cases, and there was no clear notion of where to put it. Was complaining more associated with management? Marketing? Public relations? Quality control? Research and development? Engineering? Legal? The answer is yes, some of each. So should there be a separate department, or complaint-handling functions within some or all of these other departments? Or should we just let some part-time secretary handle it on his or her lunch hour, the way we did in the past?

Clearly there is no simple or common answer. Landon looks at four of the variables and finds no common threads:

1. The addressee deals with it, no matter what. Whoever is sent a complaint, whether the president or the mail room clerk, responds to it. This method, not uncommon, tends to be inefficient and complex, and when the complainer communicates a second time, it may go to another person entirely, who is unfamiliar with the first go-round.

2. The way the complaint is delivered determines where it goes: whether it comes in by mail, fax, telephone, E-mail, or the irate consumer standing there in the lobby or the aisle with the defective juicer cradled in his arms.

3. The nature of the complaint determines where it goes, within certain predefined complaint response teams or individuals. For instance, at one big oil company, one unit handles only credit card complaints, another deals with physical injuries on company facilities, one handles warranties, one deals with environmental concerns, and one deals only with dealers and wholesalers.

4. The "Complaint Central" system, in which there is one person, or a team, who initially handles all complaints and makes the decision on what to do next: immediately handle it through a form letter or a phone call, or pass it along to the appropriate predesignated specialist who deals with that kind of complaint.

There is no "best" way of doing this, and if we really knew what went on at all of the Fortune 500 companies, we'd probably find 500 different approaches. Some advance knowledge of the way your complaint will be handled could be helpful in choosing how it will be delivered, but in most cases, you will have to depend on the general wisdom offered here, based on a combination of academic research and popular press articles.

WHO HANDLES THE COMPLAINTS

In her doctoral dissertation, Kathleen Morrow at Oklahoma State University looked at *The Role of the Consumer Affairs Professional* as perceived by him or herself, and by the head of the organization. She points out that complaint-handling, or customer service, is now a career in itself, and not just something that others do in their spare time. Morrow determined that the most limiting job factor for the complaint handler is lack of growth on the job; there is nowhere higher to go in this field in the company. A major frustration was lack of interdepartment cooperation. And, revealingly, the main source of job satisfaction was in helping the *company*, not in helping the *customer*.

THE LIKELIHOOD OF GETTING ANY RESPONSE

In a rational and harmonious world, everyone who complained would get not only a response, but a *satisfactory* response. There aren't a lot of real-world data here. There have been quite a few surveys in which people were asked, long after the fact, whether they had ever complained, and if so, whether they got a reply, and if so, if the result was satisfactory. These surveys typically report numbers like these:

- Anywhere from 56 percent to 82 percent of the people surveyed said they had received a response to a complaint. Milla Boschung reports an average of 74 percent. Other research suggests that packaged-goods companies are at the top of the heap (82 percent responding) with automobile manufacturers at the bottom (56 percent).

- Of those getting a response, 53 percent to 77 percent (depending on the research) say they are satisfied, with packaged goods again at the top of the list. Of such companies, 87 percent use product replacement, and 64 percent refund money or provide discount coupons or gift certificates as well.

- In about a third of the cases the response was by impersonal form letter, about half got a personal (or at least personalized) letter, while the rest received either a telephone call or, in 3 or 4 percent of the cases, a personal visit from a company representative.

RESEARCH ON RESPONSES

Whether because of budget constraints, ethical considerations, or diminished imagination, there have been no research studies, as best I can determine, in which someone sent out hundreds or even thousands of complaint letters to real companies and agencies, and analyzed the response, in terms of speed, quality, helpfulness, and satisfaction.

We must settle, instead, for a few modest real-world studies, and a lot of surveys asking people what they did in the past, or what they *would* have done, if such-and-such had happened.

C. L. Kendall and Frederick Russ at the University of North Carolina wrote to 100 consumer packaged goods companies, with a simple complaint. Seventy-nine percent of them replied, and 70 percent of the replies were satisfactory. In another study, similar results were obtained with complaint letters to the manufacturers of insecticides, oil additives, cereals, shampoos, and deodorants. Of the 82 percent of these who responded, 68 percent were deemed satisfactory, with 48 percent offering a cash refund, 5 percent coupons, 35 percent merchandise, and the balance asking for further information on the complaint.

Milla Boschung tested the general appearance of a letter and learned, in letters to sixty-three companies complaining about products bought in a supermarket, that the typed and literate letter was more likely to get a satisfactory response than the handwritten and poorly worded one.

A Canadian researcher learned that complaints that appeared to come from wealthier and better-educated consumers were more likely to get an inconclusive response, either asking questions or asking for more information, while the letters from "ordinary folks" got a prompt clear answer, whether positive or negative. This is possibly because of a feeling that a more articulate writer is more of a threat, and if the response is not "just so," that person may be more likely to go to third-party sources and make more trouble.

◆ ◆ ◆ ◆ ◆ ◆ ◆ ◆ ◆ ◆ ◆   *CASE STUDY*

Why Professor John Selwyn Marsh wanted to burn down your house

As indicated, very few research studies in the world of complaining and consumer behavior make use of real-world data. Some years ago, a major study was conducted that may have been the only time that a true measure of how people feel about their possessions was ever investigated.

The only problem is that the study was a complete and total hoax, here revealed for the first time.

My advertising mentor, the famous copywriter Howard Gossage, was invited to speak at the national convention of the Association for Education in Journalism. Gossage had no wish to travel from San Francisco to North Carolina, nor did he wish to offend the well-meaning academics who had invited him. In the privacy of his office, he and I concocted an elaborate hoax.

Gossage sent his regrets, but told the Association that he had been able to persuade his friend, the well-known consumer researcher Dr. John Selwyn Marsh, to appear in his stead. Marsh was described so glowingly, no one bothered to check his credentials, which was fortunate, since he didn't have any (other than his full professorship at the non-existent Bering Straits University, Cape Prince of Wales, Alaska). Marsh, in fact, did not exist.

In the guise of Dr. Marsh, I traveled to Chapel Hill, North Carolina, to deliver a speech entitled The Thermodynamic Theory of Brand Selection. Marsh's theory—probably quite accurate—was that it is impossible to find out how people really feel about various products, since they will either lie on their questionnaire, or tell the interviewer what they think he or she wants to hear.

In order to determine the true importance of various consumer goods, Dr. Marsh reported, he and his graduate students went around to people's houses at two in the morning and pounded on the doors, shouting "Fire! Fire! Your house is on fire!" Then they stood back, clipboards poised, to see which items people would choose to save, believing their house was about to burn down, for of course they would only save the things that were most important to them.

The problem with this method, he reported, is that people quickly discovered their house was not on fire, and so a true measure of their behavior was not observed. Therefore, the good doctor continued, for Phase II of the project, he and his graduate students again went out at two in the morning, but this time, they actually did burn people's houses down, and noted which things people chose to save.

The audience of academics sat through the talk quietly and politely asked a few routine questions, then dutifully assigned a copy of the paper to the oblivion of their briefcases. "Dr. Marsh" was prepared to say that Phase III of his project was never undertaken, because the balance of his government grant had to be used for bail, but no one asked.

◆ ◆ ◆ ◆ ◆ ◆ ◆ ◆ ◆ ◆ ◆ ◆

BUT DO YOU REALLY LOVE ME?
HOW SOME COMPANIES REALLY THINK
ABOUT COMPLAINERS

To be sure, there are many companies that are genuinely helpful and genuinely compassionate and genuinely believe that the complaint process can benefit *them* as well as help the complainer. But at some companies, whether or not it reflects company policy, there are people who range from mildly annoyed to downright hostile about those customers who have the temerity actually to file a complaint. And some of these people are remarkably candid in expressing their feelings, especially to academic researchers, perhaps lulled into forgetting that their words and opinions will end up in publicly accessible print.

What, for instance, could a Frigidaire appliance complaint handler be thinking when he told an academic interviewer (as reported in Arthur Best's book *When Consumers Complain),* that he hears from "three kinds of complainants: hysterical women, drunks, and people who are unwilling to pay for a product or service." He says he tries to calm down the hysterical women, hangs up on drunks, and explains to others why their complaints are not justified.

Best suggests that business complaint handlers often express general hostility to *all* complainers. A manager at Korvette's: "What'll happen if everyone finds out you can get what you ask for?" A big furniture manufacturer says: "We don't need people [complaining about] flammable fabrics...; we need people who don't smoke in sofas."

A Ford regional service manager says customers with complaints "should not try to dictate to me or be emotional. Then consideration will be given. I spend 99 percent of my time trying to help customers. They spend 1 percent of their time trying to cooperate."

A Sears executive says consumers should not argue emotionally. "A lot of them curse at you or scream at you. If they meet us halfway, we're more than willing to meet them halfway." A J. C. Penney executive politely suggests people are not as accurate as they might be; he says one should complain promptly because "the more time a customer delays and thinks about the problem, the more distorted it becomes." A major appliance company's complaint handler says that "consumers should understand the problems businesses face. Chief among these is that no one wants to pay for a product any more; people expect good performance but won't pay higher prices."

THAT'S NOT A RAT, IT'S A PANTRY PEST

People who handle complaints—not all of them, thank goodness—seem to have these beliefs and assumptions about those who complain:

1. People who complain are just trying to get free products. A major canned food company's only complaint files are lists of people who were sent replacements, to monitor those who make multiple requests. The assumption is that anyone who complains more than once must be lying.

2. People who complain have only themselves to blame. If they used the product properly and read the instructions, they wouldn't have a problem. A Mazda customer relations manager blames consumer complaints about poor gas mileage on their driving habits. A laundry that destroyed some fancy dress shirts chastised the customer for bringing such elegant things to a laundry like theirs. A man who tried to return a $3 "spill proof" coffee mug for use in a car was told he must be driving erratically.

3. People who complain just don't understand that they really don't have a problem. Jargon can be used to redefine a "situation." A Ford service manager says that the complaints he gets about vibration in a certain model are not a problem, it is "a manufacturing characteristic." Arthur Best reports that General Mills has told callers complaining about worms or insects in cereal or cake mix that these are merely harmless "pantry pests."

4. There isn't time or motivation to deal with chronic or difficult complainers. Some consumers who complain are faced with aggressive responses by businesses, including intimidation, threatened retaliation, and stonewalling. The CEO of a large embroidering firm said (I'd like to think just a little wistfully) that he takes a tough stand with complainers because "we're past the point where we're in business because we love embroidery."

COMPLAINERS AS ACTUAL OR PSYCHOLOGICAL CAPTIVES

The seller or service provider who has a monopoly, or is seen to have great power, has the best of both worlds. As Arthur Best puts it,

> if the seller treats consumers unfairly, a small number of "sophisticated elites" will leave, while the rest of the captive market will remain and more or less servilely accept the unfair treatment. The seller loses a few sales to the decamping elites but is spared their vocal abuse while at the same time reaping excessive profits from docile masses.

This is especially likely to be true with utility and telephone companies, transportation companies, and, in the matter of psychological captivity, doctors and dentists. Some people despair of the logistics, the complexities, or the loss of face in switching medical providers, and so they suffer abuse without complaining.

STONEWALLING AS COMPANY POLICY

Some companies and organizations don't respond to complaints because they do not have the staff or the budget or their act together. And there are doubtless others who choose, as their unwritten policy, remaining silent. They can use silence with impunity because, as the bumper sticker goes, "We don't care. We don't have to. We're [name of company]."

BULLDOGGING AS COMPANY POLICY

Some companies and organizations choose, as their written or unwritten policy, never giving up to a complainer. They know that they are far more powerful, that they can persevere through a prolonged conflict, that they have greater financial resources, and that they have access to information that the complainer might not have.

COMPANIES THAT INVITE CONSUMERS TO COMPLAIN

While there are those companies that clearly wish all complainers would just shrivel up and blow away, there are those who actually invite their customers and clients to complain, believing that it is good for business to do so.

Whirlpool ran advertisements consisting of a blank letter, so that people could fill in their complaints and mail it in to the company. About 3,000 people did so, and the company credits this approach, combined with accompanying quality control measures, in reducing the number of complaints from nine per thousand sales to one per thousand sales, in nine years.

USA Today sent a survey to 30,000 subscribers, inviting their complaints and offering a free key chain for responding. Based on the results, they redesigned their systems for handling complaints, including a policy of calling complainers back in a few weeks to see if they had been satisfied.

Schlage Electronics ran an ad in trade publications giving the president's private unlisted number, inviting people with complaints to call him. Of the company's 20,000 customers only five took them up on this offer. Two had genuine problems that were dealt with; the other three were unhappy because they expected more of their system than it was designed to do.

Reader's Digest created the job of customer advocate, whose "job is to represent the best interests of our customers to management without regard for the company's interest." The customer advocate regularly convenes focus groups to discuss complaint matters and randomly calls customers to see if they are satisfied.

...BUT IT DOESN'T ALWAYS WORK THE WAY THEY EXPECTED

Chrysler, in a major ad campaign, told people to send their complaints to "Your Man in Detroit," whom they identified as one Byron Nichols. Many people called instead instead of writing; the switchboard was swamped, and thousands didn't get through. Chrysler canceled the ads and began putting information in the owner's manual of new cars, offering a P.O. box to complain to, but no telephone number. The Center for Auto Safety reports that if Byron Nichols really exists, he can never be reached by telephone, does not answer his letters, and has himself become the source of growing consumer irritation.

Travelers Insurance introduced an 800-number hotline for consumer complaints on a Sunday afternoon television spot. They had apparently expected a few dozen calls, and when they received thousands on the next day, they were quite unprepared and unequipped to handle them. (They also reported many calls from people who believed Travelers had something to do with the travel industry and were complaining about an airline or a hotel.)

General Motors was embarrassed when, as the *Washington Post* reported, a Chevrolet dealer in a Washington suburb handed a pair of prospective buyers a customer satisfaction questionnaire with all the "completely satisfied" boxes already checked. A spokesman for the dealership confirmed the staff gives filled-in questionnaires to all customers. He said that General Motors uses the customer satisfaction to allocate its cars in the Washington area. "It's just super important to us to get a good rating. Most customers don't realize the difference that a 'completely satisfied' and 'somewhat satisfied' rating has on the dealership."

SOME COMPANIES' POLICIES ON COMPLAINTS

The academic and business literature on complaining offers a bit of reassurance that there really are companies and organizations that care about complainers and complaints. These companies have a clear policy in that direction that allows them to hear complaints and respond to them, both in terms of the complainer and in terms of adjusting company policies, when appropriate, to reduce the need for complaining in the future. Here are some of those satisfying situations.

Quill Corporation

Customers of America's largest independent office supplies company used to complain about waiting too long on hold. Now no one ever waits more than 55 seconds. In busy times, calls are routed from the order taker to customer service reps to supervisors and, if necessary, back to the switchboard to arrange for a callback.

When Quill began enclosing an authorized return form with every order, people predicted they'd get more returns than before, but that didn't happen.

Chevrolet

Former complaint-producing problem: Because of decentralization, files on complainers might be kept in any of a number of places: headquarters, regional or branch offices, or dealerships. The solution was to create a centralized complaint office in Troy, Michigan, with 200 service advisors fielding upwards of 5,000 calls a day, 40 percent of them complaints. The goal is to answer 80 percent of calls on the first ring, and there are no time pressures. "Angry customers are given the opportunity to ventilate."

L. L. Bean

The large mail-order company was founded on complaints. Leon Leonhart Bean invented the Maine hunting shoe, with rubber bottoms and leather tops. He got a list of out-of-staters with a Maine fishing license and sent them a brochure. One hundred pairs were sold, and 90 were returned with defects. Bean refunded their money, then got a loan to improve the product, which became the cornerstone of his company and which remains on sale today.

"Bean purposely teaches its customers how to complain," said Bill Shea, director of Customer Service. "Research has shown that customers who complain tend to be your most loyal customers....If they have problems and don't bother to complain, they usually won't bother to reorder either."

Complaining customers are asked, "What will satisfy you?" Employees have the authority, without going to higher-ups, to do whatever the customer wants. They only need to get management permission to say "No" to a customer, which doesn't happen often.

Wal-Mart

They take to heart founder Sam Walton's statement that "the greatest measurement of our success is how well we please the customer, Our Boss. Let's all support 'aggressive hospitality' and have our customers leave 100 percent satisfied every day." This is achieved by extensive "courtesy training," a "no hassle" satisfaction guarantee, and lots of good public relations, including the highly visible in-store service representatives on roller skates.

On the other hand, ten years of good public relations may have been undone when Mike Royko, in December 1995, wrote his nationally syndicated column about a man who brought his car to Wal-Mart for tires. While it was there, a dishonest employee stole it and virtually destroyed it. Wal-Mart, says Royko, disclaimed any responsibility, saying they were not accountable for what their employees do.

Ciba-Ceigy

The big pharmaceuticals company did research that persuaded them they had "low level complaint residue," which they defined as a lot of customers who were not fully satisfied, but not unhappy enough to complain. Yet, as the low-level incidents added up, eventually they took their business elsewhere. After soliciting complaints, they identified several matters that were especially annoying to these "low level" complainers, such as a policy requiring a 48-hour notice to pick up goods at a warehouse. Changes were made, and sales improved.

Good Samaritan Hospital

The huge Cincinnati hospital, with 3,200 employees, decided that complaint resolution was number two in priorities, right after medical and fire emergencies. Most complaints were made by phone. Instead of being logged in for later action, they are routed to supervisors or managers who must respond within thirty minutes, either by resolving the complaint or proposing an alternative. Shortly after the thirty minutes have elapsed, another employee calls the complainer to see if matters *have* been resolved. A money-back guarantee reinforces the hospital's commitment to prompt complaint resolution.

Holiday Inn

They promote the fact that if a complaint is not resolved by checkout time, a portion of the stay is free. With appropriate staff training, less than 2 percent of "room nights" yielded complaints, and about half of those turned out to be from "chronic complainers" who eventually get flagged, so their complaints are scrutinized especially closely, and often turn out to be nonexistent or frivolous. Holiday Inn will *not* give guests a free night if the bath towel is not exactly centered on the towel rack, as one complainer pointed out.

Ryder Truck Rental

With many employees in relatively low-level jobs, the concept of complaint-handling was sometimes hard to get across. The solution was a point system, where employees earned points for solving problems and resolving complaints. The points can be converted into banquets and free trips. When complaints are resolved in unusual ways, as with an employee who helped a customer make deliveries until three in the morning after a truck broke down, the company public relations department makes sure the story gets out.

Marshall Field

The Chicago department store also makes use of points, but awards them in the form of "frangloons," a pewter coin, awarded to employees who help resolve complaints, either by the way they deal with customers or by suggesting new policies. For instance, a salesperson pointed out that the policy of requiring a second employee to verify a check-using customer's driver's license didn't cut down on bad checks, it just slowed down the transaction and annoyed the customer. Frangloons can be converted into candy, a discount on store purchases, or days off with pay. After more than 70,000 Frangloons had been dispensed, one of the tangible results was that the time between a customer's arrival and "being noticed" was reduced from ten minutes to four, with a goal of further reduction to two minutes.

Racing Strollers

In a charming article entitled "Tom Peters Ruined My Life," Mary Bachler, president of a high-end stroller company, said that she runs her business differently with regard to complaints after hearing Peters point out that the customer *is* always right, in the sense that he or she votes by spending dollars, and simply goes away if not treated right.

Now at Racing Strollers, any employee can spend up to $300 without permission to resolve a problem, including sending a stroller by overnight delivery. Bachler writes that "I view myself and my staff as people with a religious devotion to our customers. The annoying businesses I run into are the Heathen. If they understood this love of customers, they'd be doing it. But they just don't know any better, poor things."

Cellular One

The problem was that customers kept getting lost in voice mail and referrals to other numbers, and whenever they surfaced, they were complaining vigorously. The company's solution involved "cross-training" their customer service representatives, so that each one could handle a much wider range of complaints: billing, troubleshooting, operating the equipment, and so on. Further, they installed a "silent radio" message board in their complaint department where every operator could see it, and operators could post messages like, "This customer is having problems and won't pay his bill until they are resolved. Don't cut off his service now."

Nashua Corporation

In their computer products division, complaints were categorized and sorted into piles. The easy complaints were dealt with at once, and the bigger problems were set aside to be dealt with later. But there was a tendency to delay attending to the big problems. The solution was a policy of dealing with all complaints in the order received, thereby eliminating the "problem piles."

Charles Schwab

The brokerage firm aggressively takes the position that if it doesn't make mistakes, there will be no complaints. Their "zero defects" program is focused on five basic potential problem areas of customer needs: accurate information, timely delivery, accessibility of people, reliability of information, and knowledgeable staff. Performance is measured carefully and discussed in a monthly half-day meeting, with the president presiding and all key executives present. The company does not pay commissions, but employees are rewarded with individual and group bonuses for low-complaint performance.

HOW COMPANIES USE COMPLAINTS IN THEIR OWN PLANNING

While many of the above companies make use of complaint information to help improve their own services to the public and enhance company performance and profits, that is not the mainstream position.

In a nationwide survey of firms with formal complaint-handling units, Claes Fornell and Robert Westbrook asked the question: Do complaint departments provide input into other aspects of corporate decision making? They learned that 75 percent of the firms used complaint data to improve customer service departments, but beyond that,

- only 54 percent made use of the data in their warranty department
- 49 percent passed the information along to quality control
- 44 percent made use of complaint data in packaging and labeling
- 47 percent used it for new product concepts
- 43 percent said it had an effect on advertising copy
- 21 percent used it in the consumer credit department
- 15 percent said it had an effect in price determination

So apart from the obvious customer service and warranty matters, complaint data have not had a major impact on the way big companies are run. Out of 128 companies that supplied such information, only 12 percent made product changes, 15 percent made packaging changes, 14 percent changed quality control processes, and 5 percent changed their advertising because of information learned from complaints.

THE DOG ATE YOUR COMPLAINT LETTER: RESPONSE BY EXCUSE

To what extent is old-fashioned excuse making used in responding to complaints? Robert Baer and Donnal J. Hill of Bradley University looked into this, in a study called "Excuse Making: A Prevalent Company Response to Complaints?" The question was, is organizational excuse making a usual part of the complaint management process?

They examined many companies' responses to complaint letters. Based on the literature from a field of psychology actually called "excuse theory," they studied common kinds of excuses.

A crash course in excuse theory

Excuse theory flows from the work of C. R. Snyder, R. L. Higgins, and R. J. Stucky, as published in a book called *Excuses: Masquerades in Search of Grace*. They define an excuse as "a motivated process of (a) diminishing the perceived negativity of events and (b) shifting the causal attribution for negative events away from oneself." To be effective, an excuse must diminish one's perceived connection to the act or lessen perceived negativity of the event. In other words, either "I didn't do it," or "I did it, but it's not so bad."

There are two basic categories of excuse, which the authors call "linkage" and "valence."

The three main linkage excuses are

1. Denial: I had nothing to do with it; it wasn't us; we have no record of this; you have called the wrong department or company.

2. Deflection: Someone else did it, not I; it was due to bad weather; it must have been exposed to the heat; the salesperson must have forgotten to tell you.

3. Explanation: There were extenuating circumstances that were: unusual, rare, inevitable, unintentional, uncontrollable; everyone makes mistakes.

The two main valence excuses are

1. Minimization: it was bad, but not really all *that* bad.

2. Justification: Boldly asserting that not only was it not so bad, it was even *good*, and you're better off as a result. The half-filled containers prevent breakage; by fixing this little problem now, it won't need repairs again for a long time.

In dealing with complaints, the authors found that companies and organizations are most likely to use deflection (blaming someone else) and explanation (minimizing the problem).

Those 50 percent of companies that practice regular excuse making believe (compared with those companies that don't make excuses) they really could not control or avoid the problem, and therefore it was necessary to make excuses.

Do customers buy this approach? Only partially. In an article called "Consumer Complaints and Managerial Response: A Holistic Approach," Alan Resnik and Robert Harmon report that while 52 percent of managers thought an excuse was necessary in responding to a complaint, only 34 percent of complaining customers thought an excuse was necessary.

IN CONCLUSION

Some companies, from Nordstrom to L. L. Bean, are legendary for the high quality and level of their complaint handling; others are notorious for the miserable way they deal with their customers and their customers' complaints, and most are somewhere in between. Many in the worst group have perfectly fine products or services, they just have a different attitude. If the attitude is intentional and reflects the true feelings of the owners or managers, then there is little that consumers can do, other than "voting with their feet" by marching over to a friendlier place. If it is unintentional, then there is always hope, as in the Case of the Dropped Disk.

◆ ◆ ◆ ◆ ◆ ◆ ◆ ◆ ◆ ◆ ◆ ◆

CASE STUDY

The case of the dropped disk, the compassionate president, and the Oak Ridge Boys

For our home accounting, we were using MacOneWrite, a program for which you had to insert the original disk into the computer at various times. Then the original disk went bad. Fortunately, a backup had been provided. We attempted to make a copy of this, but it was utterly uncopyable. Sometime later, by accident, we dropped the backup disk. It would not work any more. Now we could no longer access our own accounting.

We made an urgent phone call to the company from which we bought it. Sorry, they said, they no longer "support" that program; they sold the rights to another company.

Urgent call to the new company. The product has been changed and upgraded, and there no longer are available disks of the sort we need. We could buy the new version for about $400, with no guarantee that it will work on our old data.

I wrote a long and anguished letter to the president of the new company, setting forth all that had happened and stating how desperate we were. I offered to pay any reasonable price to get what really should have been free or nearly so.

The president wrote back that she is very glad we called this to her attention, because she does not wish to be the president of the sort of company that treats people the way her company had treated me. She said she would be sending a disk that will unlock our files (see, it did exist!), and, to make up for our anguish, she was also sending a complete set of their high-end accounting software, designed to handle companies doing up to $50 million a year in sales.

The disk arrived the next day, and a few days later there came a huge carton with the high-end stuff. Its list price was in the vicinity of $4,000 (although, as with most software, the actual manufacturing price was probably well under $100).

I told this story at the monthly meeting of MacInteresteds, my local computer users group, and a hand goes up: What are you planning to do with the $4,000 software? I had no plans, and so I sold it to the hand-raiser, who turned out to be the manager of the Oak Ridge Boys. He got a terrific deal, I made some money, and I got a personally autographed picture of the Boys to boot (which I keep on my wall, even after I read that they are all Republicans).

◆ ◆ ◆ ◆ ◆ ◆ ◆ ◆ ◆ ◆ ◆ ◆

For the last word on these matters, let me offer an only slightly convoluted rewrite of the Chinese aphorism about people who are awake or asleep:

> The organization that does things right, and knows that it does things right, is a model for us all. Emulate them.
>
> The organization that does things right, but doesn't know that it does things right, is a sleeper. Buy their stock.
>
> The organization that does things wrong, but doesn't know that it is doing things wrong, is in trouble. Alert them.
>
> The organization that does things wrong, and knows it does things wrong, is an abomination. Pity them, but avoid them.

CHAPTER 17

How Companies *Should* Handle Complaints

IN 1992, THE U.S. GOVERNMENT'S Office of Consumer Affairs issued a set of guidelines for how the responsible business should deal with consumer complaints. The manuscript was reviewed by the Federal Trade Commission and the National Coalition for Consumer Education. The guidelines say:

> Complaints are a critical form of communication between buyer and seller. They offer business an opportunity to correct immediate problems and they frequently provide constructive ideas for improving products, adapting marketing practices, upgrading servicing, or modifying promotional material and product information....
>
> Not all companies have made effective complaint management a routine part of their business operations. Within any industry, those companies with a positive philosophy and reputation for fair complaint management have a competitive edge. Effective complaint management leads to increased customer satisfaction, which in turn yields greater loyalty.

The report goes on to offer seven recommendations—six of them things that any business or agency can do itself, in house; the last one involves the use of outside agencies. Since these recommendations are a joint venture between government and private consumer-oriented organizations, and since they seem eminently reasonable, it seems appropriate to present them pretty much as they were published, with some editing for clarity, and, at the end, some additional suggestions culled from other writers on this topic, as well as the fount of common sense.

RECOMMENDATION 1: A STRATEGY IS NEEDED

Every company, regardless of its size or the price of its products, needs an effective strategy for managing consumer complaints.

Complaints are an inexpensive source of market research. They reveal how customers understand advertising, how products or services meet their needs, whether the instruction manuals are satisfactory, and whether the products or services need improvement.

Not dealing well with complaints can be expensive. Not only do customers leave and tell others, but if they complain effectively, it can be expensive to handle their complaints properly, whether in the courts or before third-party agencies.

RECOMMENDATION 2: A CLEAR POLICY IS NEEDED

Company management should establish the capacity, policies, and procedures necessary to provide effective complaint review and resolution.

There should be written policies and procedures, and well-trained staff. Management should closely supervise and review complaint resolution. The system should be well publicized, accessible, prompt, personal, simple, clear, objective, flexible, with good record keeping, no cost for filing complaints, and minimal cost, if any, for obtaining redress.

RECOMMENDATION 3: THERE NEED TO BE CLEAR STEPS TO FOLLOW

The basic steps of complaint management are the same, regardless of company type or size. They can always be adapted to the special needs of an organization. They are

a. Make it clear to the consumers how and where to complain (800 or 888 numbers recommended).

b. Have a system for record keeping. Information should be accessible to management and reported to other departments and outside agencies (for example, the Consumer Product Safety Commission) as needed.

c. Record and categorize the complaint, and assign it to one person for handling.

d. Acknowledge the complaint. Talk by phone or in person when possible. Don't use impersonal form letters.

e. Investigate and analyze. Be fair; get both sides; keep accurate records.

f. Resolve the complaint swiftly and fairly. Empower front-line employees to propose solutions.

g. Follow up. Ask the consumer if he or she is satisfied. Refer to a third party if needed.

h. Record the disposition of the complaint. Keep statistics.

RECOMMENDATION 4: COMPLAINING PROCEDURES SHOULD BE PUBLICIZED

Complaint procedures should be well publicized to employees and to the public. Typical methods of doing this could involve

a. posters and signs in the sales and service area

b. appropriate information on contract forms, sales slips, charge account mailings

c. use and care manuals

d. advertising

e. product packaging and labeling

f. consumer information programs: videos, booklets, educational activities

RECOMMENDATION 5: COMPLAINTS SHOULD BE ANALYZED

Effective complaint management should reduce the number of complaints. Complaints can be analyzed for these five factors:

a. Was the advertising clear?

b. Was the product or service oversold?

c. Were product disclosures, labeling, warranty information, and service agreements appropriate?

d. Are the users manuals clear, complete, and easy to read?

e. Is the warranty fair?

RECOMMENDATION 6: COMPLAINTS SHOULD BE RESOLVED AT THE LOWEST LEVEL POSSIBLE

Complaints should be resolved when possible at the point of sale: the retailer or the service provider. If that is difficult or impossible, then the manufacturer should help in the process.

Keep all levels informed. Coordinate complaint management with others in the network: retail, wholesale, manufacturer, service outlets.

Manufacturers should encourage consumers and retailers to contact them directly if the complaint cannot be promptly resolved.

RECOMMENDATION 7: USE THIRD-PARTY RESOLUTION MECHANISMS TO SUPPLEMENT THE EFFORTS

They are

a. Conciliation. A neutral conciliator brings parties together and encourages them to find a solution.

b. Mediation. A neutral mediator becomes actively involved in negotiation between the parties. The mediator can propose a solution but not enforce it.

c. Arbitration. An independent person or panel hears the facts on both sides and reaches a decision that both parties (or, sometimes, only the business party) agree to abide by.

AND FURTHERMORE...

Here are some additional points that companies and organizations might wish to bear in mind.

- Use experienced people. Dave Power of J. D. Power & Associates, the company that pioneered in rating automobile buyer attitudes and now deals with other goods and services, finds it odd that "companies often assign their greenest or least-valued personnel as gatekeepers to the public...."

- If A is broken, don't fix B. Power wonders about car dealers who spend a lot of money sprucing up their waiting lounge, when the fact is that clients would rather not stay there at all. Similarly, there is the example of the corner grocer who prided himself on knowing all his customers by name—and so he could say "bye-bye" to them as they fled to the supermarkets with their bigger selection, lower prices, and free parking.

- Be sincere. No, be *really* sincere. The Hollywood line, "Don't worry about sincerity, we can fake it," rarely works.

- Apologize. There is nothing wrong with saying, "I'm sorry, I blew it. What can I do to make things better?"

- Full disclosure. Customers like to be, in Erving Goffman's model, taken backstage, to learn a little more about how things work, and why they happened as they did.

- But not *overly* full disclosure. Backstage, yes, but not into the dressing rooms. The mail-order catalogue company that apologized for late delivery because, the owner wrote, "My husband died suddenly, and then the house burned down," was telling people more than they wanted, much less needed, to know.

- Pay attention to customers' emotional reactions as well as their satisfaction. Susan Morris points out that it is important to address underlying feelings of complainants. Responses that are OK for content but not for style and tone may cause subtle dissatisfaction and subsequent grudge-holding.

- As Susan Greco writes, in "Real World Customer Service," "Take a deep breath and don't panic. You'll never win them all."

Here are two excellent short summaries of what organizations should do about complaints.

In "Better Aimed to Please," Tom Ferguson writes, in the *Wall Street Journal*, "Promptness and courtesy are just part of what keeps us coming back to a business." We also want reliability, technical parity, economy in price and operation. In the service sector we want knowledge, a range of choices, and adaptability to our needs.

In *The Role of the Administrative Conference*, Roger Cramton characterizes ideal complaint-handling as "widely available, highly visible, client centered, independent, expert within its sphere of competence, and capable of developing general recommendations for the improvement of complaint-producing situations."

And finally, here is Allan Milham, vice president of TMI North America, a firm that offers seminars in handling customer complaints: "You've got to think of a complaint as a gift. It's the biggest bargain there is in market research."

CHAPTER 18

Buying Smart

E ACH OF THE FIFTY U.S. STATES has its own laws and regulations. One state's laws are often quite different from those of other states. In some cases, federal or national law takes precedence over the state laws, especially when matters involve something or someone crossing a state line (as with businesses that operate by mail, telephone, or computer modem, or ship goods from one state to another). In the following excerpt from the federal government's *Consumer Resource Handbook,* there is an ample amount of excellent advice combined with information on those relevant federal laws, and suggestions about situations where there may be relevant state laws.

PROTECTING YOURSELF

Consumers are faced with a marketplace full of decisions. Ask the right questions before and after you buy and avoid consumer fraud and ripoffs.

Before you buy

- Take advantage of sales, but compare prices. Do not assume an item is a bargain just because it is advertised as one.

- Don't rush into a large purchase because the "price is only good today."

- Check to see if the company is licensed or registered at the local or state level.

- Contact your consumer protection office or Better Business Bureau (BBB) for any complaint recorded against the company. Request any consumer information they might have on the type of purchase.

- Be aware of such extra charges as delivery fees, installation charges, service costs, and postage and handling fees. Add them into the total cost.

- Ask about the seller's refund or exchange policy.

- Read the warranty. Note what is covered and what is not. Find out what you must do and what the manufacturer or seller must do if there is a problem.

- Don't sign a contract without reading it. Don't sign a contract if there are any blank spaces in it or if you don't understand it. In some states, it is possible to sign away your home to someone else.

- Before buying a product or service, contact your consumer protection office to see if there are automatic cancellation periods for the purchase you are making. In some states, there are cancellation periods for dating clubs, health clubs, and time-share and campground memberships. Federal law gives you cancellation rights for certain door-to-door sales.

- Walk out or hang up on high-pressure sales tactics. Don't be forced or pressured into buying something.

- Only do business over the telephone with companies you know.

- Be suspicious of P.O. box addresses. They might be mail drops. If you have a complaint, you might have trouble locating the company.

- Do not respond to any prize or gift offer that requires you to pay even a small amount of money.

- Use unit pricing in supermarkets to compare what items cost. Unit pricing allows you to compare the price ounce-for-ounce, pound-for-pound, etc. As an example, bigger packages are not always cheaper than smaller ones.

- Use coupons carefully. Do not assume they are the best deal until you've compared them to the prices of competitive products.

- Make sure all documents you sign are in a language you understand.

- Don't rely on a salesperson's promises. Get everything in writing.

After you buy

- Read and follow product and service instructions.

- Be aware that how you use and take care of a product might affect your warranty rights.

- Keep all sales receipts, warranties, service contracts and instructions.

- If you have a problem, contact the company as soon as possible. Trying to fix the product yourself might cancel your right to service under the warranty.

- Keep a written record of your contact with the company.

- If you have a problem, check with your consumer protection office to find out about the warranty rights in your state.

- If you paid for your purchase with a credit card, you have important rights that might help you dispute charges.

- Check your contract for any statement about your cancellation rights. Contact your consumer protection office to see if a cancellation period applies.

- If you take the product in for repair, be sure the technician understands and writes down the problem you have described.

Red flags of fraud

Consumer protection offices urge consumers to be aware of the red flags of fraud. Walk away from bogus offers. Toss out the mail or hang up when you hear:

- "Sign now or the price will increase."

- "You have been specially selected..."

- "You have won..."

- "All we need is your credit card (or bank account) number—for identification only."

- "All you pay is for postage, handling, taxes..."

- "Make money in your spare time—guaranteed income..."

- "We need you to buy magazines (or a water purifier, or office products) from us because we can earn credits..."
- "I just happen to have some leftover paving material from a job down the street..."
- "Be your own boss! Never work for anyone else again. Just send in $50 for your supplies and..."
- "A new car! A trip to Hawaii! $2,500 in cash! Yours, absolutely free! Take a look at our..."
- "Your special claim number entitles you to join our sweepstakes..."
- "We just happen to be in your area and have toner for your copy machine at a reduced price."

Remember, the smart consumer always looks at the total price before deciding and checks out the company and product before buying.

Stay away from telemarketers who want to

- send a courier service for your money
- have you send money by wire
- automatically withdraw money from your checking account
- offer you a free prize, but charge handling and shipping fees
- ask for your credit card number, checking or savings account number, social security number, or other personal information
- get payment in advance, especially for employment referrals, credit repair, or providing a loan or credit card

Stay away from lotteries, pyramid schemes, and multilevel sales schemes. They are all good ways to separate you from your money.

COMPLAINING EFFECTIVELY

Remember:

1. First contact the seller if you have a complaint.
2. If that does not resolve your problem, contact the company headquarters.

3. If your problem is still unresolved, refer to the subject index for the organizations, or local, state and Federal offices that provide help in cases like yours.

4. Taking legal action should be the last resort. However, if you decide to exercise this right, be aware that you might have to act within a certain time period. Check with your lawyer about any statutes that apply to your case.

Save all purchase-related paperwork in a file. Include copies of sales receipts, repair orders, warranties, canceled checks, contracts, and any letters to or from the company. When you have a problem:

- Contact the business that sold you the item or performed the service. Calmly and accurately describe the problem and what action you would like taken.

- Keep a record of your efforts to resolve the problem. When you write to the company, describe the problem, what you have done so far to try to resolve it, and what solution you want. For example, do you want your money back, the product repaired, or the product exchanged?

- Allow time for the person you contacted to resolve your problem. Keep notes of the name of the person you spoke with, the date, and what was done. Save copies of all letters to and from the company. Don't give up if you are not satisfied.

- Contact the company headquarters if you have not resolved your problem at the local level. Many companies have a toll-free 800 number. Look for it on package labeling, in a directory of 800 telephone numbers (available at your local library), by calling (800) 555-1212 (toll free), or by writing or phoning the company. Address your letter to the consumer office or the company's president.

WRITING A COMPLAINT LETTER

Where to send it

- Check the product label or warranty for the name and address of the manufacturer.

- If you need additional help locating company information, check the reference section of your local library for the following books: *Standard & Poor's Register of Corporations, Directors and Executives; Standard Directory of Advertisers; Trade Names Dictionary;* and *Dun & Bradstreet Directory.*

- If you have the brand, but cannot find the name of the manufacturer, the *Thomas Register of American Manufacturers* lists the manufacturers of thousands of products. Check your local library.

- Each state has an agency (possibly the corporation commission or secretary of state's office) that provides addresses for companies incorporated in that state.

- Remember, do business with a company you will be able to find later. It might be difficult to find companies in other states or those listing post office boxes as addresses. Even if you have an address, it might be only a mail drop, so be sure you know where the company you are doing business with is located physically.

What to say

- Include in the letter your name, address, home or work telephone number, and account number, if any.

- Make your letter brief and to the point. Include the date and place you made the purchase, who performed the service, information about the product such as the serial or model number or warranty terms, what went wrong, with whom you have tried to resolve the problem, and what you want done to correct the problem.

- Use the sample consumer complaint letter on the following page as a guide.

- Include copies, not originals, of all documents.

- Be reasonable, not angry or threatening, in your letter.

- Type your letter, if possible, or make sure your handwriting is neat and easy to read.

- Keep a copy of all letters to and from the company.

- You might want to send your complaint letter with a return receipt requested. This will cost more but will give you proof that the letter was received and tell you who signed for it.

- If you feel you have given the company enough time to resolve the problem, send a copy of your letter to, or file a consumer complaint with, your local or state consumer protection agency; specific state agencies such as banking, insurance, and utilities; or the local Better Business Bureau. Include information about what you have done so far to try to resolve your complaint. If you think a law has been broken, contact your local or state consumer protection agency right away.

SAMPLE COMPLAINT LETTER

(Your Address)
(Your City, State, ZIP Code)
(Date)

(Name of Contact Person, if available)
(Title, if available)
(Company Name)
(Consumer Complaint Division,
    if you have no contact person)
(Street Address)
(City, State, ZIP Code)

Dear (Contact Person):
Re: (account number, if applicable)

On (date), I (bought, leased, rented, or had repaired) a (name of the product with serial or model number or service performed) at (location, date, and other important details of the transaction).

Unfortunately, your product (or service) has not performed well (or the service was inadequate) because (state the problem). I am disappointed because (explain the problem: for example, the product does not work properly, the service was not performed correctly, I was billed the wrong amount, something was not disclosed clearly or was misrepresented, etc.).

To resolve the problem, I would appreciate your (state the specific action you want—money back, charge card credit, repair, exchange, etc.). Enclosed are copies (do not send originals) of my records (include receipts, guarantees, warranties, canceled checks, contracts, model and serial numbers, and any other documents).

I look forward to your reply and a resolution to my problem, and will wait until (set a time limit) before seeking help from a consumer protection agency or the Better Business Bureau. Please contact me at the above address or by phone at (home and/or office numbers with area codes).

Sincerely,
(Your Name)
Enclosure(s)
cc: (reference to whom you are sending a
    copy of this letter, if anyone)

CONSUMER TIPS

The following sections contain a number of suggestions to help you become a smarter consumer. They include tips on how to buy a car, avoid fraud, and protect your privacy. Remember to check with your local consumer protection office and Better Business Bureau for other consumer information on a variety of topics.

Car repair

- Choose a reliable repair shop recommended to you by family or friends or an independent consumer rating organization. Check out the repair shop's complaint record with your state or local consumer protection office or Better Business Bureau.

- When you take the car to the shop, describe the symptoms. Don't diagnose the problem.

- Get more than one estimate. Get them in writing.

- Make it clear that work cannot begin until you have authorized it. Don't authorize work without a written estimate, or if the problem can't be diagnosed on the spot, insist that the shop contact you for your authorization once the trouble has been found.

- Don't sign a blank repair order. Make sure the repair order reflects what you want done before you sign it.

- Is the repair covered under warranty? Follow the warranty instructions.

- Ask the shop to keep the old parts for you.

- Get all warranties in writing.

- Some car manufacturers might be willing to repair certain problems without charge even though the warranty has expired. Contact the manufacturer's zone representative or the dealer's service department for assistance.

- Keep copies of all paperwork.

- Some states, cities and counties have special laws that deal with auto repairs. For information on the laws in your state, contact your state or local consumer protection office.

Buying a used car

- Check newspaper ads and used car guides at a local library so you know what's a fair price for the car you want. Remember, prices are negotiable. You also can look up repair recalls for car models you might be considering.

- Call the Auto Safety Hotline at (800) 424-9393 to get recall information on a car. Authorized dealers of that make of vehicle must do recall work for free no matter how old the car is.

- Shop during daylight hours so that you can thoroughly inspect the car and take a test drive. Don't forget to check all the lights, air conditioner, heater, and other parts of the electrical system.

- Do not agree to buy a car unless you've had it inspected by an independent mechanic of your choice.

- Ask questions about the previous ownership and mechanical

history of the car. Contact the former owner to find out if the car was in an accident or had any other problems.

- Check with your local department of motor vehicles to find out what you need in order to register a car.

- Ask the previous owner or the manufacturer for a copy of the original manufacturer's warranty. It still might be in effect and transferable to you.

- Don't sign anything that you don't understand. Read all documents carefully. Negotiate the changes you want and get them written into the contract.

- For information on recalls and safety issues, see page 222 under new car sales.

Buying from a private individual

- Generally, private sellers have less responsibility than dealers for defects or other problems.

- Check with your state's motor vehicle department on what you will need to register a vehicle.

- Make sure the seller isn't a dealer posing as an individual. That might mean the dealer is trying to evade the law, and might be an indicator of problems with the car. Look at the title and registration. Make sure the seller is the registered owner of the vehicle.

- Ask the seller lots of detailed questions about the car.

- Have the car inspected by your mechanic before you agree to buy it.

Buying from a dealer

- Check the complaint records of car dealers with your state or local consumer protection agency or Better Business Bureau.

- Read the "Buyers Guide" sticker required to be displayed in the window of the car. It gives information on warranties, if any are offered, and provides other information.

- In most states, used cars may be sold "as is." If the "as is" box is checked off on the "Buyers Guide," you have no warranty.

- If the "warranty" box is checked off on the "Buyers Guide," ask for a copy of the warranty and review it before you agree to buy the car.

- Have the car inspected by your mechanic before you agree to buy it.

- Some states have laws giving extra protection to used car buyers. Contact your state or local consumer protection office to find out what rights you might have.

- To order a free publication on buying a used car, contact the Federal Trade Commission, Public Reference Section, 6th and Pennsylvania Avenue, N.W., Room 130, Washington, DC 20580, (202) 326-2222.

Buying a new car

- Evaluate your needs and financial situation. Read consumer magazines and test drive several models before you make a final choice.

- Find out the dealer's invoice price for the car and options. This is what the manufacturer charged the dealer for the car. You can order this information for a small fee from consumer publications you can find at your local library.

- Find out if the manufacturer is offering rebates that will lower the cost.

- Get price quotes from several dealers. Find out if the amounts quoted are the prices before or after the rebates are deducted.

- Keep your trade-in negotiations separate from the main deal.

- Compare financing from different sources, for example, banks, credit unions, and other dealers, before you sign the contract.

- Read and understand every document you are asked to sign. Do not sign anything until you have made a final decision to buy.

- Think twice about adding expensive extras that you probably don't need to your purchase, for example, credit insurance, service contracts, or rustproofing.

- Inspect and test drive the vehicle you plan to buy, but do not take possession of the car until the whole deal, including financing, is finalized.

- Don't buy on impulse or because the salesperson is pressuring you to make a decision.

- The National Highway Traffic Safety Administration's Auto Safety Hotline at (800) 424-9393 (toll free) distributes recall and safety information on used and new cars, trucks, motorcycles, motor homes, child seats, and other motor vehicle equipment; vehicle crash test information; tire quality grading reports; child seat registration forms; and other safety literature. You should report all vehicle and child seat defect information to the Hotline.

- The Center for Auto Safety monitors auto defects. To see if there is a pattern of repeated complaints on a certain vehicle model, write the Center for Auto Safety, 2001 S Street, N.W., Suite 410, Washington, DC 20009 and include the vehicle make, model, and year, and a self-addressed stamped envelope.

- To order a free publication on how to buy a new car, contact the Federal Trade Commission, Public Reference Section, 6th and Pennsylvania Avenue, N.W., Room 130, Washington, DC 20580, (202) 326-2222.

Credit and sublease brokers

A new and rapidly growing area of consumer fraud involves con artists who prey on people who have bad credit and who are having problems getting loans to buy cars. There are two main schemes:

- The "credit broker" promises to get a loan for you in exchange for a high fee. In many cases, the "broker" takes the fee and disappears, or simply refers you to high-interest loan companies.

- The "sublease" broker charges a fee to arrange for you to "sublease" or "take over" someone else's car lease or loan.

Such deals usually violate the original loan or lease agreement. Your car can be repossessed even if you've made all of your payments. You also might have trouble insuring your car.

To protect yourself:

- Check with your state or local consumer protection agency to find out if the broker is required to be licensed.

- Do not do business with a company that does not appear to be complying with state law.

- Do not pay for services in advance.

Car leasing

- Shop around for the best leasing deal. Read lease promotions carefully. The attractive low monthly payment might be available only if you make a large down payment (capitalized cost reduction) or a balloon payment at the end of the lease.

- Beware of open-end leases. They require the consumer to pay the difference if the vehicle is worth less at the end of the lease than was estimated originally.

- The Consumer Leasing Act requires leasing companies to give you important information in writing before you sign a contract. Read the documents given to you by the leasing company and make sure you understand them before you sign anything. In particular, look for up-front costs, for example, security deposits, down payments, advanced payments, and taxes; the terms of the payment plan; termination costs, for example, excess mileage penalties, excessive wear and tear charges, and disposition charges; and penalties for early termination or default.

- When you have paid off a car loan, you own the car. When you have paid off the lease, you own nothing.

- To order a free publication on car leasing, contact the Federal Trade Commission, Public Reference Section, 6th and Pennsylvania Avenue, N.W., Room 130, Washington, DC 20580, (202) 326-2222.

Lemon laws

Almost every state has a new car "lemon law" that allows the owner a refund or replacement when a new vehicle has a substantial problem that is not fixed within a reasonable number of attempts. Many specify a refund or replacement when a substantial problem is not fixed in four repair attempts or the car has been out of service for 30 days within the first 12,000 miles/12 months. If you believe that your car is a lemon,

- contact your state or local consumer protection office for information on the laws in your state and the steps you must take to resolve the situation;

- give the dealer a list of symptoms every time you bring it in for repairs (keep copies for your records);

- get copies of the repair orders showing the reported problems, the repairs performed, and the dates that the car was in the shop; and

- contact the manufacturer, as well as the dealer, to report the problem. Some state laws require that you do so to give the manufacturer a chance to fix the problem. Your owner's manual will list an address for the manufacturer.

If the problem isn't resolved, you might have the option of participating in an arbitration program offered by the manufacturer or your state. Contact your state or local consumer protection office for information.

"Lemon Law Summary" is available upon request by sending a self-addressed, stamped (55 cents) envelope to the Center for Auto Safety, 2001 S Street, N.W., Suite 410, Washington, DC 20009.

Vehicle repossessions

When you borrow money from anyone in order to buy a car, you should know the following:

- The lender can repossess if you miss a payment or for any default (a violation of the contract).

- The lender can repossess without advance notice.

- After repossession, the lender might be able to accelerate, meaning the lender can require the borrower to pay off the entire balance of the loan in order for the borrower to get the vehicle back.

- The lender can sell the vehicle at auction.

- The lender might be able to sue the borrower for the deficiency if it sells the car for less than the borrower owes. This is true even in voluntary repossessions.

- The lender cannot commit a "breach of the peace," for example, breaking into a home or physically threatening someone, in the course of a repossession.

If you know you're going to be late with a payment, talk to the lender to try to work things out. If the lender agrees to a delay or to modify the contract, be sure you get the agreement in writing.

Some states have laws that give consumers additional rights. Contact your state or local consumer protection office for more information.

To order a free publication on vehicle repossessions, contact the Federal Trade Commission, Public Reference Section, 6th and Pennsylvania Avenue, N.W., Room 130, Washington, DC 20580, (202) 326-2222.

Renting a car

- Federal law does not cover short-term car and truck rentals. However, there are state laws that do. You should contact your state or local consumer protection office for more information on laws in your area.

- Shop around for the best rates.

- Compare all fees, in addition to the daily/weekly rate, before renting.

- Most car rental contracts make the consumer liable for all damage to the vehicle, no matter who caused it. Before buying a rental company's collision or loss damage waiver, check with your own car insurance company and your credit card company to see if they cover car rentals and to what extent. It pays to do your homework because these policies can add

$3 to $15 per day to your rental charges! Rental companies also might sell loss of use and liability insurance. Check with your insurance agent in advance, so you do not duplicate coverage you already have.

- If you pay by credit card, some rental companies will place a hold or freeze on your account during the rental period. Others might start to charge your account before the rental period is over. Find out the company's policy in advance.

- Carefully inspect the vehicle and its tires before renting, and write down all the dents and scratches you see.

- Check refueling policies. You can refill at a local gas station, you can let the car rental company refuel the car at its price, which is usually higher, or you can pay in advance for a refill which will cost you needlessly if there is any unused gas upon returning the vehicle.

- Contact your state or local consumer protection agency for information on state law or to report problems with your car rental.

- To order a free publication on car rental, contact the Federal Trade Commission, Public Reference Section, 6th and Pennsylvania Avenue, N.W., Room 130, Washington, DC 20580, (202) 326-2222.

MAIL ORDER

- Federal mail-order rules require companies that take consumers' orders by mail to

    - ship the merchandise within 30 days of receiving a completed order or within a different time frame if it is stated in their ads

    - notify consumers if shipment can't be made on time and give them the choice of waiting longer or receiving refunds

    - cancel their orders and return their money (or give them credits on their charge accounts) if the revised shipping date can't be met, unless the consumers agree to another delay.

- There also might be laws regarding mail order in your state. Contact your state or local consumer protection agency.

- Keep a record of the name, address, and phone number of the company, goods you ordered, date of your order, amount you paid, and method of payment.

- Keep a record of any delivery period that was promised.

- If you are told that the shipment will be delayed, write the date of that notice in your records and the new shipping date if you've agreed to wait longer.

- When you cancel an order that wasn't shipped on time, you have the right to get a refund within seven days or within one billing cycle for charged sales.

- When you use your credit card for mail-order purchases and you don't receive the goods or services, or they were defective or misrepresented, use the credit card protection rights described in the section on Credit Cards, page 240.

- To limit some of the mail you do not want, you can sign up with the free Mail Preference Service operated by the Direct Marketing Association, a private trade group. It will instruct its mail marketing members to take you off their lists. To join, write to the Mail Preference Service, P.O. Box 9008, Farmingdale, NY 11735.

- To report violations of the Federal mail-order rule, contact the Federal Trade Commission. For information on your state laws, contact your state or local consumer protection agency. To report a problem with mail order, contact the U.S. Postal Inspection Service or the Postal Crime Hotline at (800) 654-8896.

Mail fraud

- Read the offer carefully. Get advice from someone you trust.

- Deal only with companies or charities whose reputation and integrity are known.

- Never give your credit card number or personal, financial, or employment information unless you know with whom you are dealing.

- Never send money for any "free" merchandise or services.

- Be careful of making impulse purchases.

- Keep a record of the order, notes of the conversation, and copies of the advertisement, canceled check, receipt, letters, and envelopes.

- Take the time to shop locally and compare products, services, and prices to those in local stores.

- Check out the company with the U.S. Postal Inspection Service, your state or local consumer protection agency, or the Better Business Bureau. Mail fraud is a federal crime.

- Using your credit card or a money order might give you some recourse if you have a problem, despite your carefulness.

- Be suspicious of "free gifts" that require a "tax payment" or "registration fee"; sweepstakes requiring an entry fee or purchase; employment or work-at-home opportunities requiring a fee; offers requiring your credit card number or bank account number; loans that require you to pay a fee in advance; mailings that look like they are from official government agencies, and prize notices requiring you to call a 900 number.

TELEMARKETING

While many legitimate businesses use the telephone to make their sales, it's easy for fraudulent companies to abuse the phone. Beware of the con artists who promise anything and deliver nothing, or at least not what customers thought they were getting.

Tips for smart telephone shopping:

- Always keep a record of the name, address, and phone number of the company, goods you ordered, date of your purchase, amount you paid (including shipping and handling), and method of payment.

- Keep a record of any delivery period that was promised.

- If you are told that the shipment will be delayed, write the date of that notice in your records and the new shipping date, if you've agreed to wait longer.

- Don't give your credit card number, checking account number or other personal information to a telemarketer unless you are familiar with the company or organization, and the information is necessary in order to make your purchase.

Telephone order rights

- Some states have telemarketing laws that require written contracts, automatic cancellation periods, or registration of telemarketing companies. Contact your state or local consumer protection agency. Federal telephone order rules require companies that take consumers' orders by phone, computer, or fax to

    - ship the merchandise within 30 days of receiving a completed order or within a different time frame if it is stated in their ads

    - notify consumers if shipment can't be made on time and give them the choice of waiting longer or receiving refunds

    - cancel their orders and return their money (or give them credits on their charge accounts) if the revised shipping date can't be met, unless the consumers agree to another delay

Use caution and common sense

- Don't be pressured into acting immediately or without the full information you need.

- Shop around and compare costs and services.

- Report all fraudulent activity to your consumer agency. Check the company out with your consumer protection agency or the Better Business Bureau.

- If the solicitation came by mail, call the Postal Crime Hotline at (800) 654-8896 (toll free) for more advice on not becoming a victim.

- Call the National Fraud Information Center, administered by the National Consumers League, at (800) 876-7060 (toll free) for information about telemarketing fraud.

Blocking telemarketing calls

You have the right under federal law:

- to tell a company not to call you by phone or not to contact you in writing (the company must keep a list of these consumers and not contact them; keep a record for your file);
- not to get calls before 8 A.M. or after 9 P.M.;
- not to receive unsolicited ads by fax; and
- to be disconnected from a prerecorded machine-delivered message within five seconds of hanging up.

Some states do not allow telemarketers to call people who do not want to receive calls. Contact your state or local consumer protection agency to check your state's rights.

To reduce telephone calls you do not want, you can sign up with the free Telephone Preference Service operated by the Direct Marketing Association, a private trade group. To join, write to the Telephone Preference Service, P.O. Box 9014, Farmingdale, NY 11735.

To report violations of the telephone order rule, contact the Federal Trade Commission. If you made the telephone transaction in response to a postcard or other mailing, contact the U.S. Postal Inspection Service or the Postal Crime Hotline at (800) 654-8896 (toll free). For information on the laws in your state, contact your state or local consumer protection agency.

CALLS THAT COST

900 numbers and other pay-per-call services

Unlike 800 numbers, which are free, you pay a fee when you call a 900-type number. The company or organization you're calling sets the price, not the telephone company. Most states do not regulate the cost of these calls. Charges can vary from less than a dollar to more than $50. Federal law requires the following:

- Consumers be told the cost of calling the number and given a description of the product and service. This must appear in advertisements and, for calls costing more than two dollars, in the call's introductory message or preamble.

- The cost of calling must be disclosed by flat rate, by the minute with any minimum or maximum charge that can be determined, or by range of rates for calls with different options; all other fees charged for services and the cost of any other service to which a caller might be transferred must be disclosed.

- Consumers must be given time to hang up after the introductory message without being charged; there must be a signal or tone to let them know when the preamble ends.

- No charges can be made for calling 800 numbers unless the consumer agrees in advance to be charged.

- Any pay-per-call services offering sweepstakes, prizes, or awards must disclose the odds of winning or the factors for determining the odds.

- Ads directed to children under age twelve are not allowed unless they are for legitimate educational services.

- Ads directed primarily to people under the age of eighteen must state that parents' consent is needed to call the number.

- Ads for information about federal programs offered by private companies must state clearly that they are not endorsed, approved, or authorized by government agencies.

Protect yourself from fraud by avoiding:

- ads that don't describe clearly the goods or services or the cost of the calls

- offers of "free" gifts or prizes just for calling

- promises of jobs, loans, credit cards for people with poor credit, "credit repair" or other services aimed at consumers who are in financial hardship

- contests to win money in which little or no skill is required

- services targeted at children under twelve that don't appear to serve any legitimate educational purpose

- offers of cheap travel or any other deals that seem to be "too good to be true"

Hang up if you're being switched from an 800 number to a 900 number without your prior consent.

What you need to know about 800 numbers

Generally, you cannot be charged for 800 numbers, unless:

- You have a "presubscription arrangement" with the company (for example, with an information service); this means you already have an agreement to accept charges before you called the 800 number; or

- You agree to a credit card charge.

Your rights and recourse

- You can dispute 900-type number charges that appear on your phone bill. Your local and long-distance telephone service cannot be disconnected for disputed pay-per-call charges.

- In most cases, the charge for a pay-per-call service is collected by the local telephone company on behalf of the service provider. Follow the instructions on your bill immediately to dispute the charges. Keep a record of whom you talked to and the date, and copies of any letters you send. Pay the undisputed portion of your phone bill.

- Even if the telephone company removes the charges, the debt might be turned over to a collection agency by the service provider. Send the collection agency a letter explaining why you dispute the debt.

- To avoid problems with 900-type numbers, you can request "blocking" from your local phone company. Blocking prevents 900 numbers from being dialed from your phone.

- If you suspect a violation of pay-per-call rules, contact your state or local consumer protection agency and the Federal Trade commission. If the ad for the number came by mail, write to the U.S. Postal Inspection Service or call the Postal Crime Hotline at (800) 654-8896 (toll free). If you are not satisfied with the way the phone company handled your complaint, contact the Federal Communications Commission.

DOOR-TO-DOOR SALES

- Ask to see the salesperson's personal identification and license or registration if that is required where you live. Make note of his/her name, the name and address of the company, and whether the salesperson carries proper identification.

- Ask for sales literature and then call local stores that might sell the same merchandise to compare prices. Some door-to-door products might be overpriced.

- Don't be pressured into buying something. Watch for the warning signs: an offer of a "free gift" if you buy a product, an offer that is only good for that day, or you're told that a neighbor just made a purchase.

- If you feel threatened or intimidated, ask the person to leave. Don't leave the person unattended in any room of your home. If you are suspicious, report the incident to the police immediately.

Cancellation rights

- The "Door-to-Door Sales Rule" (or "Cooling Off Rule") gives you the right to cancel certain purchases costing $25 or more. Notify the company in writing by midnight of the third business day following the sale. Saturdays are considered business days, but Sundays and holidays are not.

- The seller must tell you about your cancellation rights and give you two dated copies of a cancellation form showing the seller's name and address and explaining your right to cancel.

- These federal cancellation rights apply to purchases made in locations outside the seller's normal place of business, in other words, at a house party, a temporarily rented room, or in your home.

- States might have additional cancellation laws that protect consumers. Check with your state or local consumer protection agency for your rights.

- To cancel a contract, sign and date one copy of the cancellation form. Mail it within the three-day limit, making sure it's postmarked before midnight of the third business day. Sending it by certified mail will show proof that it was mailed.

- Once you cancel, you have a right to a refund within ten days. The seller must let you know when the product will be picked up and must return any paperwork and trade-ins within that time. Within twenty days, the seller must pick up the item or reimburse you for any shipping expenses if you send it back yourself. If you do not return it, you still are responsible under the contract.

- Extend your rights! If you paid by credit card, canceled the contract within three days, have not yet paid the credit card bill, and still have a problem getting a refund, dispute the charges with your credit card company under the Fair Credit Billing Act.

HOME IMPROVEMENT

- Plan ahead. Know what you want or need to have done before contacting a contractor.

- Get detailed estimates from reputable contractors. Contact your local or state consumer agency and Better Business Bureau for information on contractors' licensing or registration requirements, complaint records, and for brochures containing advice.

- Contact your local building inspection department to check for permit and inspection requirements.

- Call your insurance company to find out if you are covered for any injury or damage that might occur and be sure your contractor has the required insurance for his/her workers and subcontractors.

- Insist on a complete written contract. Know exactly what work will be done, the quality of materials that will be used, timetables, the names of any subcontractors, the total price of the job, and the schedule of payments.

- You have cancellation rights (usually three business days) in many home improvement contracts. Before you sign a contract, check with your local consumer agency to find out if you have cancellation rights and how they apply.

- Understand your payment options. You can get your own loan or the contractor might arrange financing. Be sure you have a reasonable payment schedule at a fair interest rate.

- Some state laws specify payment schedules, for example, only allowing a certain percentage of the total cost to be made as a down payment. Contact your state or local consumer agency to find out what the law is in your area.

- Lien rights, which might give the contractor or subcontractors the ability to attach your home for unpaid bills, vary from state to state. Ask your local consumer agency to explain the situation where you live.

- You need to be especially cautious if the contractor
    - comes door-to-door or seeks you out
    - just happens to have material left over from a recent job
    - tells you your job will be a "demonstration"
    - offers you discounts for finding him/her other customers
    - quotes a price that's too cheap
    - pressures you for an immediate decision
    - has workers or suppliers who tell you they have trouble getting paid
    - can be reached only by leaving messages with an answering service
    - drives an unmarked van or has out-of-state plates on his/her vehicle

HOME FINANCING

- Check the real estate or business sections in the newspaper for information on current interest rates. Call several lenders for rates and terms based on the type of mortgage you want.

- When buying a newly constructed home, compare the interest rate and terms offered through the builder's sales office with those offered by other lending institutions.

- When interest rates go down, you might save money by refinancing, but you probably should not refinance unless the new interest rate will be at least two percentage points below the rate you're paying currently.

- For an adjustable rate mortgage, or ARM, find out the "cap" or the maximum interest rate that can be charged during the life of the loan. Ask how often the rate might change and what determines the rate change.

- Get a complete list of "closing" or "settlement" costs and find out which costs will be refunded if your loan is not approved.

- Be wary of financing that is based on "negative amortization." While the payments under this sort of arrangement might be lower than in other types of loan agreements, they're not enough to cover the monthly interest charges. The portion of interest that is left unpaid is added to the principal, which means that each month, the borrower pays interest on a higher amount than before. With negative amortization, the debt actually keeps increasing rather than decreasing. You could end up owing a lot of money at the end of the loan or losing your home.

Home equity credit lines

- Although a home equity credit line might allow you to take tax deductions you could not take with other types of loans, your home will be at risk if you cannot make the monthly payments.

- Some questions to ask when comparing home equity loan offers:
    - How large a credit line can be extended?
    - How long is the term of the loan?
    - What is the minimum monthly payment? Is there a maximum?

- What is the annual percentage rate?
- If the interest rate "floats," or is adjustable, how much can it increase at one time? Is there a maximum rate?
- Are there any annual fees or transaction fees?

Reverse mortgages

- If you own your home, a reverse mortgage loan will pay you in monthly advances or through a line of credit. It lets you convert the equity in your home into cash, which you can use for any purpose, while still retaining your ownership in your home. Before you sign, be sure you understand all the terms and conditions.

- Interest rates on this type of loan might be higher and are charged on a compound basis. Application fees, points, and closing costs also might be higher than other types of loans. Interest rates are not deductible on your income taxes until you repay the loan in full. There will be less equity for you and your heirs in the future.

- For more information or to file a complaint, contact: Department of Housing and Urban Development Office of Single Family Housing, 451 Seventh Street, S.W., Room 9282, Washington, D.C. 20410, (202) 708-3175, or your state or local Consumer Protection Office.

SELECTING A FINANCIAL INSTITUTION

Carefully select a financial institution by comparing the terms and prices of all of the services you need.

- Shop around. Do not do business with the first institution that seems willing to do business with you.

- Check the front door to see if the institution displays a government logo indicating that it is insured federally. Generally, if the institution is insured federally, an individual is covered for up to $100,000 in deposits if the institution fails. Many consumers just assume they're insured, but they may not be.

Truth in Savings Act

- Requires financial institutions to disclose the "annual percent-age yield," or APY, on savings accounts. The APY tells you how much money you would earn if you kept $100 in the account for one year.

- Requires that the institution credit your entire deposit instead of crediting a portion of your deposit or using a "low balance per month" method. This increases your earnings.

- Requires that institutions have available a list of their fees for bounced checks, stop payment orders, certified checks, wire transfers, or similar items. Ask for the list.

- Prohibits institutions from advertising "free" checking if there are hidden charges or requirements, for example, having to maintain a minimum balance to qualify

Checking accounts

Before you open a checking account, find out what the fees will be for writing checks, for bounced checks, for the checks themselves, and for other services. Ask if the institution will send you the canceled checks with your monthly statement. If not, find out the cost for copies of canceled checks. You might need them for proof of payment in some situations.

Loans

- When shopping for a mortgage, check the real estate section of your local newspaper to find out the current interest rates. Check the rates for thirty-year mortgages, fifteen-year mort-gages, and adjustable rate mortgages. Ask the lending institu-tion to explain the differences.

- Most home improvement loans are secured by a mortgage on your home. It's better not to finance expensive credit life insur-ance or to consolidate other debts into this loan. Your home will be at risk for every extra dollar you borrow. If you don't make your payments, you could lose your home.

- For car loans, compare the rates offered by the car dealer with those of local lending institutions. Don't add expensive extras like credit life insurance to the total amount of the loan. You do not have to purchase credit insurance in order to get a loan.

CREDIT

Credit reporting

The three biggest credit reporting agencies, TRW, Equifax, and Trans Union, each have millions of credit files on consumers nationwide. Their toll-free numbers are

- TRW: (800) 392-1122
- Equifax: (800) 685-1111
- Trans Union: (800) 851-2674

You can find other credit bureaus in your area by looking in the yellow pages under Credit Bureaus or Credit Reporting.

If you apply for credit, insurance, a job, or try to rent an apartment, your credit record might be examined. You can make sure yours is accurate:

- Get a copy once a year or before major purchases. Your report is generally free if you've been denied credit in the past sixty days. Otherwise, the credit bureau can impose a reasonable charge.

- Read the report carefully. The credit bureau must provide trained personnel to explain the information in the report.

- Dispute any incorrect information in your credit record. Write to the credit bureau and be specific about what is wrong with your report. Send copies of any documents that support your dispute.

In response to your complaint, the credit bureau

- must investigate your dispute and respond to you, usually within 30–35 days; information that is inaccurate or cannot be verified must be corrected or taken off your report; and

- cannot be required to remove accurate, verifiable information that is less than seven years old (ten years for bankruptcies).

If you are dissatisfied with the results of the reinvestigation, you can have the credit bureau include a 100-word consumer statement, giving your version of the disputed information. You also can contact the source of the disputed information and try to resolve the matter.

If there is an error on a report from one credit bureau, the same mistake might be on others as well. You might want to contact the three major bureaus, as well as any local bureau listed in the yellow pages of your telephone book.

Credit bureaus sometimes sell your name to banks or others who want to send you offers for credit cards or other forms of credit. If you don't want your name included on such lists, write or call the three major credit bureaus and tell them not to release your name.

Credit repair

You might see or hear ads from companies that promise to "clean up" or "erase" your bad credit and give you a fresh start. They charge high fees, usually hundreds of dollars, but do not deliver on their promises.

If you are thinking of paying someone to "repair" your credit, remember this:

- Negative credit information can be reported for seven years (ten years for a bankruptcy).

- No one can require a credit bureau to remove accurate negative information before that period is up.

- There are no "loopholes" or laws that credit repair companies can use to get correct information off your credit report.

- No credit repair company can do anything you can't do for yourself. (See the section on credit reporting, page 240.)

- A "money-back guarantee" does you no good if the company has gone out of business or refuses to make good on its refund promise.

- The only way to "repair" bad credit is by good credit practices over a period of time.

Some credit repair companies promise not just to clean up your existing credit record, but to help you establish a whole new credit identity. Remember, it is illegal to make false statements on a credit application or to misrepresent your Social Security number. If you use such methods, you could face fines or even prison. Beware of any company or method that

- encourages you to omit or lie about bad credit experience when you apply for new credit

- tells you to use a new name or address or a new number, for example, an employer identification number (EIN), in place of your Social Security number, in applying for credit

- says it is legal to establish a new credit identity

You can rebuild your good credit by handling credit responsibly. You might want to contact a Consumer Credit Counseling Service (CCCS) office. This is a nonprofit organization that will provide help at little or no cost to you. For a CCCS office in your area, call (800) 388-CCCS.

Credit billing and disputes

The Fair Credit Billing Act applies to credit card and charge accounts and to overdraft checking. It can be used for

- billing errors

- unauthorized use of your account

- goods or services charged to your account, but not received or not provided as promised

- charges for which you request an explanation or written proof of purchase.

To protect your rights:

- Write to the creditor or card issuer within sixty days after the first bill containing the disputed charge is mailed to you. (Even if more than sixty days have passed since you were billed for the item, you still might be able to dispute the charge if you only recently found out about the problem.)

- Send your letter to the address provided on the bill; do not send the letter with your payment.

- In your letter, give your name and account number, the date and amount of the charge disputed, and a complete explanation of why you are disputing the charge. Be specific.

- To be sure your letter is received, and so you will have a record, you might wish to send it by certified mail, with a return receipt requested.

If you follow these requirements, the creditor or card issuer must acknowledge your letter in writing within thirty days after it is received and conduct an investigation within ninety days.

While the bill is being disputed and investigated, you need not pay the amount in dispute. The creditor or card issuer may not take action to collect the disputed amount, including reporting the amount as delinquent, and may not close or restrict your account.

If there was an error or you do not owe the amount, the creditor or card issuer must credit your account and remove any finance charges or late fees relating to the amount not owed. For any amount still owed, you have the right to an explanation and copies of documents proving you owe the money.

If the bill is correct, you must be told in writing what you owe and why. You will owe the amount disputed, plus any finance charges. You may ask for copies of relevant documents.

Debt collection

The Fair Debt Collection Practices Act applies to those who collect debts owed to creditors for personal, family, and household debts, including car loans, mortgages, charge accounts, and money owed for medical bills. A debt collector may not

- contact you at unreasonable times or places, for example, before 8 A.M. or after 9 P.M., unless you agree, or at work if you tell the debt collector your employer disapproves

- contact you after you write a letter to the collection agency telling them to stop, except to notify you if the debt collector or creditor intends to take some specific action

- contact your friends, relatives, employer, or others, except to find out where you live and work or tell such people that you owe money

243

- harass you by, for example, threats of harm to you or your reputation, use of profane language or repeated telephone calls
- make any false statement, including that you will be arrested
- threaten to have money deducted from your paycheck or sue you unless the collection agency or creditor actually intends to do so, and it is legal to do so.

If you are contacted by a debt collector, you have a right to a written notice, sent within five days after you are first contacted, telling you

- the amount owed
- the name of the creditor
- what action to take if you believe you don't owe the money.

If you believe you do not owe the money or don't owe the amount claimed, contact the creditor in writing and send a copy to the debt collection agency with a letter telling them not to contact you.

If you do owe the money or part of it, contact the creditor to arrange for payment.

Equal Credit Opportunity Act

The Equal Credit Opportunity Act guarantees you equal rights in dealing with anyone who regularly offers credit, including banks, finance companies, stores, credit card companies, and credit unions. A creditor is someone to whom you owe money. When you apply for credit, a creditor may not

- ask about or consider your sex, race, national origin, or religion
- ask about your marital status or your spouse, unless you are applying for a joint account or relying on your spouse's income or you live in a community property state (Arizona, California, Idaho, Louisiana, Nevada, New Mexico, Texas, and Washington)
- ask about your plans to have or raise children
- refuse to consider reliable public assistance income or regularly received alimony or child support

- discount or refuse to consider income because of your sex or marital status or because it is from part-time work or retirement benefits.

You have the right to

- have credit in your birth name, your first name and your spouse's last name, or your first name and a combined last name

- have a co-signer other than your spouse if one is necessary

- keep your own accounts after you change your name or marital status or retire, unless the creditor has evidence you are unable or unwilling to pay

- know why a credit application is rejected. The creditor must give you the specific reasons or tell you of your right to find out the reasons if you ask within 60 days.

- have accounts shared with your spouse reported in both your names.

Credit cards

- For a small fee, you can purchase a list of the most competitive interest rates and credit cards in the country and find out how to qualify for the lowest rate possible by contacting Bankcard Holders of America, 560 Herndon Parkway, Suite 120, Herndon, VA 22070, (703) 481-1110.

- If you cannot pay off your full credit card balance each month, a lower interest rate will save you money. If you do pay off your balance in full each month, choose a card with no annual fee.

- Report billing errors and unauthorized charges to your credit card company right away. Keep a list of credit card numbers and card company phone numbers to alert a credit card company immediately if a card is stolen or missing. If you report the incident immediately, the most you will have to pay for any unauthorized charges is $50 on each card, regardless of how high the total unauthorized charges go before you report your card missing.

- Don't give your credit card number over the phone to unfamiliar companies or to people who say they need it to "verify" your identity in order to give you a prize.

- After signing your name on a credit card charge slip, pull out the carbons and rip them up.

- A federal law gives all consumers equal access to credit. The Equal Credit Opportunity Act makes it illegal for creditors to discriminate against applicants on the basis of race, sex, national origin, marital status, age, or religion, or because of public assistance income.

- Be cautious of offers for "secured" credit cards. These cards usually require you to set aside money in a separate bank account in an amount equal to the line of credit on the card to guarantee that you will pay the credit card debt. Some of these offers advertise that secured cards can be used to "repair" a bad credit record, but you should know that no matter how well you handle this account, your payment history on your past debts still will be taken into consideration when you apply to other lenders for credit or for employment or housing.

For more information or to file a complaint, contact:

Federal Deposit Insurance Corporation
Office of Consumer Affairs
550 17th Street, N.W.
Washington, DC 20429
(202) 898-3536
(202) 898-6726 (voice/TDD)
(800) 934-3342 (toll free)

Sources of more information:

Board of Governors of the Federal Reserve System
Division of Consumer and Community Affairs
20th and C Streets, N.W.
Mail Stop 198
Washington, DC 20551
(202) 452-3693
(202) 898-6726 (FDIC voice/TDD)

Comptroller of the Currency
Consumer Affairs
250 E Street, S.W.
Washington, DC 20219
(202) 874-4820

Bankcard Holders of America
560 Herndon Parkway, Suite 120
Herndon, VA 22070
(703) 481-1110

National Credit Union Administration
1775 Duke Street
Alexandria, VA 22314-3428
(703) 518-6300

You can also contact state banking authorities or state and local Consumer Protection Offices.

Choosing a credit card

Credit card issuers offer a wide variety of terms. Consider and compare all the terms, including the following, before you select a card:

- Annual percentage rate (APR)—the cost of credit as a yearly rate.

- Free or grace period—allows you to avoid any finance charge by paying your balance in full before the due date. If there is no free period, you will pay a finance charge from the date of the transaction, even if you pay your entire balance when you receive your bill.

- Fees and charges—most issuers charge an annual fee; some also might charge a fee for a cash advance or if you fail to make a payment on time or go over your credit limit.

Shop around for the terms that are best for you. Before giving money to a company that promises to help you get a credit card:

- Find out who the card issuer is and get the credit card terms in writing, including all the fees and whether a deposit is required.

- Try to apply to a card issuer directly, rather than giving money to a third party; if you don't get the credit card, you might not be able to get your money back.

- Beware of "credit cards" that only allow you to buy from certain overpriced, restricted goods catalogs.

- Beware of companies that promise "instant credit" or guarantee you a credit card "even if you have bad credit or no credit history"; no one can guarantee you credit in advance.

Using a credit card

- Know your credit card protections. When you have used your card for a purchase and you don't receive the goods or services as promised, you might be able to withhold payment for the goods or services. Card issuers must investigate billing disputes.

- If your card is lost or stolen, you are not liable for any charges if you report the loss before the card is used. If the card is used before you report it missing, the most you will owe is $50.

- Protect your credit record. Pay bills promptly to keep finance charges low and to protect your credit rating. Keep track of your charges and don't exceed your credit limit. Report any change of address prior to moving so that you receive bills promptly.

Preventing credit card fraud

- Sign cards when they arrive, so no one can forge your signature on the cards and use them.

- Keep copies of all sales slips. Open credit card bills promptly and compare the sales slips with the charges on your bill.

- Promptly report any suspicious or unauthorized charges to the card issuer.

- Never give your credit card number over the phone unless you have made the call and you know the company is reputable.

- Draw a line through blank spaces on charge slips. Do not sign a blank charge slip.

- Destroy carbons and incorrect charge slips.

- Keep a record of your card numbers and expiration dates and the phone number of the card issuer in a safe place.

For more information

To order free brochures on credit, contact the Federal Trade Commission, Public Reference Section, 6th and Pennsylvania Avenue, N.W., Suite 130, Washington, DC 20580, (202) 326-2222. To file a complaint, contact your state or local consumer protection agency, your state attorney general, or your Better Business Bureau.

CONSUMER PRIVACY

How to reduce unwanted solicitations and guard your privacy:

- Pay for local purchases with cash, rather than by check or credit card.

- Ask manufacturers, catalogue or magazine subscription companies, charities, and others with whom you do business not to sell your name to others for marketing purposes.

- Don't release your Social Security number except to an employer, government agency, lender, or credit bureau that requires it to identify you.

- Don't give anyone your credit card or checking account numbers unless you're making purchases with them, and don't put credit card numbers on your checks.

- When filling out warranty or other information cards, don't include optional or unnecessary personal information.

- Federal law gives you the right to ask telemarketers to take your name off of their lists and not to call you again. Keep records of their names, addresses, and the dates of your requests. File a complaint with the Federal Communications Commission if they don't remove your name from their marketing lists once you have made your request.

- Personal information is easily obtained by companies promoting sweepstakes, contests, and prize offers. Be careful to check out the companies before deciding to do business with them or releasing personal or financial information. Contact your state or local consumer agency or Better Business Bureau. These three types of promotions are in the top ten consumer complaints nationwide.

Review files that contain information about you

The Medical Information Bureau (MIB) is a data bank used by insurance companies. You might want to obtain a copy of your file and make sure the information it contains is correct. Write to the Medical Information Bureau, P.O. Box 105, Essex Station, Boston, MA 02112.

Credit bureaus keep records about your credit history. You should periodically review your credit reports for accuracy. (See the section on credit reporting, beginning on page 240.) To limit mail or telephone calls you do not want, you can sign up at no cost for a service that tells some of the telephone or mail marketing companies not to contact you.

Many states have their own privacy laws concerning telemarketing; employment; the use of social security, credit card, or checking account numbers; medical records; mailing lists; credit reports; debt collection; computerized communications; insurance records; and public data banks. Check with your state or local consumer agency about specific privacy rights or a referral to the appropriate agency.

ADVANCE FEE SCAMS

- Be wary of ads promising guaranteed jobs, guaranteed loans, credit repair, debt consolidation, or similar claims. Many of these are only a way to get you to send money in exchange for little or no service.

- Be cautious when responding to advertisements that use 900 telephone numbers. You can be charged substantial and differing amounts for calls to 900 numbers.

- Be careful with your personal information, including Social Security number, credit card numbers, and bank account numbers, among others. Fraudulent businesses could use this information to make an unauthorized charge to your credit card or to withdraw money from your bank account.

- Before you make any payment, ask the business to send you a contract and other information stating the terms of the service and whether you can cancel the service and get a refund.

- Ask how long the firm has been in business and if it is licensed properly. Request that the company send you copies of its business or other licenses. Review all contracts carefully.

- Contact your state or local consumer protection agency and the Better Business Bureau to find out a company's complaint record.

- Some states have enacted laws banning or regulating these types of businesses. To find out the law in your state or to report a fraud, contact your state or local consumer protection agency.

- For information on the dangers of these types of scams, call the nonprofit National Fraud Hotline at (800) 876-7060 (toll free).

SPECIAL CONTRACTS

Health clubs

When you are considering whether to join a health club, be cautious of:

- joining clubs that have not opened—they might never open
- low-cost "bait" ads—many "switch" you to expensive long-term contracts
- promises that you can cancel anytime and stop paying—check the written contract for the terms of membership and any other promises
- the fine print—many low-cost ads and contracts severely restrict hours of use and services
- signing long-term contracts—consumer protection agencies report that many consumers quit using the club within a few months
- automatic monthly billing to your charge card or debit from a checking account—these are easier to start than to stop
- unbelievably low one-time fees with no monthly dues.

Before you sign, be sure to:

- check with your doctor before you begin an exercise program

- visit the club at the hours you will be using it
- check to see that promised equipment/services are actually available
- talk to current members regarding their satisfaction with the club
- check out several clubs before you sign a contract
- consider your commitment to a long-term program—good intentions seem to fade as the reality of the hard work sets in
- read the contract carefully before you sign. Is interest charged for a payment plan? Are all promises in writing?
- Check with your local or state consumer agency or Better Business Bureau for any laws in your state, cancellation rights or complaints against the company.

Dating clubs/matchmakers

When you choose to deal with a dating service, be sure to check:

- from how far away the referrals might come
- the economic/professional status of dates
- that dates are club members
- your ability to review the video/profile/picture, etc., of a proposed date before your phone number is given or a meeting is arranged
- that the information in your file is clear, e.g., wishes, interests, requirements, "won't accepts"
- the length of the contract and the number of dates/introductions promised
- the cost of any additional fee to extend/renew/continue the membership
- any extra costs associated with club functions (parties, picnics, trips)
- what the club promises to do for the basic fee. There might be little relationship between the cost and performance of the club; beware of very high-priced companies.
- that all "guarantees" are in writing

- for figures on its percent of success and the average length of time needed to locate an acceptable spouse if the club promises to find you a spouse

- the cancellation policy. Check with your state or local consumer agency for your legal rights; contact your consumer agency or the Better Business Bureau to file a complaint.

Time-shares/campgrounds

- Prizes and awards might be used in promoting time-shares and campgrounds. They sometimes are overvalued or misrepresented. Free awards might "bait" you into driving a long distance to the property, only to attend a long, high-pressure sales pitch to obtain your prize.

- Be realistic. Make your decision based on how much you will use it and if it provides the recreational and vacation purposes you want. Don't decide to purchase based on an investment possibility. It might be difficult or almost impossible to resell.

- Ask about such additional costs as finance charges, annual fees and maintenance fees. Maintenance fees can go up yearly.

- Compare your total annual cost with that of hotels or your normal vacation expenses.

- Ask about availability during your vacation periods. Ask what other time-shares or campgrounds you may use with your membership.

- Talk to individuals who already purchased from the company about the services, availability, upkeep, and reciprocal rights to use other facilities.

- Get everything in writing and make sure verbal promises are in the written contract. Have an attorney review any contracts/documents and make sure there are no blanks on the papers you sign.

- Do you have cancellation rights? State laws vary. Check with your local or state consumer agency.

- Check for any complaints against the company, seller, developer, and management company with your consumer agency or the Better Business Bureau.

- To order a free publication on time-shares and health clubs, contact the Federal Trade Commission, Public Reference Section, 6th & Pennsylvania Avenue, N.W., Suite 130, Washington, DC 20580, (202) 326-2222.

Travel scams

- Don't be taken by solicitations by postcard, letter, or phone claiming you've won a free trip or can get discounts on hotels and airfares. These offers usually don't disclose the hidden fees involved, for example, deposits, surcharges, excessive handling fees, or taxes.

- Some travel scams require you to purchase a product to get a trip that's "free" or "two-for-one." You'll end up paying for the "free" trip or more for the product than the trip is worth, and the two-for-one deal might be more expensive than if you had arranged a trip yourself by watching for airfare deals.

- Be wary of travel offers that ask you to redeem vouchers or certificates from out-of-state companies. Their offers are usually valid only for a limited time and on a space-available basis. The hotels are often budget rooms and very uncomfortable. The company charges you for the trip in advance, but will the company still be in business when you're ready to take the trip?

- Check the reputation of any travel service you use, especially travel clubs offering discounts on their services in exchange for an annual fee. Contact your state or local consumer protection agency or the Better Business Bureau.

- Request copies of a travel club's or agent's brochures and contracts before purchasing your ticket. Don't rely on oral promises. Find out about cancellation policies and never sign contracts that have blank or incomplete spaces.

- Never give out your credit card number to a club or company with which you're unfamiliar or that requires you to call 900 numbers for information.

- Don't feel pressured by requests for an immediate decision or a statement that the offer is only good "if you act now." Don't deal with companies that request payment in advance or that don't have escrow accounts where your deposit is held.

- Research cut-rate offers, especially when dealing with travel consolidators who might not be able to provide your tickets until close to your departure date.

- You can protect yourself by using a credit card to purchase travel services. If you don't get what you paid for, contact the credit card issuer and you might be able to get the charges reversed. Be aware that you have sixty days to dispute a charge.

Rent-to-own

Although buying in a rent-to-own transaction sounds like a simple solution when you are short of cash, rent-to-own can be expensive. The rental charge can be three or four times what it would cost if you paid cash or financed the purchase at the highest interest rate typically charged in installment sales. Before signing a rent-to-own contract, ask yourself the following questions:

- Is the item something I absolutely have to have right now?

- Can I delay the purchase until I have saved enough money to pay cash or at least make a down payment on an installment plan?

- Does a retail store offer a layaway plan for the item?

- Have I considered all my credit options, including applying for retail credit from the merchant or borrowing money from a credit union, bank, or small loan company?

- Would a used item purchased from a garage sale, classified ad, or secondhand store serve the purpose?

If you decide that rent-to-own is the best choice for you, here are some questions you should ask before you sign on the dotted line.

- What is the total cost of the item? The total cost can be determined by multiplying the amount of each payment by the number of payments required to purchase the item. Make sure to add in any additional charges, for example, finance, handling, or balloon payments at the end of the contract.

- Am I getting a new or used item?

- Can I purchase the item before the end of the rental term? If so, how is the price calculated?

- Will I get credit for all of my payments if I decide to purchase the item?

- Is there a charge for repairs during the rental period? Will I get a replacement while the rented item is not in my possession?

- What happens if I am late on a payment? Will the item be repossessed? Will I pay a penalty if I return the item before the end of the contract period?

Comparison shop among various rent-to-own merchants. Contact your local or state consumer protection agency to find out if there are any complaints on record against the business. Check for any specific state laws. Read the contract carefully and make sure you understand all the terms and get all promises in writing.

Remember, know what you are paying. Compare the cash price plus finance charges in an installment plan with the total cost of a rent-to-own transaction.

Long-term rent-to-own contracts cost so much more than installment plans that you could rent an item, make a number of payments, return the item, buy it on an installment plan and still come out ahead.

PRODUCT SAFETY AND RECALLS

- Knowing how to use products correctly, reading instructions and being alert to hazards will help to ensure a safe environment around you. You also should pay attention to product recalls in the news and consumer magazines. Several federal government agencies provide recall information on a variety of products, including toys, cars, child safety seats, food, and health and beauty aids.

- Read about major appliances, tools, and other items before you buy. There are several consumer magazines at the library that give detailed information on the prices, features, and safety of various products.

- Learn to use power tools and electrical appliances safely. If you don't know what a ground fault circuit interrupter (GFCI) is, find out. Read the instructions carefully before using the equipment.

- Don't use things for purposes the manufacturer never intended. Tools aren't kids' toys.

- Poolside safety demands nonclimbable fencing, CPR training, a poolside phone, a GFCI, and constant adult supervision to help ensure the protection of children. Some building codes require some of these safety features.

- Make sure toys are age appropriate. A baseball bat can be a lethal weapon in the hands of a three-year-old slugger.

- Kids should always wear bicycle helmets. Some states now require it. When shopping for helmets, look for the ANSI and/or SNELL sticker to ensure the safest helmet.

- Small parts can present choking hazards to children who put things in their mouths. Beware of balloons, balls, marbles, and older children's toys.

- Baby items demand special attention. Cribs, baby walkers, and baby gates have changed dramatically as the result of new safety requirements. Don't buy used baby items that don't comply with current standards.

- Garage and tag sales are places where small appliances, power tools, baby furniture, and toys with safety defects, lead paints, or other hazards get passed along to new owners. Make sure these types of items meet current safety requirements.

- If you spot a product defect, design flaw, allergic reaction, or hidden hazard, contact the U.S. Consumer Product Safety Commission or your state or local consumer protection agency.

- Read product labels. Some products can turn into deadly poisons when mixed with other products, stored improperly, or used in poorly vented areas.

- Keep all medicines, cleaning products, wood finishes, toxic art supplies, and paints out of the sight and reach of young children. Keep leftover products in their original containers. Have the poison control emergency number near your phone. Get rid of old and dated products.

- Look for tamper-resistant packaging on foods and medicine.

- Watch out for dinnerware decorated with lead paint or glaze and lead crystal decanters. If there's no way to ensure the items are lead-free, don't buy them.

- Contact the Auto Safety Hotline at (800) 424-9393 (toll free) to report safety problems, and to obtain recall and safety information on new and used cars, trucks, motorcycles, motor homes, child seats, and other motor vehicle equipment.

For consumer education material or to file a complaint, contact:

Consumer products, other than cars, food, or drugs:
Product Safety Hotline
U.S. Consumer Product Safety Commission
Washington, DC 20207
1 (800) 638-CPSC (toll free)
1 (800) 492-8104 (toll free TDD in MD)
1 (800) 638-8270 (toll free TDD outside of MD)

Vehicles, child safety seats, and other motor vehicle equipment:
Auto Safety Hotline
National Highway Traffic Safety Administration
Department of Transportation
Washington, DC 20590
(202) 366-0123
(202) 366-7800 (TDD)
1 (800) 424-9393 (toll free outside DC)
1 (800) 424-9153 (toll free TDD outside DC)

Food, drugs, medical devices, such radiological products as microwave ovens, televisions, and sunlamps:

U.S. Food and Drug Administration

Recall and Emergency Coordinator

(Refer to the white pages of your local telephone book for your regional FDA office.)

Recalls

Federal Information Center

Pueblo, CO 81009

(Write to this address to receive a free publication 595Z prepared by the U.S. Office of Consumer Affairs that explains which federal agencies issue consumer product recalls, the kinds of products each of them covers, how to report product safety problems, and how to find out about warnings or recalls that have been announced.)

NUTRITION LABELING

The new food label format offers more complete, useful, and accurate nutrition information than has been available in the past. Shoppers can compare the nutritional value of every packaged food on the grocery shelf.

Nutrition labeling panel—content

The revamped nutrition panel on each food product is called "Nutrition Facts" and lists the following mandatory dietary components:

- total calories
- calories from fat
- total fat
- saturated fat
- cholesterol
- sodium
- total carbohydrates

- dietary fiber
- sugars
- protein
- vitamins A and C
- calcium
- iron

Voluntary dietary components that can be listed on the label include calories from saturated fat, polyunsaturated fat, monosaturated fat, potassium, soluble fiber, insoluble fiber, sugar alcohol, other carbohydrates, and essential vitamins and minerals.

Nutrition labeling—format

All nutrients must be stated as a percentage of their "Daily Value" (the daily nutrient intake level recommended by public health authorities) to show how much of a day's ideal total of a particular nutrient a consumer is getting. For example, if a serving of soup contains half the amount of sodium that is recommended for consumers daily, the food label shows the "Daily Value" of sodium in that soup as 50 percent. These percentages are based on a daily intake of 2,000 calories.

Serving sizes

Serving sizes are standardized and will reflect more closely the amount of food usually eaten at one time. The serving size for similar products from different manufacturers will be comparable.

Nutrient content descriptors

Food manufacturers are required to use standardized definitions when making claims concerning the nutrient contents of foods, for example, "light," "low-fat," "free," "reduced calories" and "high fiber."

Health claims

Product claims about the relationship between a nutrient or food and the risk of a disease are limited to specific types of claims in seven areas. For example, if a product makes a health claim related to the link between calcium and osteoporosis, the product must contain at least 200 milligrams of calcium and must be a form of calcium that can be absorbed easily by the body. The claims must be stated so that the consumer can understand the relationship between the nutrient and the disease.

For more information

Food and Drug Administration
Consumer Affairs and Information
Department of Health and Human Services
5600 Fishers Lane, Room 16-85 (HFE-88)
Rockville, MD 20857
(301) 443-3170

Department of Agriculture
Human Nutrition Information Service
Federal Building Rooms 360 and 364
6505 Belcrest Road
Hyattsville, MD 20782
(301) 436-8617

Detailed Case Studies

These are full versions of the case histories briefly described starting on pages 13.

---

1. Big deal, strong commitment, few complaints, low quality

"Get this *#?@!# off the shelves."
The case of the the "dirty dictionary"

The *American Heritage Dictionary* was the first popular dictionary to include most of the "four-letter" words. Several "decency" groups organized complaint-letter drives, both to the publisher (to eliminate that filth) and to school districts (urging them to take the foul volume from their shelves). The publisher, with a strong commitment to a major publishing venture, was unmoved by the modest number of form letters received, and said they found them to be "somewhere between amusing and scary." From time to time, school boards with less commitment to such matters do heed complaints to ban this reference work, along with the works of Mark Twain, John Steinbeck, Alice Waters, and others.

Incidentally, California School Superintendent Max Rafferty's staunch support for the campaign to ban the dictionary contributed to his defeat at the next election. (Rafferty then took a school job in Alabama, "thereby," according to California politician Jess Unruh, in one of the nastier political jibes of our time, "raising the IQ level in both states.")

2. Small deal, strong commitment, few complaints, low quality

The case of the American Legion versus UNICEF

For the first ten years of its existence, UNICEF, the United Nations Children's Fund, was virtually unknown, and averaged no more than half a dozen letters a year from the general public. It was an active but, it seemed, quite uncontroversial organization. Then a Seattle printer named Lawrence Timbers decided UNICEF was a very bad thing. He was vice-chairman of the Anti-Subversive Committee of the American Legion in Washington. On his own press, he began printing anti-UNICEF tracts, urging that letters of complaint be showered on Congress, so that the United States would no longer support this subversive organization.

An analysis of the modest number of letters received by legislators showed that virtually 100 percent had the same gross errors of fact, and even the misspellings of Timbers' tracts. Although UNICEF was a tiny matter in the U.S. budget, there was a strong commitment to its goals, and the small number of form letters had no effect at all.

3. Big deal, weak commitment, few complaints, low quality
"Sho 'nuff, Massa Colgate"
The case of the darkie on the tube

Companies can get complaints when they enter the international marketplace and discover that what was just fine in Podunk or Peoria turns out to be offensive, controversial, or possibly even illegal in Hong Kong or Tokyo. Colgate found itself in deep fluoride when it took over a company that marketed a very popular brand of toothpaste called Darkie, which featured, on the tube and in the ads, a widely grinning top-hatted blackface minstrel man. Colgate, backpedaling furiously, insisted that the logo symbolizes nothing more than a man with clean white teeth. Bring up the banjo music, maestro. Colgate hastens to point out that people in Hong Kong don't complain about their Darkie toothpaste; they've loved it for years. It is only a small number of pesky westerners traveling in Asia who write the complaint letters.

As the *Wall Street Journal* puts it, "Colgate has tried to find a way to silence American critics...while sustaining the 60-year-old brand's appeal to Asians." They considered renaming it. Darbie and Hawley were rejected, and Dakkie was test-marketed without success.

As the controversy marched on, Colgate's sincerity was brought into question. While the Darkie complaints poured in, they launched a new toothpaste in Japan, where Darkie had never been sold. The Japanese brand, by an amazing coincidence, used the same minstrel logo, and was called Mouth Jazz. A Colgate executive, Gavin Anderson, assures us that "there is no reason to associate the two products." Yassuh, Mistuh Gavin.

The company finally gave in and changed the name. Their weak commitment to the notion of refusing to change strategy for a major product resulted in the change, despite a modest number of what the company regarded as irrelevant complaints.

4. Small deal, weak commitment, few complaints, low quality
The case of the DAR and the patriotic panty girdles

The Treo Company of New York is a large manufacturer of underwear, well known in the trade as much for the quality of its products as for its outrageous advertising, especially in trade publications. The focal points of their ads have been improbable (or impossible) items of underwear, which the company had no intention of manufacturing, such as the two-cup jock strap and the three-cup brassiere.

When Andy Warhol and pop art were at their peak, Treo ran a tongue-in-cheek ad for "Pop Pants," a series of wildly decorated panty girdles. They received so many serious inquiries and favorable comments, they decided actually to go into production with four designs, including Stars 'n Stripes (a border of white stars in a blue field, with vertical red and white stripes down the legs). A major advertising campaign was prepared, with ads to run in *Vogue, Seventeen, Mademoiselle*, and comparable magazines.

A Treo representative told me that the company anticipated some complaints, probably from what he called the "smut nuts." The company had decided, even before Pop Pants went into production, that if there were serious complaints raised, either of the advertising or the pants themselves, the whole project would be canceled.

But no one had anticipated a patriotic objection by the Daughters of the American Revolution. A small number of members responded to a plea to write, including the national chairman of the DAR Flag of the United States of America Committee, who said, "Patriotism should be encouraged by proper respect of the Stars and Stripes, the symbol of this great country."

Because of the company's weak commitment to this small deal, they gave in and recalled 3,000 pairs of Stars 'n Stripes girdles and the campaign was discontinued. What then of the thousands of pairs of Star 'n Stripes? "We'll probably burn the damn things," a Treo spokesman said.

5. Big deal, strong commitment, many complaints, low quality
"Don't give in, Xerox, don't give in."
The case of Xerox versus the John Birch Society

Xerox Corporation announced that a significant portion of its advertising budget for one year would be devoted to producing and sponsoring some television programs about the work of the United Nations. This simple announcement provoked one of the largest complaint letter campaigns in history. The John Birch Society took this on as their major cause for the year and managed to generate more than 60,000 complaint letters. The vast majority of them were easily identifiable as form letters. The expenditure was a big deal, and the company's commitment was strong, and so a great many low-quality complaints had no effect at all. When word of the scope of the anti-UN campaign got out, pro-UN groups countered with a massive "write to Xerox" campaign of their own, resulting in 15,000 letters urging the company to ignore those 60,000 letters, but the company resolve was already firm.

6. Small deal, strong commitment, many complaints, low quality

The case of the communist front called
the *Ladies Home Journal*

The *Ladies Home Journal* published a short story called "The Children's Story." It told of what could happen in a classroom after the Communists took over the U.S. The new Communist teacher slyly and charmingly wins the affections and finally the minds of her class. While it might have been assumed that anyone with the IQ of mashed potatoes would see this as a strong anti-Communist message, Robert Welch of the John Birch Society concluded that the story was "the most brazen, and also the most infuriating, piece of propaganda against God and Country that I have ever read." Members were urged to flood the *Ladies Home Journal* with complaint letters.

The *Journal* logged in 2,378 letters about this story. Forty-nine were favorable; 233 wrote diverse and mild letters saying they didn't like it. (This is a typical number for a *Journal* story.) Two thought the story was *too* anti-Communist. And 2,096 either were exact copies of the "sample" letter Welch offered (1,371), or reflected Welch's remarks, but gave some indication that the writer had at least looked at the story (725). Even the form letters with return addresses got a polite form-letter reply from the *Journal,* and those produced fifty-eight new responses, "even more hysterical than the first," the editor reported. "It was as if, in explaining that the *Journal* was not part of a Communist plot, we had robbed them of a bone of hatred that they had to gnaw lest they starve and die."

Although a single story was a small deal, the *Journal* was committed to it, and a flood of low-quality complaints had no effect at all.

7. Big deal, weak commitment, many complaints, low quality
The case of United Airlines reneging on its promise to the hero pilot

A United Airlines pilot named Charles Dent made a difficult and complex landing, demonstrating great skill and bravery. United rewarded him with a cash bonus, which Captain Dent donated, publicly, to the United Nations Association of the United States. Captain Dent took advantage of the press's interest in this act to lobby for his employer to make a public statement of support for the United Nations. United Airlines readily agreed to apply the UN emblem to all its planes, with the subscript "We Believe," and to make UN literature available on the planes. A major press conference was called to announce this matter.

Three months later, *Saturday Review* reported that United had quietly removed the UN emblem from its planes and the UN literature from its magazine racks because of complaints received from anti-UN organizations. Many letters from anti-UN writers were received, most of them form letters, and, since the airline had, as it turned out, a very weak commitment to this big idea, this large volume of low-quality response was sufficient to bring about the changes. The president of the airline stated that he had to question if he had "the right, legally or morally, to use the facilities of the stockholders to engage in such controversy."

8. Small deal, weak commitment, many complaints, low quality
The case of the slave-labor hams

The Jewel Tea Company, a Midwestern chain of supermarkets, was urged, in a pressure-group-organized complaint-letter campaign, not to sell "slave-labor Polish hams" in their stores. The letters struck a respondent chord with Jewel's meat buyer, and ham sales were curtailed. It was a small deal to the market, and there was no real commitment to those products, and a flurry of form letters was enough to bring about the action the complainers desired.

After the hams had been removed, there was then a small number of high-quality complaints from Jewel customers, and, since it was still a small deal and one of weak commitment, the company reversed its policy and restocked the slave-labor hams.

9. Big deal, strong commitment, few complaints, high quality

"But for seventeen miles, it was one helluva fine car." The case of the flaming Cadillac

A man in the Midwest purchased a lovely new Cadillac from his local dealer. After only seventeen miles of driving, the car burst into flames and was badly damaged. General Motors offered to repair the car without charge, but refused to replace it with a new one. Despite the sincere and anguished complaint, the company was strongly committed to its policy of not replacing defective cars, perhaps for fear of the problems they would face if "everyone" wanted them to do this.

The Cadillac owner took GM and the dealer to court, where the judge ruled that Cadillac advertising creates a certain confidence level in the quality of the car, and "once such confidence is shaken, a repair is not proper tender of the goods purchased." The company was ordered to replace the car.

10. Small deal, strong commitment, few complaints, high quality

"I cooked it for twelve hours and now it doesn't taste right." The case of the all-day turkey

Stew Leonard's in Connecticut is one of the largest dairy stores in the country. There is a six-ton boulder at the entrance, engraved: "Rule 1: the customer is always right. Rule 2: if the customer is ever wrong, reread Rule 1."

The policy was put to the test when a woman came in with her Thanksgiving turkey, which had been cooked so long it was shriveled and leathery. She complained that it was too dry. It was a small deal in an organization with a strong commitment to policy, so this sincere, if misguided, complaint resulted in an immediate offer of either a new turkey or a $20 refund. Wisely, the woman chose the money.

11. Big deal, weak commitment, few complaints, high quality

Time-Warner and "Cop Killer"

The huge Time-Warner was earning profits from the sale of rap music by a record company of which they were a part-owner. Some newspaper columnists and others suggested, in a small number of high-quality complaints, that it was inappropriate for Time-Warner to be reaping profits from an album including the selection called "Cop Killer." The company clearly felt that it was inappropriate to give in on matters of editorial policy, and their record business was a big deal, so they held firm. But their resolve was not that strong and they sold their interest in that particular record company, claiming the deal was just good business and unrelated to the earlier flap.

12. Small deal, weak commitment, few complaints, high quality
"Oh that's all right. I'll just sleep in the lobby."
The case of the weary (but crafty) businessman

Salesman Albert G. had had a long tiring day on the road, and when his twice-delayed flight finally got him to Chicago near midnight, he made his weary way to the Holiday Inn, where he was told, "Sorry, we only held your room until 6 P.M.; it has been rented to someone else, and the hotel is completely full." Albert pointed out that he had guaranteed the room with his credit card. But the number the hotel had was one digit off, and they couldn't get approval from Visa. Because of a major convention in town, there were no vacancies at any nearby hotels. Holiday Inn did find a vacancy way out in the suburbs, but the prospect of another hour on the road was unacceptable to Albert.

Eying the large and soft sofas in the lobby, Albert had an idea. Without a word to the night clerk, he repaired to the men's room, and emerged a few minutes later in his pajamas. He padded over to a large sofa and settled in, using his overcoat as a blanket. Within minutes, he was being tapped on the shoulder by a security guard, who told him he would have to leave. Albert said he would be delighted to leave, as soon as they found a room for him; otherwise, they would have to carry him bodily from the hotel, and if they did that, please carry him to a phone booth, so he could phone his lawyer, the two local newspapers, and the headquarters of Holiday Inn.

It was now one in the morning, and the hotel somehow managed to find a room for Albert—more than likely, one guaranteed by some other traveler, whom they started praying would never show up. It was a small deal for the big hotel (booking problems happen all the time), and there was no major commitment to a "resettlement" policy, so Albert's innovative high-quality complaint did the job.

13. Big deal, strong commitment, many complaints, high quality

"Bed companies do the darnedest things." The case of Art Linkletter and Craftmatic beds

For years, the smiling face of Art Linkletter, on television and in people's mailboxes, was instrumental in selling hundreds of thousands of Craftmatic electric folding beds, mostly to senior citizens, who were visited by aggressive salespeople representing independent distributors. Thousands complained to the company, the Better Business Bureau, their attorney general, and to Art Linkletter. In various lawsuits, it was alleged that unprovable medical claims were made, Medicare reimbursement possibilities were misstated, and there was "bait and switch" to the $6,000 top-of-the-line model.

For years, the company blamed its independent distributors for the problems, but since hundreds of thousands of people wrote or called the main office, at the urging of Mr. Linkletter, the blame clearly was shared. Craftmatic finally evolved a strong commitment to make things right. They got a toll-free complaint phone line (located in their lawyer's office!) and agreed to binding arbitration for all complaints that could not otherwise be settled.

14. Small deal, strong commitment, many complaints, high quality

"Pink birds, si; golf, no." The case of the Venezuelan flamingos

A Venezuelan government agency announced plans to do major industrial development right in the middle of an area inhabited by a large flock of flamingos. The Audubon Society of Venezuela put out a call for help, and an answer came from Global Response, a Colorado-based international letter-writing network. Even though the government was strongly committed to the project, it was a relatively small deal in the grander scheme of things. And Global Response was able to generate hundreds of high-quality complaint letters that, a government official said, proved "an embarrassment to Venezuela." They decided that the new golf course, highway, and factory area were not too important after all, and the project was canceled.

15. Big deal, weak commitment, many complaints, high quality
"Excuse me, but half my parts are missing." The case of Classic Motor miscarriages

Classic Motor Carriages was a large Florida manufacturer of elaborate kits that enabled people to build exact replicas of famous sports cars onto the chassis of inexpensive and reliable American cars. More than 20,000 kits were sold at prices well up into the thousands of dollars. The kits had many flaws, as did the advertising, which suggested that anyone with modest mechanical skills and simple tools could successfully build a kit. There were even bigger flaws in the way the company handled complaints or, more accurately, didn't handle them.

After a huge flurry of complaints in the early and mid 1980s from people whose kits took many months to arrive (after being promised four to six weeks), were missing 30 to 50 percent of the parts when they did arrive, and that assumed a level of skill far beyond that of the weekend tinkerer, regulators in Florida secured an assurance of voluntary compliance from Classic. This was a big deal—the company had only one product—but, as it turned out, they had a weak commitment to making things right.

Seven years passed, during which the complaints kept pouring in, often accompanied by photographs and videos. "Classic had wonderful products," wrote Bill Moore, former editor of *Kit Car Illustrated*. "They had the production capability and the marketing ability. They had it all. But when consumers started complaining, it was a clarion call. They didn't act to solve the problems. If they had acted properly, they would have risen even higher." Instead they sank lower and lower. Classic finally threw in the towel, fading away, leaving a wake of anger, hostility, and unsettled claims.

16. Small deal, weak commitment, many complaints, high quality
"Oh, did we say a free television? We meant to say 'a useless little coupon book.'"
The case of the time-share resort scam

Nearly every homeowner in America has gotten them: the lavish invitation to visit a nearby vacation resort, have a lovely day, listen to a short sales presentation, and come home with a free television set or other significant gift. Michael and Tina P., living in a Boston suburb, received such an invitation to a time-share resort in the Berkshires and decided to accept. The literature assured them that after attending a one-hour sales presentation, they would receive either a color television or, if they were extremely fortunate, a new car.

Problem one was that the sales presentation was extremely high pressure, and lasted four hours, not one. They stayed because of the promise of the gift at the end. When the end finally came, they were handed a coupon book good for some discounts in Hawaii. What about the television or the car? "So sorry," they were told, "there must have been a misprint in our brochure."

Michael and Tina complained, along with many others, to the Office of Consumer Affairs. The perpetrators had many other schemes going, so closing down this one and making good was no big deal. Facing the possibility of criminal charges, they retroactively offered a 13-inch color television to everyone who had suffered through their sales pitch, and agreed to advertise and behave responsibly from now on.

National Consumer Organizations

THESE ORGANIZATIONS DEFINE their missions as consumer assistance, protection, and/or advocacy. The descriptions below are based on information they provided. The services they provide vary. Those that assist individuals with marketplace problems are specified clearly. Otherwise, these organizations do not assist consumers with individual complaints, although many are interested in hearing from consumers about problems, issues, trends, and so on, in connection with their advocacy and consumer education activities. Most, though not all, develop and distribute consumer education and information materials; several are professional associations primarily or exclusively concerned with improving consumer protection or customer service; and many are engaged in advocacy of consumer interests before government, the courts, and the news media. Where information or educational materials are offered, there might be a charge; contact the organization to find out.

Alliance Against Fraud in Telemarketing
c/o National Consumers League
815 15th Street, N.W., Suite 928-N
Washington, DC 20005
(202) 639-8140
(202) 347-0646 (fax)

American Association of Retired Persons
Consumer Affairs Section
601 E Street, N.W.
Washington, DC 20049
(202) 434-6030
(202) 434-6466 (fax)

American Council on Consumer Interests
240 Stanley Hall
University of Missouri–Columbia
Columbia, MO 65211
(314) 882-3817
(314) 884-4807 (fax)

Serving the professional needs of consumer educators, researchers, and policy makers.

American Council on Science and Health
1995 Broadway, 2nd Floor
New York, NY 10023-5860
(212) 362-7044
(212) 362-4919 (fax)

Bankcard Holders of America
Suite 120
560 Herndon Parkway
Herndon, VA 22070
(703) 481-1110
(703) 481-6037 (fax)

A nonprofit organization, BHA assists consumers in saving money on credit, getting out of debt, and resolving credit problems.

Call for Action
3400 Idaho Avenue, N.W.
Suite 101
Washington, DC 20016
(202) 537-0585
(202) 244-4881 (fax)

An international nonprofit hotline to assist consumers. Affiliated with radio and television stations.

Center for Auto Safety
2001 S Street, N.W., Suite 410
Washington, DC 20009
(202) 328-7700

CAS assists consumers with auto-related problems. CAS advocates on behalf of consumers in auto safety and quality, fuel efficiency, emissions, and related issues. For advice on specific problems, CAS requests that consumers write, including a brief statement of the problem or question; year, make, and model of the vehicle; and a stamped self-addressed envelope.

Citizen Action
1120 19th Street, N.W.
Suite 630
Washington, DC 20036
(202) 775-1580
(202) 296-4054 (fax)

Citizen Action works on behalf of its 3 million members and 32 state organizations on health care reform, environment, and energy issues.

Congress Watch
215 Pennsylvania Avenue, S.E.
Washington, DC 20003
(202) 546-4996
(202) 547-7392 (fax)

An arm of Public Citizen, Congress Watch works for consumer-related legislation, regulation and policies.

Consumer Action (CA)
116 New Montgomery, Suite 233
San Francisco, CA 94105
(415) 777-9635 (consumer complaint
    hotline, 10 A.M.–3 P.M., PST)
(415) 777-5267 (fax)

Consumer Action assists consumers with marketplace problems. An education and advocacy organization specializing in banking and telecommunications issues, Consumer Action offers a consumer complaint hotline, free information on its surveys of banks and long-distance telephone companies, and consumer education materials in as many as eight languages.

Consumers Union of U.S., Inc.
101 Truman Avenue
Yonkers, NY 10703-1057
(914) 378-2000
(914) 378-2900 (fax)

A nonprofit, independent organization, CU researches and tests consumer goods and services, and publishes *Consumer Reports* magazine.

National Consumers League
815 15th Street, N.W., Suite 928-N
Washington, DC 20005
(202) 639-8140
(202) 737-2164

Founded in 1899, NCL is America's pioneer consumer advocacy organization. The league is a nonprofit, membership organization working for consumer health and safety protection and fairness in the marketplace and workplace. Current principal issue areas include consumer fraud, food and drug safety, fair labor standards, child labor, health care, the environment, and telecommunications.

National Foundation For Consumer Credit, Inc. (NFCC)
8611 2nd Avenue, Suite 100
Silver Spring, MD 20910
(301) 589-5600
(800) 388-2227
(301) 495-5623 (fax)

The foundation does advise consumers on credit problems. The goals are to educate and counsel consumers on credit issues and problems and promote the intelligent use of credit in individual and family financial planning.

National Fraud Information Center (NFIC)
c/o National Consumers League
815 15th Street, N.W., Suite 928-N
Washington, DC 20005
(800) 876-7060 (toll free—TDD available)
(202) 347-0646 (fax)

NFIC assists consumers with recognizing and filing complaints about fraud. A project of the National Consumers League, the center's toll-free hotline assists consumers with information to help them avoid becoming victims of fraud, and provides referral to appropriate law enforcement agencies and professional associations, and assistance in filing complaints.

National Institute for Consumer Education (NICE)
207 Rackham Building
College of Education
Eastern Michigan University
Ypsilanti, MI 48197
(313) 487-2292
(313) 487-7153 (fax)

A consumer education resource and professional development center. Manages a national clearinghouse of consumer education materials, including videos, software programs, textbooks, and curriculum guides.

Public Citizen, Inc.
2000 P Street, N.W.
Washington, DC 20036
(202) 833-3000

Probably the best way to reach Ralph Nader.

U.S. Public Interest Research Group
(U.S. PIRG)
215 Pennsylvania Avenue, S.E.
Washington, DC 20003
(202) 546-9707

The national lobbying office for state groups. PIRG does not handle individual consumer complaints directly, but measures complaint levels to gauge the need for remedial legislation.

State Consumer Protection Offices

THESE ARE, AT THE VERY LEAST, a place to start. Some of these offices are free-standing state agencies, while others are departments or divisions of the attorney general's office of the state. All of them have listed telephone numbers (that's good), but not all of them are necessarily easy to reach by telephone (that's bad). Most of the toll-free numbers work only in the state in question.

Alabama

Consumer Protection Division
Office of the Attorney General
11 S. Union St.
Montgomery, AL 36130
(334) 242-7334 or (800) 392-5658

Alaska

The Consumer Protection Section was closed in 1995. The state suggests turning to lawyers, small claims court, the BBB, or, presumably, grinning and bearing it. Those who wish to complain about not being able to complain should complain to:

Attorney General
1031 W. Fourth Ave., Suite 200
Anchorage, AK 99501
(907) 276-3550

Arizona

Consumer Protection Division
Office of the Attorney General
1275 W. Washington St., Room 259
Phoenix, AZ 85007
(602) 542-3702 or (800) 352-8431

Arkansas

Consumer Protection Division
Office of the Attorney General
200 Tower Building
4th and 323 Center St.
Little Rock, AR 72201
(501) 682-2341
(800) 482-8982

California

Department of Consumer Affairs
1020 N Street
Sacramento, CA 95814
(916) 445-0660
(800) 344-9940

Colorado

Consumer Protection Unit
Office of the Attorney General
110 16th St., 10th Floor
Denver, CO 80202
(303) 620-4581

Connecticut

Department of Consumer Protection
State Office Building
165 Capitol Ave.
Hartford, CT 06106
(203) 566-4999
(800) 842-2649

Delaware

Division of Consumer Affairs
Department of Community Affairs
820 N. French St., 4th Floor
Wilmington, DE 19801
(302) 577-3250

District of Columbia

Department of Consumer and
    Regulatory Affairs
614 H St., N.W.
Washington, DC 20001
(202) 727-7000

Florida

Division of Consumer Services
Mayo Building
407 S. Calhoun St.
Tallahassee, FL 32399
(904) 488-2226
(800) 327-3382

Georgia

Office of Consumer Affairs
2 Martin Luther King Jr. Drive
Plaza Level, East Tower
Atlanta, GA 30334
(404) 656-3790
(800) 869-1123

Hawaii

Office of Consumer Protection
Department of Commerce and
    Consumer Affairs
828 Fort Street Mall
Honolulu, HI 96813
(808) 587-3222

(Note: During the two years I lived in Hawaii, I found this to be the least responsive and most annoying public agency I have ever tried to deal with for any reason, ever.)

Idaho

Consumer Protection Unit
Office of the Attorney General
700 W. Jefferson, Room 119
Boise, ID 83720
(208) 334-2424
(800) 432-3545

Illinois

Governor's Office of Citizen
    Assistance
222 S. College, 401 FLR
Springfield, IL 62706
(217) 782-0244
(800) 642-3112

Indiana

Consumer Protection Division
Office of the Attorney General
219 State House
Indianapolis, IN 46204
(317) 232-6330
(800) 382-5516

Iowa

Citizens' Aid Ombudsman
Capitol Complex
215 E. 7th St.
Des Moines, IA 50319
(515) 281-3592 or
(800) 358-5510

Kansas

Consumer Protection Division
Office of the Attorney General
Kansas Judicial Center
301 W. 10th St.
Topeka, KS 66612
(913) 296-3751
(800) 432-2310

Kentucky

Consumer Protection Division
Office of the Attorney General
209 St. Clair St.
Frankfort, KY 40601
(502) 564-2200
(800) 432-9257

Louisiana

Consumer Protection Section
Office of the Attorney General
State Capitol Building
P.O. Box 94005
Baton Rouge, LA 70804
(504) 342-7013

Maine

Consumer Assistance Service
Office of the Attorney General
State House Station No. 6
Augusta, ME 04333
(207) 289-3716

Maryland

Consumer Protection Division
Office of the Attorney General
200 St. Paul Place
Baltimore, MD 21202
(301) 528-8662 or
(202) 727-7000

Massachusetts

Consumer Protection Division
Office of the Attorney General
131 Tremont St.
Boston, MA 02111
(617) 727-7780

Michigan

Consumer Protection Division
Office of the Attorney General
P. O. Box 30213
Lansing, MI 48909
(517) 373-1140

Minnesota

Office of Consumer Services
Office of the Attorney General
117 University Ave., Room 124
St. Paul, MN 55155
(612) 296-2331

Mississippi

Consumer Protection Division
Office of the Attorney General
P.O. Box 22947
Jackson, MS 39225
(601) 354-6018

Missouri

Public Protection Division
Office of the Attorney General
P.O. Box 899
Jefferson City, MO 65102
(314) 751-3321
(800) 392-8222

Montana

Office of Consumer Affairs
Department of Commerce
1424 9th Ave.
Helena, MT 59620
(406) 444-4312

Nebraska

Consumer Protection Division
Department of Justice
2115 State Capitol, Room 2115
Lincoln, NE 68509
(402) 417-4723

Nevada

Consumer Affairs Division
Department of Commerce
4600 Kietezke Lane, Bldg. M,
    Suite 245
Reno, NV 89502
(702) 688-1800
(800) 992-0900

New Hampshire

Consumer Protection and Antitrust
   Bureau
Office of the Attorney General
25 Capitol St.
Concord, NH 03301
(603) 271-3641

New Jersey

Department of the Public Advocate
25 Market St., CN850
Trenton, NJ 08625
(609) 292-7087
(800) 792-8600

New Mexico

Consumer and Economic Crime
   Division
Office of the Attorney General
P.O . Drawer 1508
Santa Fe, NM 87504
(505) 827-6060
(800) 432-2070

New York

Bureau of Consumer Frauds and
   Protection
Office of the Attorney General
The Capitol
Albany, NY 12224
(518) 474-5481

North Carolina

Consumer Protection Division
Office of the Attorney General
P.O. Box 629
Raleigh, NC 27602
(919) 733-7741

North Dakota

Consumer Fraud Division
Office of the Attorney General
600 East Blvd.
Bismarck, ND 58505
(701) 224-3404
(800) 472-2600

Ohio

Consumer Frauds and Crimes
   Section
Office of the Attorney General
30 E. Broad St., 25th Floor
Columbus, OH 43266
(614) 466-4986
(800) 282-0515

Oklahoma

Consumer Protection Unit
Office of the Attorney General
112 State Capitol Building
Oklahoma City, OK 73105
(405) 521-3921

Oregon

Financial Fraud Section,
   Consumer Complaints
Department of Justice
Justice Building
Salem, OR 97310
(503) 378-4320

Pennsylvania

Bureau of Consumer Protection
Office of the Attorney General
Strawberry Square, 14th Floor
Harrisburg, PA 17120
(717) 787-9707
(800) 441-2555

Puerto Rico

Department of Consumer Affairs
Minillas Station, P. O. Box 41059
Santurce, PR 00940
(809) 722-7555

Rhode Island

Consumer Protection Division
Office of the Attorney General
72 Pine St.
Providence, RI 02903
(401) 277-2104
(800) 852-7776

South Carolina

Department of Consumer Affairs
P.O. Box 5757
Columbia, SC 29250
(803) 734-9452
(800) 922-1594

South Dakota

Division of Consumer Affairs
Office of the Attorney General
500 East Capitol Building
Pierre, SD 57501
(605) 773-4400

Tennessee

Division of Consumer Affairs
500 James Robertson Parkway,
5th Floor
Nashville, TN 37243
(615) 741-4737
(800) 342-8385

Texas

Consumer Protection Division
Office of the Attorney General
Capitol Station
P. O. Box 12548
Austin, TX 78711
(512) 463-2070

Utah

Division of Consumer Protection
Department of Commerce
160 East 3rd South
Salt Lake City, UT 84145
(801) 530-6601

Vermont

Public Protection Division
Office of the Attorney General
109 State St.
Montpelier, VT 05609
(802) 828-3171

Virgin Islands

Department of Licensing and
Consumer Affairs
Property and Procurement Building
Subbase #1, Room 205
St. Thomas, VI 00802
(809) 774-3130

Virginia

Division of Consumer Affairs
P.O. Box 1163
Richmond, VA 23209
(804) 786-2042

Washington

Consumer and Business Fair
Practice Division
Office of the Attorney General
900 4th Ave., Suite 2000
Seattle, WA 98164
(202) 464-6684
(800) 551-4636

West Virginia

Consumer Protection Division
Office of the Attorney General
812 Quarrier St., 6th Floor
Charleston, WV 25301
(304) 348-8986
(800) 368-8808

Wisconsin

Office of Consumer Protection and
Citizen Advocacy
Department of Justice
P.O. Box 7856
Madison, WI 53707
(608) 266-1852
(800) 362-8189

Wyoming

Consumer Affairs
Office of the Attorney General
123 State Capitol Building
Cheyenne, WY 82002
(307) 777-7841

Better Business Bureaus

ETTER BUSINESS BUREAUS are described in some detail, starting on page 131. They are not always wonderful, but in many situations, they may be well worth a try, as part of a complaining process. BBBs are nonprofit organizations sponsored by local businesses. They can provide consumer education materials, answer consumer questions, mediate and arbitrate complaints, and provide general information on companies' consumer complaint records. Each BBB has its own policy about reporting information. It might or might not tell you the nature of the complaints against a business, but all will tell you if a complaint has been registered. Many of the BBBs accept written complaints and will contact a firm on your behalf. BBBs do not judge or rate individual products or brands, handle complaints concerning the prices of goods or services, or give legal advice. However, many bureaus do offer binding arbitration, a form of dispute resolution, to those who ask for it. You should find your local BBB in the telephone book. To learn about BBBs in other locations, ask the national headquarters. There is also an informative and often helpful Internet area where you can get information on local BBBs and their work. The BBB's World Wide Web home page can be found at http://bbb.com.

National Headquarters
Council of Better Business Bureaus, Inc.
4200 Wilson Boulevard
Arlington, VA 22203
(703) 276-0100

Trade Associations and Other Resolution Programs

COMPANIES THAT MANUFACTURE similar products or offer similar services often belong to industry associations. These associations help resolve problems between their member companies and consumers. Depending on the industry, you might have to contact an association, service council, or consumer action program. If you have a problem with a company and cannot get it resolved with the company, ask if the company is a member of an association. Then, check this list to see if the association is listed. If the name of the association is not included on this list, check with a local library. This list includes the names and addresses of the associations and other dispute resolution programs that handle consumer complaints for their members. In some cases, the national organizations listed here can refer you to dispute resolution programs near you. These programs are usually called alternative dispute resolution programs.

Generally, there are three types of programs: arbitration, conciliation, and mediation. All three methods of dispute resolution vary. Ask for a copy of the rules of the program before you file your case. Generally, the decisions of the arbitrators are binding and must be accepted by both the customer and the business. However, in other forms of dispute resolution, only the business is required to accept the decision. In some programs, decisions are not binding on either party. Remember, before contacting one of these programs, try to resolve the complaint by contacting the company.

American Apparel Manufacturers Association
2500 Wilson Boulevard, Suite 301
Arlington, VA 22201
(703) 524-1864

American Arbitration Association
140 West 51st Street
New York, NY 10020-1203
(212) 484-4006

American Bar Association
Section on Dispute Resolution
1800 M Street, N.W.,
Suite 790
Washington, DC 20036
(202) 331-2258

American Collectors Association
P.O. Box 39106
Minneapolis, MN 55439-0106
(612) 926-6547

American Council of Life Insurance
Communications Department
1001 Pennsylvania Avenue, N.W.
Washington, DC 20004-2599
(800) 942-4242 (toll free,
    8 A.M.–8 P.M., EST, M–F)

American Gas Association
Consumer and Community Affairs
1515 Wilson Boulevard
Arlington, VA 22209
(703) 841-8583

American Health Care Association
1201 L Street, N.W.
Washington, DC 20005-4014
(202) 842-4444
(800) 321-0343 (toll free,
    publications only)

American Hotel and Motel Association
1201 New York Avenue, N.W.,
    Suite 600
Washington, DC 20005-3931
(written inquiries only)

American Institute of Certified Public Accountants
Professional Ethics Division
Harborside Financial Center
201 Plaza III
Jersey City, NJ 07311-3881
(201) 938-3175

American Orthotic and Prosthetic Association
1650 King Street, Suite 500
Alexandria, VA 22314-1885
(703) 836-7116

American Society of Travel Agents, Inc.
Consumer Affairs
1101 King Street
Alexandria, VA 22314
(703) 739-2782

American Textile Manufacturers Institute
1801 K Street, N.W., Suite 900
Washington, DC 20006
(202) 862-0552

Automotive Consumer Action Program (AUTOCAP)
8400 Westpark Drive
McLean, VA 22102
(703) 821-7144

BBB AUTO LINE
Council of Better Business
    Bureaus, Inc.
4200 Wilson Boulevard, Suite 800
Arlington, VA 22203-1804
(800) 955-5100

Better Hearing Institute
P.O. Box 1840
Washington, DC 20013
(703) 642-0580
(800) EAR-WELL

Blue Cross and Blue Shield Association
Consumer Affairs
1310 G Street, N.W., 12th Floor
Washington, DC 20005
(202) 626-4780

Boat Owners Association of the United States
Consumer Protection Bureau
Boat/U.S.
880 South Pickett Street
Alexandria, VA 22304-0730
(703) 823-9550

Career College Association
Accrediting Commission for Trade and Technical Schools
Accrediting Commission for Independent Colleges and Schools
First Street, N.E.
Washington, DC 20002
(202) 336-6700

Carpet and Rug Institute
Ms. Sarah Hicks
Director of Public Relations
Box 2048
Dalton, GA 30722
(written inquiries only)

Cemetery Consumer Service Council
Mr. Robert M. Fells, Assistant Secretary
P.O. Box 3574
Washington, DC 20007
(703) 379-6426

Children's Advertising Review Unit (CARU)
Council of Better Business Bureaus, Inc.
845 Third Avenue
New York, NY 10022
(212) 754-1354

Chrysler Corporation
Chrysler Customer Center
12000 Chrysler Drive
Highland Park, MI 48288-0001
(800) 992-1997

Consumer Insurance Interest Group
400 North Washington Street
Alexandria, VA 22314

Department of Defense
Office of National Ombudsman
1555 Wilson Boulevard
Suite 200
Arlington, VA 22209-2405
(800) 336-4590

Direct Marketing Association (DMA)
Ethics and Consumer Affairs
1101 17th Street, N.W., Suite 705
Washington, DC 20037
(written complaints only)

Direct Selling Association
1776 K Street, N.W.
Suite 600
Washington, DC 20006-2387
(written inquiries only)

Distance Education and Training Council
1601 18th Street, N.W.
Washington, DC 20009
(202) 234-5100

Ford Dispute Settlement Board
P.O. Box 5120
Southfield, MI 48086-5120
(800) 392-3673

Hearing Industries Association
515 King Street
Suite 320
Alexandria, VA 22314
(703) 684-5744

Insurance Information Institute
Public Relations & Consumer Affairs
110 William Street
New York, NY 10038
(800) 942-4242

International Association for Financial Planning
2 Concourse Parkway
Suite 800
Atlanta, GA 30328
(404) 395-1605

Major Appliance Consumer Action Panel (MACAP)
20 North Wacker Drive
Chicago, IL 60606
(312) 984-5858
(800) 621-0477

Media Advertising Credit Services
11600 Sunrise Valley Drive
Reston, VA 22091-1412
(703) 648-1248

Monument Builders of North America
1740 Ridge Avenue
Evanston, IL 60201
(708) 869-2031

Mortgage Bankers Association of America Media Relations Coordinator/ Consumer Affairs
1125 15th Street, N.W., 7th Floor
Washington, DC 20005
(202) 861-1929

National Advertising Division (NAD)
Council of Better Business
    Bureaus, Inc.
845 Third Avenue
New York, NY 10022
(212) 754-1320

National Association of Home Builders
Consumer Affairs/Public Liaison
1201 15th Street, N.W.
Washington, DC 20005
(800) 368-5242

National Association of Personnel Services
3133 Mt. Vernon Avenue
Alexandria, VA 22305
(703) 684-0180

National Association of Professional Insurance Agents
Consumer Affairs
400 North Washington Street
Alexandria, VA 22314

National Association of Securities Dealers, Inc.
Arbitration Department
33 Whitehall Street, 8th Floor
New York, NY 10004
(212) 858-4000

National Food Processors Association
Government Affairs
1401 New York Avenue, N.W.
Washington, DC 20005
(202) 639-5939

National Futures Association
Public Affairs & Education
200 West Madison Street
Chicago, IL 60606-3447
(800) 621-3570

National Tire Dealers and Retreaders Association
1250 Eye Street, N.W., Suite 400
Washington, DC 20005
(202) 789-2300
(800) 876-8372

National Turkey Federation
Department of Consumer Affairs
11319 Sunset Hills Road
Reston, VA 22090-5227
(written inquiries only)

Photo Marketing Association
3000 Picture Place
Jackson, MI 49201
(written complaints only)

The Soap and Detergent Association
Consumer Affairs
475 Park Avenue South
New York, NY 10016
(212) 725-1262

Tele-Consumer Hotline
1910 K Street, N.W., Suite 610
Washington, DC 20006
(202) 223-4371

Toy Manufacturers of America
200 Fifth Avenue
Room 740
New York, NY 10010
(212) 675-1141

U.S. Tour Operators Association (USTOA)
211 East 51st Street
Suite 12-B
New York, NY 10022
(212) 944-5727

Corporate Complaint-Line Phone Numbers

THIS SECTION LISTS THE NAMES and telephone numbers of 725 corporations. Toll-free numbers are provided when the company gives them out. Bear in mind that when you call a toll-free number, the company you are calling can determine your number whether or not you have caller ID blocking. A few companies specifically say that collect calls are accepted. Other say to write only, in which case the address is provided. You may eventually wish to write in most instances, but you can begin with the telephone, to learn the proper address and the name of the relevant person. In some cases, you will see a company name or brand name listed with the instructions to see another company listed elsewhere in this section, for example, "Admiral, see Maycor." This means that questions about Admiral appliances should be directed to the Maycor company. If you do not find the product name in this section, check the product label or warranty for the name of the manufacturer. Public libraries also have various books (and librarians) that might be helpful. *Standard & Poor's Register of Corporations, Directors and Executives; Trade Names Dictionary; Standard Directory of Advertisers;* and *Dun & Bradstreet Directory* are four sources that list information about most firms. If you cannot find the name of the manufacturer, the *Thomas Register of American Manufacturers* lists the manufacturers of thousands of products, and the directory called *Who Owns Whom* tells which companies are owned by which other companies.

AAMCO Transmissions, Inc.
(800) 523-0401

ABC Television
see Capital Cities

Ace Hardware Corporation
(708) 990-6600

Admiral
see Maycor

AETNA Life and Casualty
(800) US-AETNA

Airwick Industries, Inc.
see Reckitt & Colman, Inc.

AJAY Leisure Products
(800) 558-3276

Alamo Rent A Car
(800) 445-5664

Alaska Airlines
(206) 431-7286

Alberto Culver Company
(708) 450-3394

Allied Van Lines
(800) 470-2851

Allstate Insurance Company
(708) 402-5448

Aloha Airlines
(800) 803-9454

Alpo Pet Foods
(800) 366-6033

Amana Refrigeration, Inc.
(800) 843-0304

American Airlines, Inc.
(817) 967-2000

American Automobile Association
Mailspace 15
1000 AAA Drive
Heathrow, FL 32746-5063
(written complaints only)

American Cyanamid Company
see Lederle Consumer Health

American Express Company
(800) 528-4800

American Family Publishers
(800) AFP-2400

American Greetings Corporation
(800) 321-3040

American Home Food Products, Inc.
(800) 544-5680

American Standard, Inc.
(800) 223-0068

American Stores Company
(800) 541-2863

American Tourister, Inc.
(800) 635-5505

**America's Favorite Chicken
Corporation**
(404) 391-9500

America West Airlines
(800) 235-9292

Ameritech
(202) 326-3814

Amoco Oil Company
(800) 333-3991

Amtrak
(800) USA-RAIL

Amway Corporation
(800) 548-3878

Andersen Windows, Inc.
(612) 430-5564

Anheuser-Busch, Inc.
(314) 577-3093

Apple Computer, Inc.
(800) 776-2333

Aramis, Inc.
see Estee Lauder Companies

Arizona Mail Order
(520) 748-8600

Arm & Hammer
see Church & Dwight Co., Inc.

Armorall Products Corporation
(800) 747-4104

Armour Swift Eckrich
(800) 325-7424

Armstrong Tire Division
(800) 243-0167

Armstrong World Industries
(800) 233-3823

AT&T
(908) 221-5311

Atari Video Game Systems
(800) GO-ATARI

Atlantic Richfield Company
(800) 322-ARCO

Atlas Van Lines
(800) 252-8885

Avis Rent-A-Car System
(800) 352-7900

Avon Products, Inc.
(800) 367-2866

Bacardi Imports Inc.
(800) BACARDI

Bali
(800) 654-6122

Bally Manufacturing Corporation
(312) 399-1300

Bank of America, NT & SA
(415) 241-7677

The Bank of New York Company
(212) 495-2066

Barnett Banks, Inc.
(904) 791-7720

Bass Pro Shop
(800) BASS-PRO

Eddie Bauer
(800) 426-6253

Bausch and Lomb
(800) 553-5340

Bayer Corporation
(800) 331-4536

L.L. Bean, Inc.
(800) 341-4341

Bear Creek Corporation
(503) 776-2400

Beatrice Cheese, Inc.
(414) 782-2750

Becton Dickinson
(201) 847-6618

Beiersdorf, Inc.
(800) 233-2340

Bell Atlantic Corporation
(202) 392-1358

BellSouth
(800) 346-9000

Benihana of Tokyo
(800) 327-3369

Best Foods
(201) 894-2324

Best Western International
(800) 528-1238

BIC Corporation
(203) 783-2000

Birds Eye
see General Foods

Black and Decker Household Products
(800) 231-9786

Black and Decker Power Tools
(800) 762-6672

Blockbuster Entertainment Corporation
(305) 832-3000

Block Drug Company, Inc.
(800) 365-6500

Bloomingdale's by Mail, Ltd.
(800) 366-9921

Blue Bell, Inc.
see Wrangler

Blue Cross and Blue Shield Association
(202) 626-4780

Bojangles
(800) 366-9921

Borden, Inc.
(614) 225-4511

Boyle-Midway Household Products, Inc.
see Reckitt & Colman Inc.

Bradlees Discount Department Stores
(617) 380-5377

Breck Hair Care Products
see the Dial Corporation

Bridgestone/Firestone, Inc.
(800) 367-3872

Brights Creek
(804) 827-1850

Bristol-Myers Products
(800) 468-7746

British Airways
(718) 397-4000

Brown-Forman Beverage Company
(800) 753-1177

Brown Group, Inc.
(800) 766-6465

Budget Rent-A-Car Corporation
(800) 621-2844

Bull & Bear Group, Inc.
(800) 847-4200

Bulova Watch Company
(718) 204-3300

Burlington Coat Factory Warehouse Corporation
(609) 387-7800

Burlington Hosiery
see Kayser-Roth Corporation

Burlington Industries
(910) 379-2276

Burroughs Wellcome Company
(919) 248-3000, ext. 4511

CBS Television
(212) 975-3166

CIBA Consumer Pharmaceuticals
(908) 277-5000

CIGNA Property and Casualty Companies
(215) 761-4555

CPC International Inc.
(201) 894-4000

C&R Clothiers
(310) 559-8200

CVN
see QVC Network

CVS
(800) 555-0475

Cabela's, Inc.
(800) 237-8888

Cadbury Beverages, Inc.
(800) 426-4891

Caloric Modern Maid Corporation
see Amana Refrigeration, Inc.

Campbell Soup Company
(800) 257-4883

Canandaigua Wine Company
(716) 394-7900

Canon U.S.A., Inc.
(800) 828-4040

Capital Cities/ABC Inc.
(212) 456-7477

Carnival Cruise Lines
(800) 438-6744

Carrier Air Conditioning
(800) 227-7437

Carte Blanche
see Diners Club

Carter Hawley Hale Stores, Inc.
(213) 227-2422

Carter-Wallace Inc.
(212) 339-5000

Carvel Corporation
20 Batterson Park Road
Farmington, CT 06032-2502
(written inquiries only)

Casio, Inc.
(800) 962-2746

Ceridian Corporation
(612) 853-8100

Champion Spark Plug Company
(419) 535-2458

Chanel, Inc.
(212) 688-5055

Chattem, Inc.
(800) 745-2429

Cheesebrough-Pond's, USA
(800) 243-5804

Chemical Bank
(212) 310-5286

ChemLawn Services Corporation
see TruGreen Limited Partnership

Chevron U.S.A. Inc.
(800) 962-1223

Chi-Chi's, Inc.
(502) 426-3900

Chuck E. Cheese
(214) 258-8507

Church & Dwight Company, Inc.
(800) 524-1328

Church's Fried Chicken, Inc.
see America's Favorite Chicken Corp.

Cincinnati Microwave
(800) 433-3487

Circuit City Stores, Inc.
(800) 251-2665

Citicorp/Citibank
(212) 559-0043

Citizen Watch Company
(800) 321-1023

Clairol, Inc.
(800) 223-5800
(800) HISPANA (Spanish)

Clinique Laboratories, Inc.
see Estee Lauder Companies

Clorox Company
(800) 292-2200

Club Med Sales, Inc.
(212) 977-2100

The Coca-Cola Company
(800) 438-2653

Coldwell Banker Corp.
(714) 367-1800

Colgate-Palmolive Company
(800) 221-4607

Colonial Penn Group, Inc.
(800) 523-1700

Columbia House (SONY Music)
(800) 457-0500

Combe Incorporated
(800) 431-2610

Commodore Business Machines, Inc.
(215) 431-9100

Compaq Computer Corporation
(800) 345-1518

Comprehensive Care Corp.
(800) 678-2273

Congoleum Corporation
(800) 274-3266

Consumers Products Group
see Commodore Business
    Machines, Inc.

Contempo Casuals
(800) 368-5923

Continental Airlines, Inc.
(713) 987-6500

Continental Baking Company
(314) 982-4953

Converse, Inc.
(800) 428-2667

Conwood Company, L.P.
(800) 642-6116

Coors
(800) 642-6116

Coppertone
see Schering-Plough HealthCare
    Products, Inc.

Corning/Revere
(800) 999-3436

Cosmair, Inc.
(800) 631-7358

Cotter & Company
(312) 975-2700

Craftmatic Organization, Inc.
(800) 677-8200

Jenny Craig International
(619) 259-7000

A.T. Cross Company
(800) 282-7677

Crown Books
(800) 831-7400

Cuisinarts Corporation
(800) 726-0190 (toll free outside NJ)

Culligan International Company
(708) 205-5757

Cumberland Packing Corporation
(718) 858-4200

Cunard
(800) 528-6273

Current, Inc.
(800) 525-7170

Curtis Mathes Corporation
(800) 657-1979

d-Con
see L&F Products

DHL Corporation
(800) CALL-DHL

Dairy Queen
see International Dairy Queen

Dannon Company, Inc.
1111 Westchester Avenue
White Plains, NY 10604
(written inquiries only)

Danskin
(800) 288-6749

Dayton's, Hudson's, Marshall Field's
Dept. Stores
(612) 375-3382

Dean Witter, Discover & Company
(800) 733-2307

Deere & Company
(309) 765-8000

Del Laboratories, Inc.
(516) 293-7070

Del Monte Foods
(800) 543-3090

Delco Remy Division, General Motors
(317) 646-3367

Delta Air Lines
(404) 715-1402

Delta Faucets
(317) 848-1812

Denny's, Inc.
(803) 596-8000

Dep Corporation
(800) 367-2855

DeVry, Inc.
(800) 225-8000

The Dial Corporation
(800) 528-0849

Diet Center, Inc.
(800) 333-2581

Digital Equipment Corporation
(800) 332-4636

Dillard Department Stores, Inc.
(501) 376-5200

Diners Club International
(800) 234-6377

Dole Packaged Foods
(800) 232-8888

Domino's Pizza, Inc.
(313) 930-3030

Doubleday Book & Music Clubs, Inc.
(516) 873-4628

Dow Brands
(800) 428-4795

Dr. Pepper/Seven-Up Companies, Inc.
(Welch's & IBC Root Beer)
(214) 360-7000

Walter Drake & Sons, Inc.
(719) 596-3140

Drug Emporium, Inc.
(614) 548-7080 - Ext. 104

Dulcolax
(908) 602-6780

Dunkin Donuts of America
(617) 961-4000

Dunlop Tire Corporation
(800) 548-4714

DuPont Company
(800) 441-7515

Duracell USA
(800) 796-4565

Durkee-French Foods
see Reckitt & Colman Inc.

Eastman Kodak Company
(800) 242-2424

Eckerd Drug Company
(813) 399-6000

Edmund Scientific Company
(609) 573-6260

Electrolux Corporation
(800) 243-9078

Emery Worldwide
(800) 227-1981

Encore Marketing International, Inc.
(800) 638-0930

Encyclopaedia Britannica, Inc.
(312) 347-7230

Equifax
(770) 612-2899

Equitable Life Assurance Society
(212) 245-4609 (collect)

Esprit de Corps
(800) 777-8765

Estee Lauder Companies
(212) 572-4200

Ethan Allen, Inc.
(203) 743-8553

The Eureka Company
(800) 282-2886

Bob Evans Farms, Inc.
(800) 272-PORK

Exxon Company U.S.A.
(713) 656-2111

Family Circle Magazine
(212) 463-1124

Faultless Starch/Bon Ami Company
(816) 842-1230

Fayva Shoe Stores
see Morse Shoe, Inc.

Federal Express Corporation
(800) 238-5355

Federated Department Stores
(513) 579-7000

Fieldcrest Cannon, Inc.
(800) 841-3336

Finast
(216) 587-7100

Fingerhut Corporation
(612) 259-2500

First Brands Corporation
(800) 835-4523

First Fidelity Bancorporation
(800) 345-9042

First Interstate Bank of California
(213) 614-3103

First Union National Bank of Florida
(800) 735-1012

Fisher
see SFS Corporation

Fisher Price
(800) 432-5437

Florida Power and Light Co.
(800) 432-6554 (toll free TDD)

Florist's Transworld Delivery
   Association (FTD)
(800) 788-9000

Florsheim Shoe Company
(800) 633-4988

Flowers Industries, Inc.
(912) 226-9110

Forbes Inc.
(212) 620-2409

Foster & Gallagher, Inc.
(309) 691-4610

The Franklin Mint
(800) 523-7622

Frank's Nursery and Crafts, Inc.
(313) 366-8400

Fretter Appliance Company
(800) 736-3430

The Frigidaire Co.
(800) 374-7714

Fruit of the Loom, Inc.
(502) 781-6400

Fuji Photo Film U.S.A., Inc.
(800) 659-3854, ext. 2571

Fuller Brush Company
(800) 523-3794

Ernest & Julio Gallo Winery
(209) 579-3161

Lewis Galoob Toys, Inc.
(415) 952-1678

Gannett Company, Inc.
(703) 284-6048

General Electric Company
(800) 626-2000

General Foods Corporation
(800) 431-1001

General Host Corporation
(203) 357-9900

General Mills, Inc.
(800) 328-6787

General Motors Acceptance
   Corporation (GMAC)
(800) 441-9234

General Tire Inc.
(800) 847-3349

Generra
(206) 728-6888

Genesee Brewing Company, Inc.
(716) 546-1030

Georgia-Pacific Corp.
(404) 652-4000

Gerber Products Company
(800) 4-GERBER

Giant Food Inc.
(301) 341-4365

Gibson Appliances
see The Frigidaire Co.

Gillette Company
(617) 463-3337

Glenbrook Laboratories
see Sterling Health

The Glidden Company
(216) 344-8818

Goodyear Tire & Rubber Co.
(800) 321-2136

Gordon's Jewelers
(214) 580-4924

Greensweep
(800) 225-2883

Greyhound Lines, Inc.
(214) 419-3914

GTE Corporation
(203) 965-2000

Guess? Inc.
(213) 765-3100

Guinness Import Company
(800) 521-1591

H&R Block, Inc.
(800) 829-7733

HVR Company
see Clorox Company

Hallmark Cards, Inc.
(816) 274-5697

Halston Borghese, Inc.
(212) 572-3100

Hanes
see L'eggs Products

Hanover-Direct Inc.
(717) 637-6000

Hardwick
see Maycor

Harry and David
see Bear Creek Corporation

Hartz Mountain Corporation
(201) 481-4800

Hasbro, Inc.
(800) 255-5516

Hathaway Shirts
see Warnaco Men's Apparel

Heath Company
(616) 925-6000

G. Heileman Brewing Company
(708) 292-2100

Heinz U.S.A.
(412) 237-5740

Helene Curtis, Inc.
(312) 661-0222

Hershey Foods Corporation
(800) 468-1714

Hertz Corporation
(800) 654-3131

Hewlett-Packard Company
(800) 752-0900

Hilton Hotels Corporation
(310) 278-4321

Hit or Miss
(617) 344-0800

Hitachi Home Electronics
(America), Inc.
(800) 241-6558

Holiday Inn Worldwide
(404) 604-2000

Home Depot Inc.
(404) 433-8211

Home Owners Warranty
Corporation (HOW)
(800) CALL-HOW

Home Shopping Network
(800) 753-5353

Honeywell, Inc.
(800) 468-1502

Hoover Company
(800) 944-9200

The Horchow Collection
(800) 395-5397

Hormel Foods Company
(507) 437-5395

Hostess Cakes
see Continental Baking Co.

Huffy Bicycle Company
(513) 866-6251

Humana Inc.
(502) 580-1000

Hunt-Wesson, Inc.
(714) 680-1431

Hyatt Hotels & Resorts
(800) 228-3336

IBC Root Beer
see Dr. Pepper/Seven-Up
    Companies, Inc.

IBM
(800) 426-3333

Illinois Bell
(312) 727-2293

Indiana Bell
(317) 265-5965

Integra
(214) 233-0966

International Dairy Queen, Inc.
(612) 830-0200

International Service Specialists, Inc.
see The Bohannon Group

JRT
(804) 827-6000

JVC Company of America
(800) 252-5722

Jackson & Perkins Nursery Stock
(800) 872-7673

James River Corporation
(800) 243-5384

Jenn-Air Company
see Maycor

Jockey International, Inc.
(414) 658-8111

John Hancock Financial Services
(617) 572-6272

Johnny Appleseed's, Inc.
(800) 225-5051

Johnson & Johnson Consumer Products, Inc.
(800) 526-3967

Johnson Publishing Company, Inc.
820 South Michigan Avenue
Chicago, IL 60605
(written complaints only)

S.C. Johnson and Sons
(800) 558-5252

Howard Johnson, Inc.
(602) 389-5555

Jordache Enterprises, Inc.
(800) 289-5326

K-III
(212) 745-0500

Kmart Corporation
(800) 63-KMART

Karastan Rugmill
(800) 476-7113

Carl Karcher Enterprises
(714) 774-5796

Kawasaki Motor Corporation, U.S.A.
(714) 770-0400

Kayser-Roth Corporation
(910) 229-2224

Keebler Company, Inc.
(708) 833-2900

Kellogg Company
(800) 962-1413

The Kelly Springfield Tire Company
(301) 777-6635

Kelvinator Appliance Company
see The Frigidaire Company

Kemper National Insurance Company
(800) 833-0355

Kenner Products
(800) 327-8264

Kimberly-Clark Corporation
(800) 544-1847

Kinetico, Inc.
(216) 564-9111

Kingsford Products Company
see Clorox Company

KitchenAid
(800) 422-1230

Calvin Klein Industries, Inc.
(800) 326-6800

Kodiak Smokeless Tobacco
see Conwood Co., L.P.

Kohler Company
(414) 457-4441

Kraft, Inc.
(800) 323-0768

Kroger Company
(800) 632-6900

Krystal Company
(615) 757-1550

LA Gear
(213) 822-1995

La-Z-Boy Chair Company
(313) 242-1444

L&F Products
(800) 888-0192

LaCoupe
see Playtex Family Products Group

Land O'Lakes, Inc.
(800) 328-4155

Lands' End
(800) 356-4444

Lane Furniture
(804) 369-5641

Lechmere
(800) 733-4666

Lederle Consumer Health
(800) 282-8805

Lee Company
(913) 384-4000

L'eggs Products
(919) 519-2529

Leichtung, Inc.
(800) 654-7817

Lennox Industries
(214) 497-5000

Lever Brothers Company
(800) 598-1223

Levi Strauss & Co.
(800) USA-LEVI

Levitz Furniture Corporation
(800) 631-4601

Levolor Corporation
(800) LEVOLOR

Liberty Mutual Insurance Group
(800) 225-2390, ext. 41015

Life Fitness
(800) 351-3737

Lillian Vernon Corporation
(804) 430-1500

Eli Lilly & Company
(317) 276-8588

The Limited, Inc.
(614) 479-7000

Little Caesar Enterprises
(800) 7-CAESAR

Lone Star Brewing Company
see G. Heileman Brewing Company

Long John Silver's
(606) 263-6000

L'Oreal
see Cosmair, Inc.

Lorillard Tobacco Company
(910) 373-6669

Los Angeles Times
(213) 237-5000

Lucky Stores, Inc.
(415) 833-6000

MAACO Enterprises, Inc.
(800) 523-1180

MCA Inc.
(818) 777-3591

MCI Consumer Markets
(703) 415-3195

M&M/Mars, Inc.
(201) 852-1000

MTV Networks
see Viacom International Inc.

R.H. Macy & Company, Inc.
(212) 695-4400

Magic Chef
see Maycor

Magnavox
see Phillips Consumer Electronics

Mannington Resilient Floors, Inc.
(800) 356-6787

Manor Care Corporation
(800) 833-7696

**Manufacturers Hanover Trust
Company**
(212) 270-7370

**Manville Corporation/Schuller
International, Inc.**
(800) 654-3103

Marine Midland Bank, N.A.
(716) 841-2424

Marion Merrell Dow Inc.
(800) 552-3656

Marriott Corporation
(301) 380-7600

**Massachusetts Mutual Life Insurance
Company**
(800) 828-4902

MasterCard International
(800) 826-2181

Matsushita Services Company
(201) 348-7000

Mattel Toys, Inc.
(800) 524-TOYS

Max Factor
see Procter & Gamble Company

Maxicare Health Plans, Inc.
(213) 742-0900

Maxwell House
see General Foods

May Department Stores Co.
(314) 342-4336

Maybelline Inc.
(901) 320-2166

**Maycor Appliance Parts and Service
Company**
(615) 472-3333

Mayflower Transit, Inc.
(800) 428-1200

Maytag
see Maycor

McCormick & Company, Inc.
(800) 632-5847

McCrory Stores, Inc.
(717) 757-8181

McDonald's Corporation
(708) 575-6198

McGraw-Hill, Inc.
(800) 262-4729

McKee Foods Corporation
(800) 522-4499

McKesson Water Products Company
(818) 585-1192

McNeil Consumer Products Company
(215) 233-7000

Medco Containment Services, Inc.
(201) 358-5530

Media General, Inc.
(804) 649-6000

Meineke Discount Muffler
(704) 377-3070

Melitta USA, Inc.
(800) 451-1694

Mellon Bank Corporation
(412) 234-8552

Melville Corporation
(914) 925-4000

Mem Company, Inc.
(201) 767-0100

Mennen Company
(800) 228-7408

Mentholatum Company, Inc.
(716) 882-7660

Mercruiser
(405) 377-1200

Mercury, Mariner, and Force Outboards
(414) 929-5000

Merillat Industries
(517) 263-0771

Merrill Lynch Pierce Fenner & Smith
(908) 563-8777

Mervyn's
(415) 786-8337

Metromedia Steakhouses Company, L.P.
(513) 454-2400

Metropolitan Life Insurance Company
(212) 578-2544

Michelin Tire Corporation
(800) 847-3435

Michigan Bell Telephone Co.
(313) 223-7224

Michigan Bulb Company
(616) 771-9500

Midas International Corporation
(800) 621-8545

Mid-Michigan Surgical Supply
(800) 445-5820

Miles Kimball
41 West 8
Oshkosh, WI 54906
(Written inquiries only)

Milton Bradley Company
(413) 525-6411

Minolta Corporation
(201) 825-4000

Minwax, Inc.
(800) 523-9299

Miracle Gro Products, Inc.
(516) 883-6550

Mitsubishi Electronics America, Inc.
(800) 332-2119

Mobil Oil Corporation
(800) 662-4592

Mobil Oil Credit Corporation
(913) 752-7000

Monet, Trifari and Marvella Jewelry
(401) 728-9800

Monsanto Company
(314) 694-1000

Montgomery Ward
(800) 695-3553

Morse Shoe Company
(617) 828-9300

Morton Salt
(312) 807-2694

Motorola, Inc.
(708) 576-5000

Motts USA
(800) 426-4891

Murphy-Phoenix Co.
(216) 248-2411

Mutual Life Insurance Company
of New York
(201) 907-6669

Mutual of Omaha Insurance Co.
(402) 342-7600

NBC Television
(212) 664-2333

NEC Technologies Inc.
(800) 366-9500

Nabisco Foods Group
(800) NABISCO

National Amusements Inc.
(617) 461-1600

National Car Rental System, Inc.
(800) 468-3334

National Education Corporation
(714) 261-7606

National Media Corporation
(215) 772-5000

National Presto Industries, Inc.
(715) 839-2121

Nationwide Insurance Companies
(800) 622-2421

Neighborhood Periodical Club, Inc.
(513) 771-9400

Neiman-Marcus
(800) 685-6695

Nestle USA
(818) 549-6579

Neutrogena Corporation
(800) 421-6857

Nevada Bell
(800) 356-4040

The New England
(617) 578-2000

New Hampton, Inc.
(804) 827-7010

Newport News
(804) 827-7010

News America Publishing, Inc.
(800) 625-7300

Newsweek, Inc.
(800) 631-1040

New Woman Magazine
see K-III

New York Life Insurance Company
(212) 576-5081 (collect calls
accepted)

New York Magazine
see K-III

New York Times Company
(212) 556-7171

Nexxus Products
(805) 968-6900

Niagara Mohawk Power
Corporation
(315) 460-7015

Nike, Inc.
(800) 344-6453

Nintendo of America Inc.
(800) 255-3700

Norelco Consumer Products Company
(800) 243-7884

Norge
see Maycor

North American Watch Corporation
(201) 460-4800

Northwest Airlines
(800) 328-2298

Northwestern Mutual Life Insurance
   Company
(414) 271-1444299-7179

Norwegian Cruise Line
(800) 327-7030

Nu Tone, Inc.
(800) 543-8687

The NutraSweet Company
(800) 321-7254

Nutri/System Inc.
(215) 445-5300

Nynex/New York Telephone
(800) 722-2300

Ocean Spray Cranberries Inc.
(800) 662-3263

Ohio Bell Telephone Company
(216) 822-7361

O'Keefe & Merit Appliances
see The Frigidaire Company

Olan Mills, Inc.
(800) 251-6323

Olympus America
(800) 622-3263

Oneida, Ltd.
(800) 877-6667

Ore-Ida Foods
(208) 383-6800

Orkin
(800) 346-7546

Ortho Consumer Products
(415) 842-5539

OSCO Drugs
see American Stores Company

Outboard Marine Corporation
(800) 357-7662

Owens Corning World Headquarters
(419) 248-8000

Pacific Bell
(800) 697-6547

Pacific Enterprises
(213) 244-1200

Pacific Telesis Group
see Pacific Bell

PaineWebber Inc.
(800) 354-9103

Panasonic
see Matsushita Services Company

Paramount Publishing
(201) 767-5000

Parke-Davis
see Warner-Lambert Company

Pella Corporation
(515) 628-1000

J.C. Penney Company, Inc.
(214) 431-8500

Pennzoil Products Company
(800) 990-9811

Peoples Drug Stores, Inc.
see CVS

Pepperidge Farm, Inc.
(203) 846-7276

Pepsi-Cola Company
(800) 433-2652

Perdue Farms
(800) 442-2034

The Perrier Group
(203) 531-4100

Pet Incorporated
(800) 325-7130

Pfizer Inc.
(212) 573-2323

Philco
see Philips Consumer Electronics

**Philip Morris Companies
Incorporated**
(800) 343-0975

Philips Consumer Electronics
(615) 475-8869

Philips Lighting Company
(908) 563-3081

Phillips Petroleum Company
(918) 661-1215

Piaget
see North American Watch
Corporation

Piedmont Airlines
see USAir

Pillsbury Company
(800) 767-4466

Pioneer Electronics Service, Inc.
(800) 421-1404

Playskool
(800) 752-9755

Playtex Apparel, Inc.
(800) 537-9955

Playtex Family Products Corp.
(800) 222-0453

Polaroid Corporation
(800) 343-5000

Polo/Ralph Lauren Corporation
(800) 775-7656

Ponderosa
see Metromedia Steakhouses
Company, L.P.

Popeye's
see America's Favorite Chicken

Premiere Magazine
see K-III

Procter & Gamble Company
(800) 426-8374

Progresso
see Pet Incorporated

Provident Mutual Life Insurance
(800) 253-4681

**Prudential Insurance Company
of America**
(201) 802-6000

**Prudential Property & Casualty
Company**
(800) 437-5556

Prudential Securities Inc.
(800) 367-8701

Publishers Clearing House
(800) 645-9242

Publix Super Markets
(813) 688-1188

QVC Network
(610) 701-1000

Quaker Oats Company
(800) 494-7843

Quaker State Corporation
(800) 759-2525

Quasar
see Matsushita Services Company

Radio Shack
see Tandy Corporation

Ralston Purina Company
(800) 345-5678

**Ramada International Hotels and
    Resorts**
(305) 460-1900

Readers Digest Association, Inc.
(800) 431-1246

Reckitt & Colman, Inc.
(800) 232-9665

Orville Redenbacher
see Hunt-Wesson, Inc.

Reebok
(800) 843-4444

Remington Products
(800) 736-4648

Revlon
(800) 473-8566

Reynolds Metals
(800) 433-2244

Rockport
(800) 343-9255

Rodale Press
(800) 848-4735

Rolex
(212) 758-7700

Rollins, Inc.
(800) 346-7546

Ross Laboratories
(800) 227-5767

Roto Rooter
(800) 575-7737

Royal Oak Enterprises, Inc.
(800) 241-3955

Royal Silk
(800) 962-6262

Royal Viking Line
(800) 422-8000

Rubbermaid, Inc.
(216) 264-6464, ext. 2619

Rustler Jeans
see Wrangler

Ryder Truck Rental
(800) 327-7777

Ryland Group, Inc.
(800) 638-1768

SFS Corporation
(800) 421-5013

Safeway Inc.
(510) 891-3267

Saks & Companies NY
(800) 239-3089

Sandoz Company
(201) 503-7500

Sanyo Electric Inc.
see SFS Corporation

Sara Lee Corporation
(800) 621-5235

Schering-Plough HealthCare Products, Inc.
(800) 842-4090

Scholl
see Schering-Plough HealthCare Products, Inc.

Schwinn Bicycle Company
(800) 633-0231

Scott Paper Company
(800) 835-7268

Scudder Investor Services Inc.
(800) 225-5163

Joseph E. Seagram & Sons, Inc.
(212) 572-7335

Sealy Mattress Manufacturing Company
(216) 522-1310

Seamans Furniture Company, Inc.
(800) 445-2503

G.D. Searle and Company Pharmaceuticals
(800) 323-1603

Sears Merchandise Group
(800) 427-3049

Seiko Corporation of America
(201) 529-3311

Select Restaurants, Inc.
(216) 464-6606

Serta, Inc.
(800) 426-0371

7 Eleven Food Stores
see The Southland Corporation

Seventeen Magazine
see K-III

Seven-Up
see Dr. Pepper/Seven-Up Companies, Inc.

Sharp Electronics Corporation
(800) 237-4277

The Sharper Image
(800) 344-5555

Shell Oil Company
(800) 248-4257

Sherwin-Williams Company, Paint Stores Group
(216) 566-2151

Shoney's Inc.
(615) 391-5201

ShowBiz Pizza Time, Inc.
(214) 258-8507

Showtime Networks Inc.
see Viacom International Inc.

Simmons Company
(404) 512-7700

Singer Sewing Company
(800) 877-7762

Sizzler International, Inc.
(310) 827-2300

Skaggs Company
see American Stores Company

Skoal Moist Smokeless Tobacco
see UST

SlimFast Foods Company
(800) 862-4500

**Smith Barney, Harris Upham
& Co., Inc.**
(800) 421-8609

SmithKline Beecham Consumer Brands
(800) 245-1040

J.M. Smucker Company
(216) 682-3000

**Soap Opera Digest, Soap Opera
Weekly**
see K-III

**Sonesta International Hotels
Corporation**
(617) 421-5432

Sony Corporation of America
(800) 282-2848

South Central Bell
see BellSouth Telecommunications

Southern Bell Corporation
see BellSouth Telecommunications

The Southland Corporation
(800) 255-0711

Southwest Airlines
(800) 533-1305

Southwestern Bell Corporation
(210) 351-2604

Spalding & Evenflo, Inc.
(800) 225-6601

Speed Queen Company
(414) 748-3121

Spencer Gifts
(800) 762-0419

Spiegel, Inc.
(708) 986-8800

Springmaid/Performance
(212) 903-2100

Squibb
see Bristol-Myers Squibb
Pharmaceutical Group

Stanley Hardware
(800) 622-4393

**State Farm Mutual Automobile
Insurance Company**
(309) 766-2714

Sterling Health
(800) 331-4536 a

J.P. Stevens
see WestPoint Pepperell

Stokley USA, Inc.
(800) 872-1110

**Stop & Shop Supermarket
Company Inc.**
(617) 770-6040

Stouffer Foods Corporation
(216) 248-3600

Strawbridge & Clothier
(215) 629-6722

The Stroh Brewery Company
(313) 446-2000

Sunbeam/Oster Household Products
P.O. Box 247
Laurel, MS 39441-0247
(written inquiries only)

Sun-Diamond Growers of California
(209) 467-6267

Sunset Magazine
(800) 777-0117

Supermarket General Corporation
(908) 499-3500

Swatch Watch USA
(800) 937-9282

The Swiss Colony
Monroe, WI 53566
(608) 324-4000

Sylvania Television
see Philips Consumer Electronics

3M
(800) 364-3577

TJX Companies (T.J. Maxx)
(800) 926-6299

TRW Information Services
(214) 235-1200

TV Guide
see News America Publishing, Inc.

Talbots
(800) 992-9010

TAMBRANDS, Inc.
(800) 523-0014

Tandy Corporation/Radio Shack
(817) 390-3218

Tappan Appliance Company, Inc.
see The Frigidaire Co.

Target Stores
(612) 370-6056

Technics
see Matsushita Services Company

Teledyne Water Pik
(800) 525-2774

Teleflora
(800) 421-2815

Tenneco, Inc.
(713) 757-2131

Tetley Inc.
(800) 732-3027

Texaco Refining and Marketing
(713) 647-1500

Texas Instruments Incorporated
(800) 842-2737

Thom McAn Shoe Co.
(508) 791-3811

Thompson & Formby, Inc.
(800) FORMBYS

Thompson Medical Company, Inc.
(407) 820-9900

Thrift Drug, Inc.
(800) 284-8212

Time Inc.
(800) 541-1000

Time Warner Inc.
(212) 484-8000

Timex Corporation
(800) 448-4639

Titleist
(800) 225-8500

Tonka Products
(800) 248-6652

The Toro Company
(612) 887-8900

Toshiba America Consumer Products, Inc.
(800) 631-3811

Totes, Incorporated
(513) 583-2300

Tourneau, Inc.
(800) 223-1288

Toys "R" Us
(201) 599-7897

Trak Auto
(800) 835-7300

Trane/CAC, Inc.
(903) 581-3200

Trans World Airlines, Inc.
(800) 421-8480

The Travelers Companies
(203) 277-3198

TruGreen Limited Partnership
(800) TRUGREEN

True Value Hardware Stores
see Cotter & Company

Tupperware
(800) 858-7221

Turner Entertainment Networks
(404) 827-1632

Turtle Wax, Inc.
(800) 323-9883

Tyco Toys
(800) 367-8926

Tyson Foods
(800) 233-6332

U-Haul International
(800) 528-0463

UST
(203) 661-1100

Uniroyal Goodrich Tire Company
(800) 521~9796

UNISYS Corporation
(215) 986-4011

United Airlines
(800) 323-0170

United Parcel Service of America, Incorporated
(404) 828-6000

United States Fidelity & Guarantee Company
(301) 547-3000

United Van Lines, Inc.
(800) 325-3870

Unocal Corporation
(800) 527-5476

The Upjohn Company
(800) 253-8600

USAir
(910) 661-0061

U.S. Shoe Corporation
(800) 284-9955

U.S. Sprint
(800) 347-8988

U S WEST, Inc.
(800) 255-6920

Valvoline Oil Company
(800) 354-9061

Van Heusen Company
(800) 777-1726

Vanity Fair
(800) 832-8662

Van Munching and Co., Inc.
(212) 332-8500

Viacom International Inc.
(212) 258-6346

Vicorp Restaurants Inc.
(303) 296-2121

Visa USA, Inc.
(415) 432-3200

Vons Companies Inc.
(818) 821-7000

Wagner Spray Tech Corporation
(800) 328-8251

Walgreen Co.
(800) 289-2273

Wal-Mart Stores, Inc.
(501) 273-4000

Wamsutta Pacific
(800) 344-2142

Wang Laboratories Inc.
(800) 639-9264

Warnaco Men's Apparel
(207) 873-4241

Warner-Lambert Company
(800) 223-0182

Welch's
see Dr. Pepper/Seven-Up
 companies, Inc.

Wells Fargo & Company
(415) 396-3832

Wendy's International, Inc.
(614) 764-6800

West Bend Company
(414) 334-2311

**Western Union Financial
 Services, Inc.**
(314) 291-8000

WestPoint Pepperell
(800) 533-8229

Whirlpool Corporation
(800) 253-1301

White Westinghouse Appliances
see The Frigidaire Co.

Williams-Sonoma
(800) 541-1262

Winn Dixie Stores Inc.
(904) 783-5000

Winnebago Industries
(515) 582-6939

Winthrop Consumer Products
see Sterling Health

Wisconsin Bell
(800) 237-8576

Wonder Bread
see Continental Baking Company

F.W. Woolworth Company
(212) 553-2000

World Book Educational Products
(800) 621-8202

Wrangler
(919) 373-3564

Wm. Wrigley Jr. Company
(312) 644-2121

Xerox Corporation
(716) 423-5480

Yamaha Motor Corporation
(714) 761-7439

The Yardley Limited Company
(901) 320-2166

Zale Corporation
(214) 580-5104

Zenith Data Systems
(800) 227-3360

Zenith Electronics Corporation
(708) 391-8100

Index

LIST OF CASE STUDIES